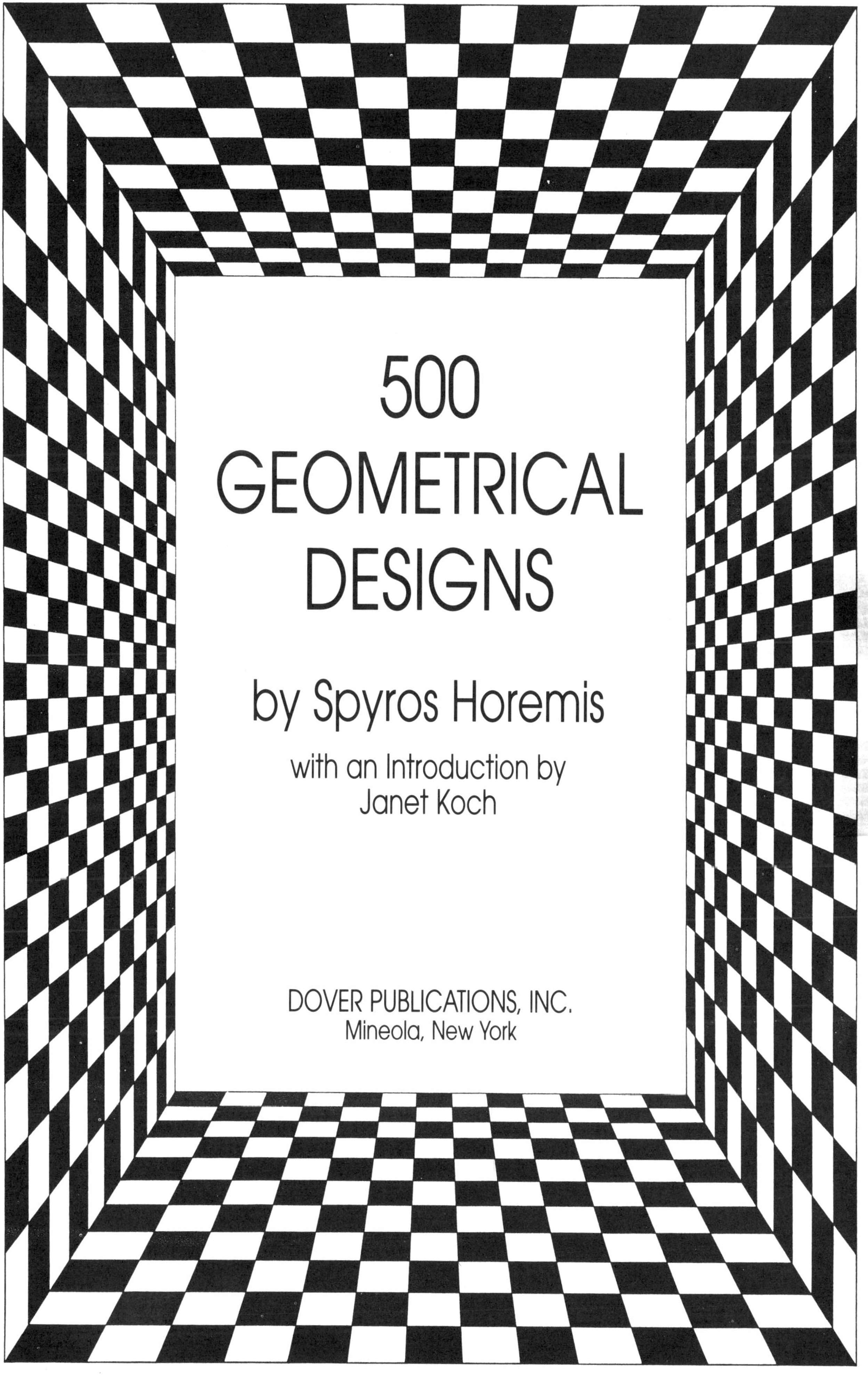

500 GEOMETRICAL DESIGNS

by Spyros Horemis

with an Introduction by
Janet Koch

DOVER PUBLICATIONS, INC.
Mineola, New York

I wish to thank Mr. Moses Capon, Miss Leta Koutsohera and Miss Rene Kapitsala for their help with this book.
S. H.

Published in Canada by General Publishing Company, Ltd., 30 Lesmill Road, Don Mills, Toronto, Ontario.

Bibliographical Note

500 Geometrical Designs is a new work, first published by Dover Publications, Inc., in 1970 under the title *Optical and Geometrical Patterns and Designs.*

International Standard Book Number: 0-486-22214-4
Library of Congress Catalog Card Number: 70-106491

Manufactured in the United States of America
Dover Publications, Inc., 31 East 2nd Street, Mineola, N.Y. 11501

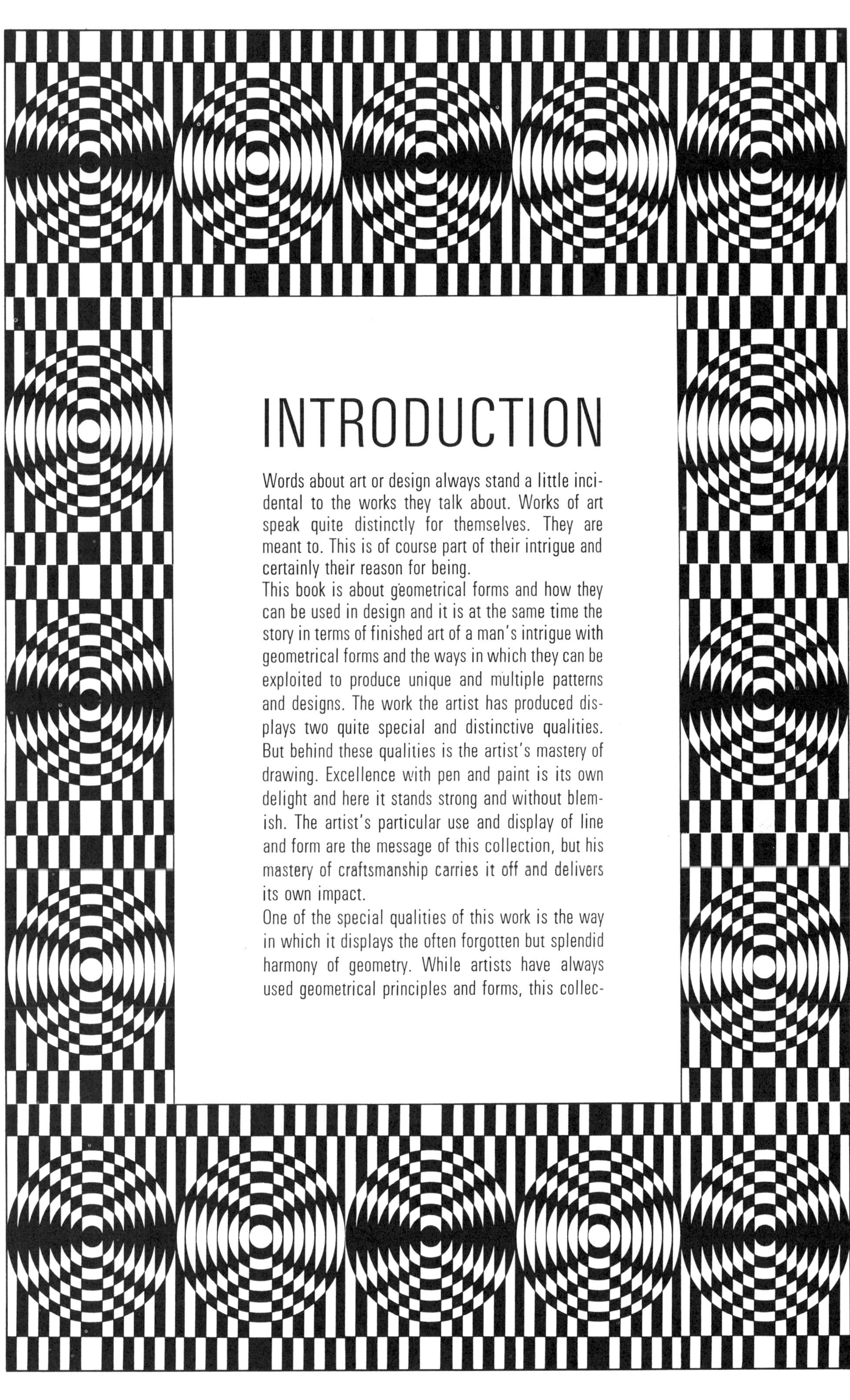

INTRODUCTION

Words about art or design always stand a little incidental to the works they talk about. Works of art speak quite distinctly for themselves. They are meant to. This is of course part of their intrigue and certainly their reason for being.

This book is about geometrical forms and how they can be used in design and it is at the same time the story in terms of finished art of a man's intrigue with geometrical forms and the ways in which they can be exploited to produce unique and multiple patterns and designs. The work the artist has produced displays two quite special and distinctive qualities. But behind these qualities is the artist's mastery of drawing. Excellence with pen and paint is its own delight and here it stands strong and without blemish. The artist's particular use and display of line and form are the message of this collection, but his mastery of craftsmanship carries it off and delivers its own impact.

One of the special qualities of this work is the way in which it displays the often forgotten but splendid harmony of geometry. While artists have always used geometrical principles and forms, this collection focuses in a particular way on geometry by and of itself. It is in a real and exciting way a pictorial display of geometry. The artist's geometrical images invite us to recall and recognize in new light the balance and harmony of geometry's precision, symmetry and mathematical exactness. Our vision is attracted by circles and squares, lines and angles, always precise and evenly structured. The forms themselves, the precision, symmetry and even the restrictiveness intrinsic to them strike chords of balance. And as the forms are set in tight and formal geometrical relationships one with another, we see a full visualization of geometry and its fascinating, innate harmony.

This virtuoso display of geometrical harmony is tremendously exciting, but the special fascination and attraction of these plates is perhaps primarily due to the artist's inventive exploration of the ways in which geometrical forms and relationships can be worked into remarkably varied and endlessly fascinating patterns and designs. There is no better word for his technique than exploitation. The artist shows how the repetition of designs, in full plates or in strips or borders, can set forth a uniform design sequence. Repetition of a pattern is conceptually the simplest, though certainly not the least appealing result of his geometrical creations. The harmony of regularity and symmetry holds fast. Each pattern or theme he plays in repetition stands for itself, but he gives us several examples and several separate themes. We see how a carefully and precisely executed basic pattern, with its special characteristics, affects the repetitive sequence. The basic themes differ one from another and accordingly so do the sequences played out. While some of the sequences are exactly repetitive, the artist in others introduces variations on the theme; some show the special effects of reversing black and white, sometimes of the whole scheme, sometimes of a minor, particular facet. Moving away from themes in repetition, the artist jumps to freer, more fascinating exploitation. Patterns appear; he cuts them apart, places sections in juxtaposition and opposition to one another, further improvising variations on his theme. A circular design, perhaps an intricate mosaic or simply a series of concentric circles, is cut along the edge or through the center. The parts are then imaginatively and sometimes chimerically fitted one to another to form a design which retains a sense of the original, master theme while also becoming a new and unique image.

One is fascinated by the effects of the breaks and splits, often along unexpected points, but there is additional fascination in being confronted with changed perspectives. Circular and square patterns are halved, shown straight and then beguile us as they are tilted top to toe.

The sense of variations on an original theme is seen too in a surprisingly different way as the artist turns to superimposing forms or facets on a thematic scheme. Again basic forms are set down. Multiple, varied, often strangely cut pieces always deriving in one way or another from the basic design are superimposed to form new patterns. When we view them in sequence we are attracted not only by the individual new patterns but by the conglomerate effect of the multiple variations on the original theme. The closer and the more frequently we examine the designs, the more we become aware of their subtleties and intricacies and of the complex system of variations. As we take second and third looks at these plates our vision is dazzled by the multiplicity of splendidly harmonious themes set forth to stand for themselves while at the same time participating in new images, displaying new intricacies of pattern and sequence. In purpose and form this book is about geometrical shapes and how they can be used in design. In spirit it is an unusual and distinctive display of virtuosity.

JANET KOCH

New York City
October, 1969

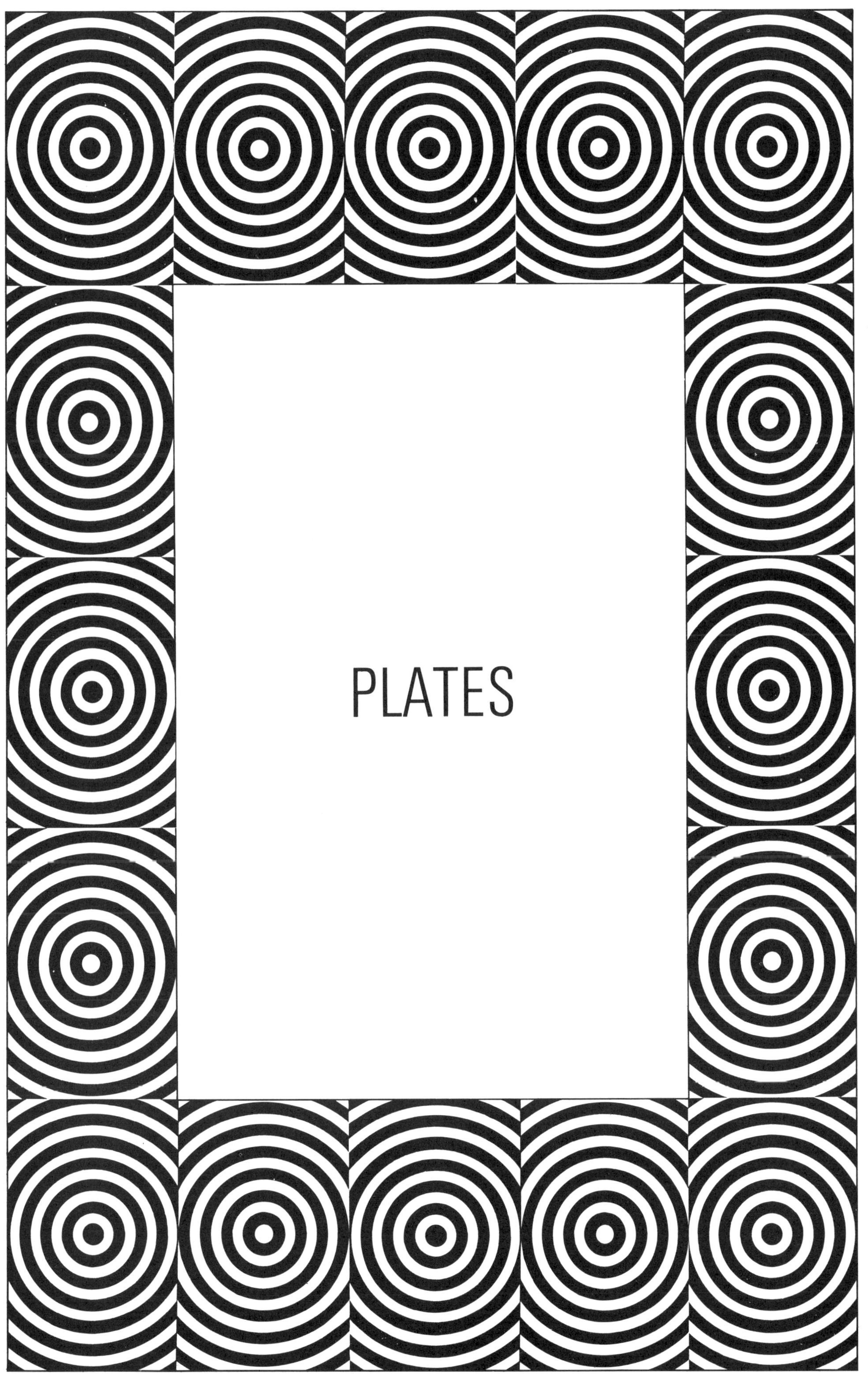

PLATES

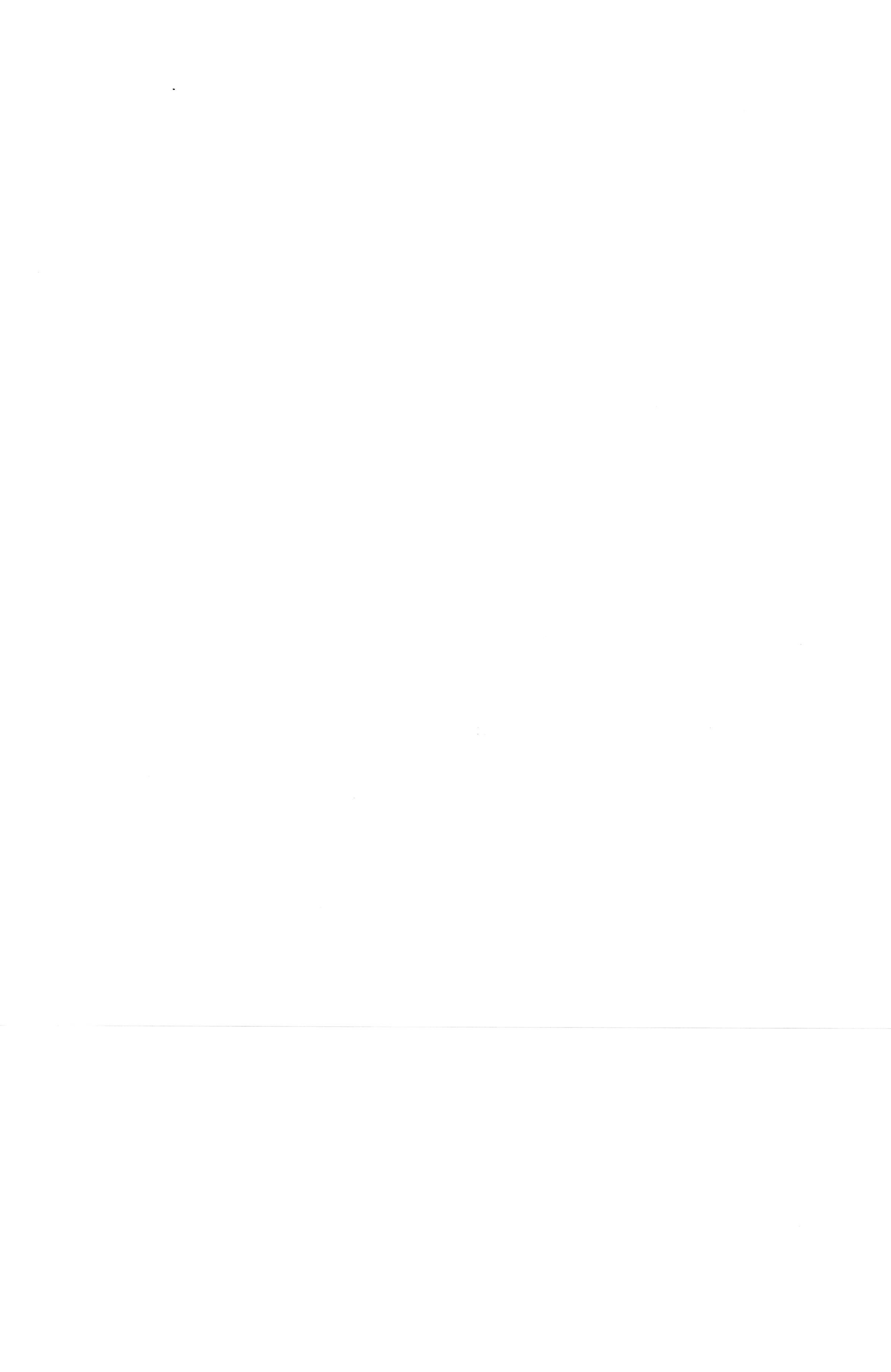

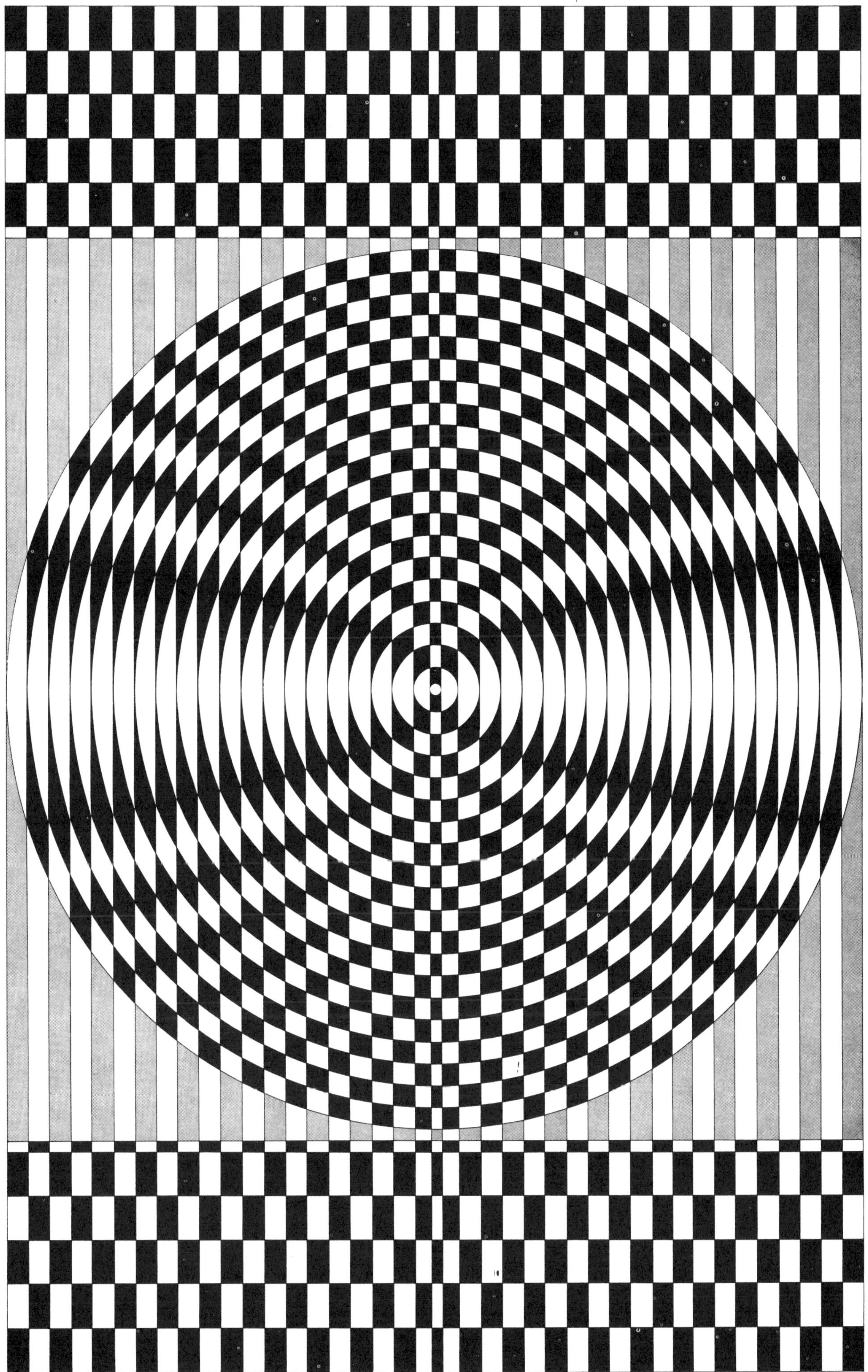

PLATE 1

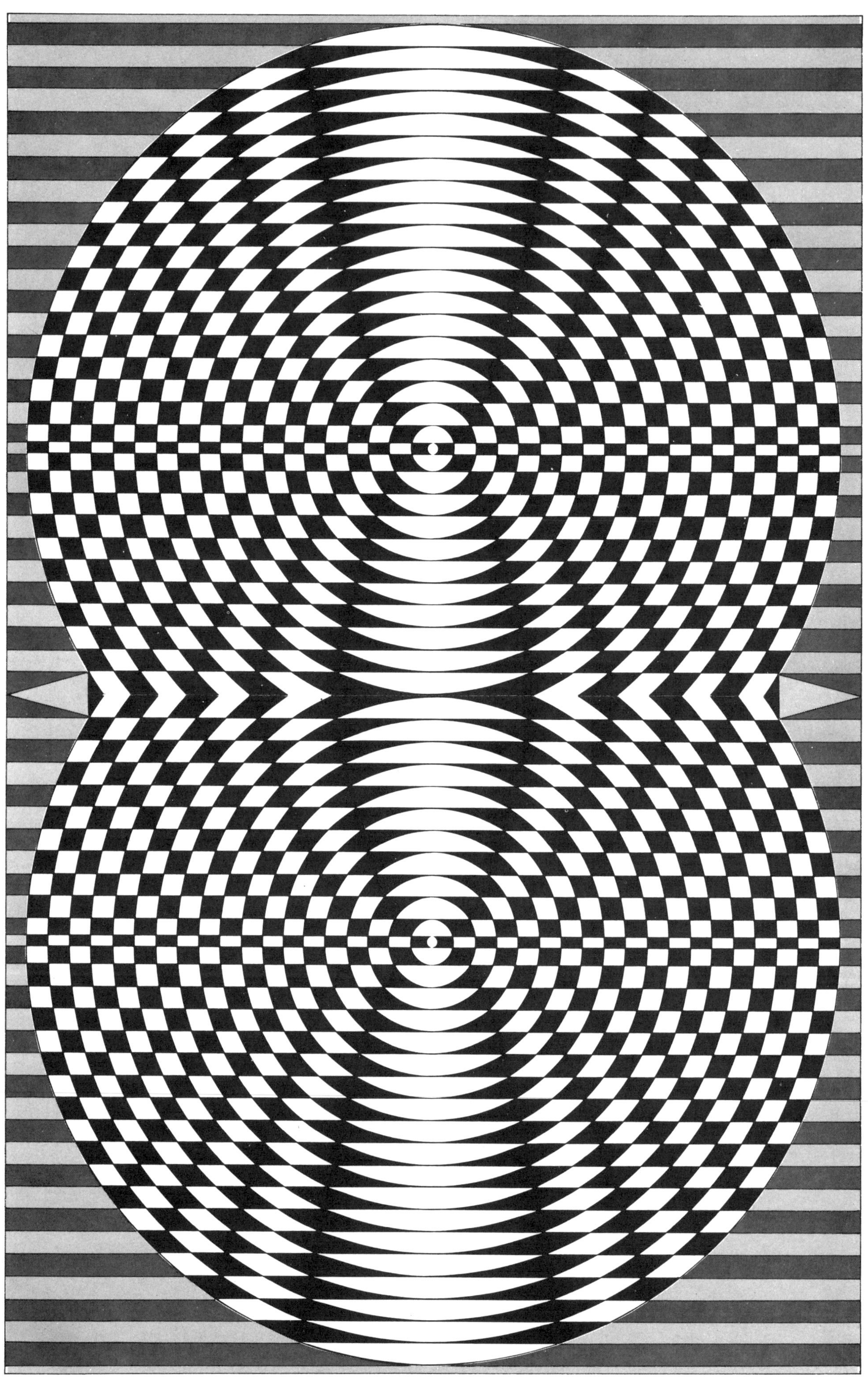

PLATE 2

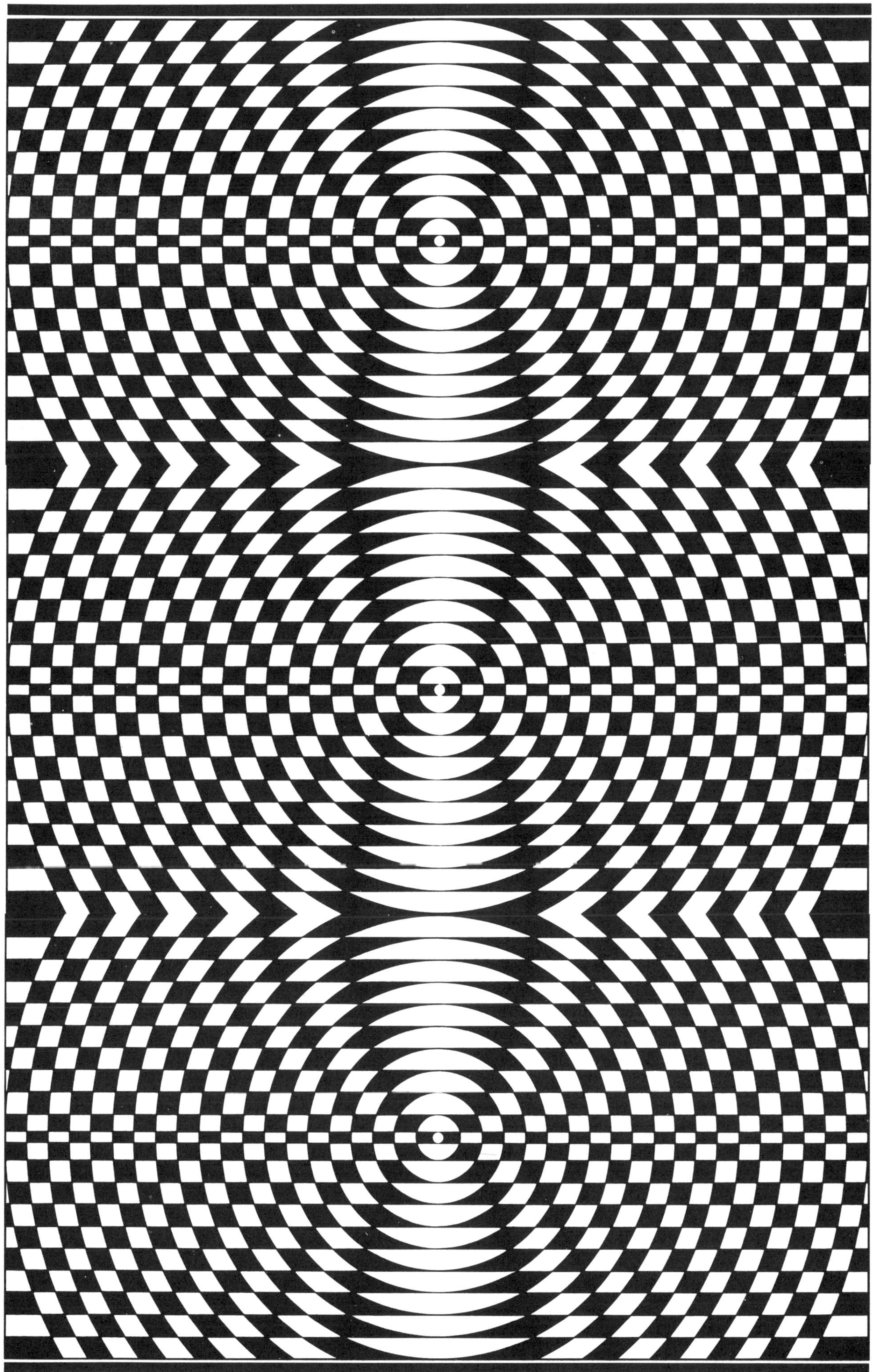

PLATE 3

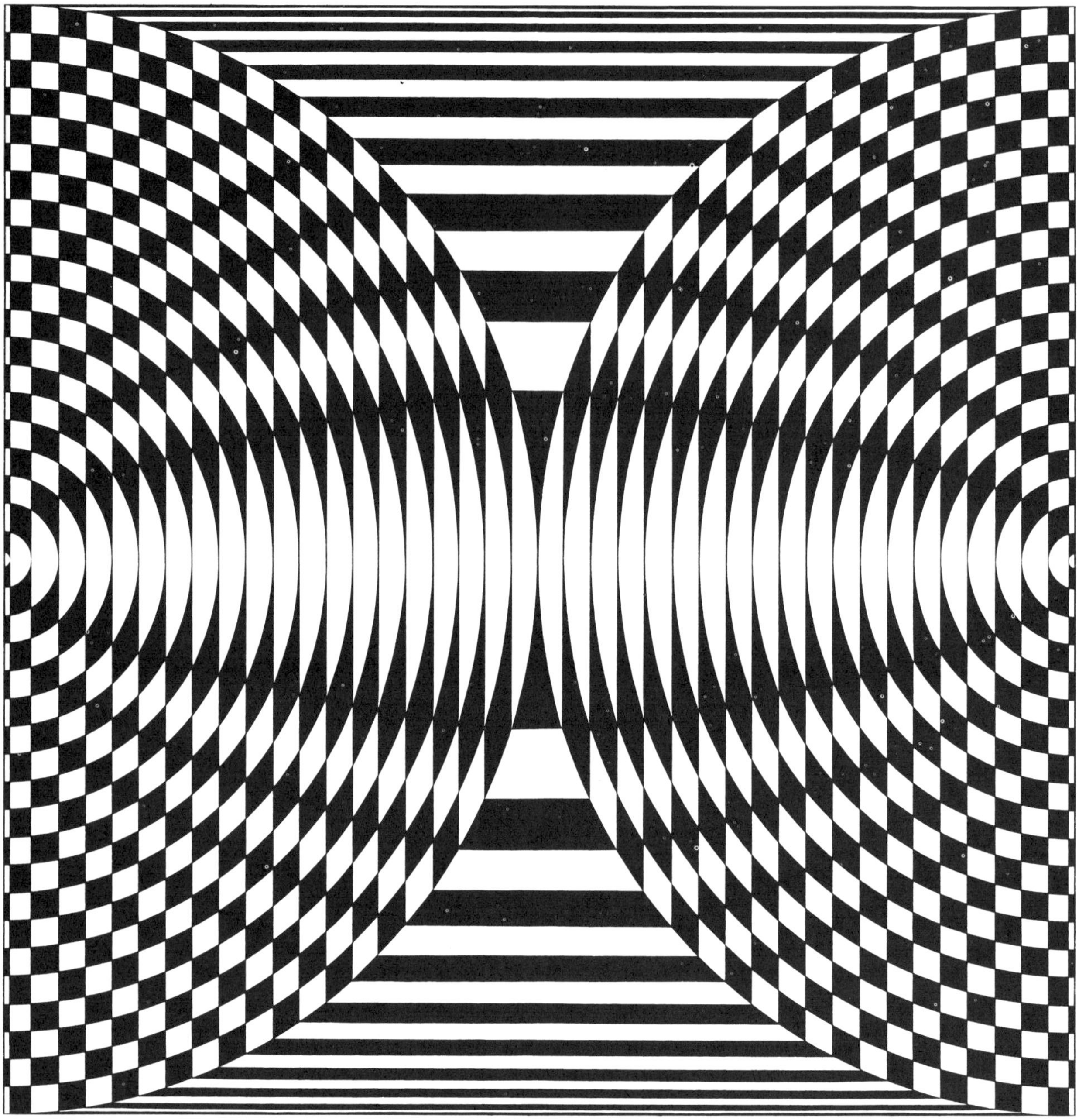

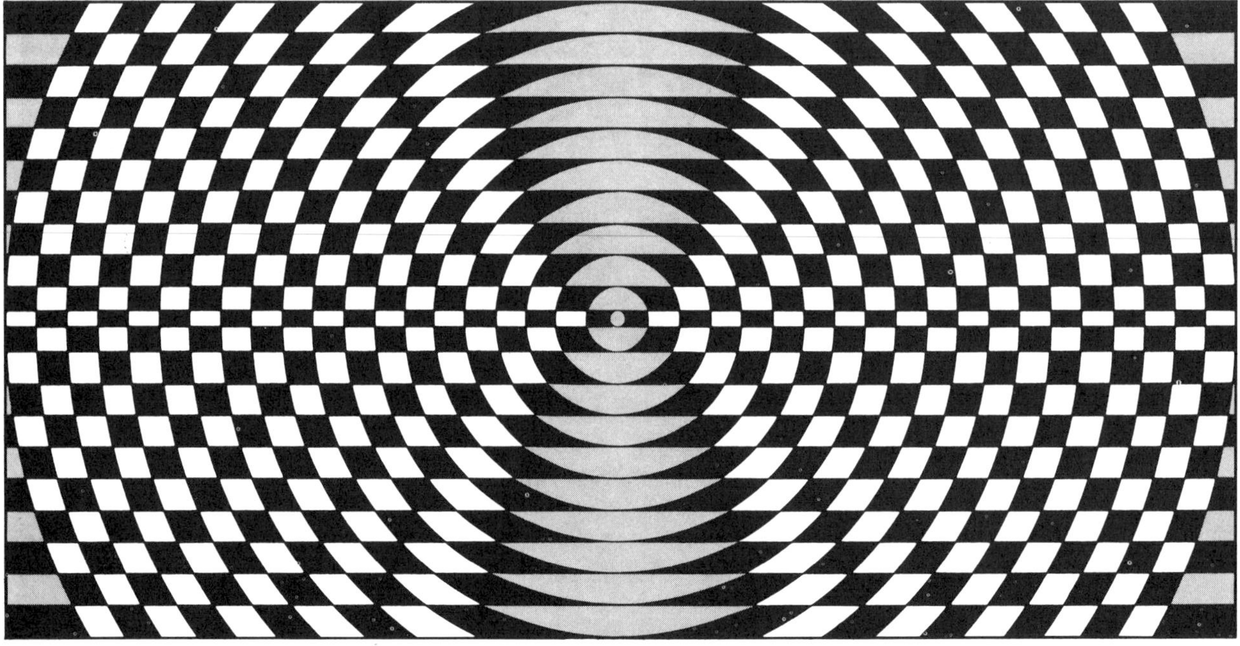

PLATE 4

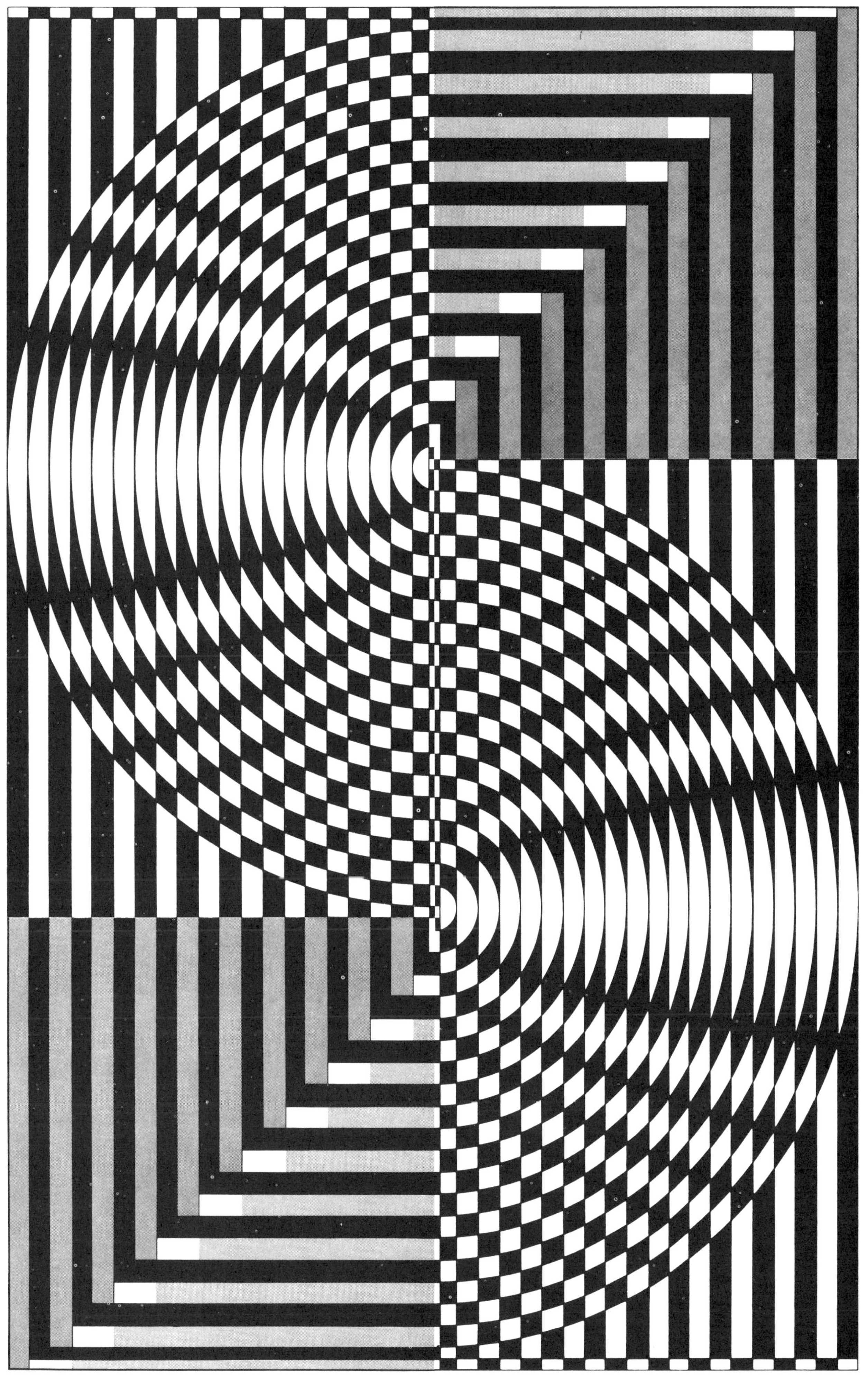

PLATE 5

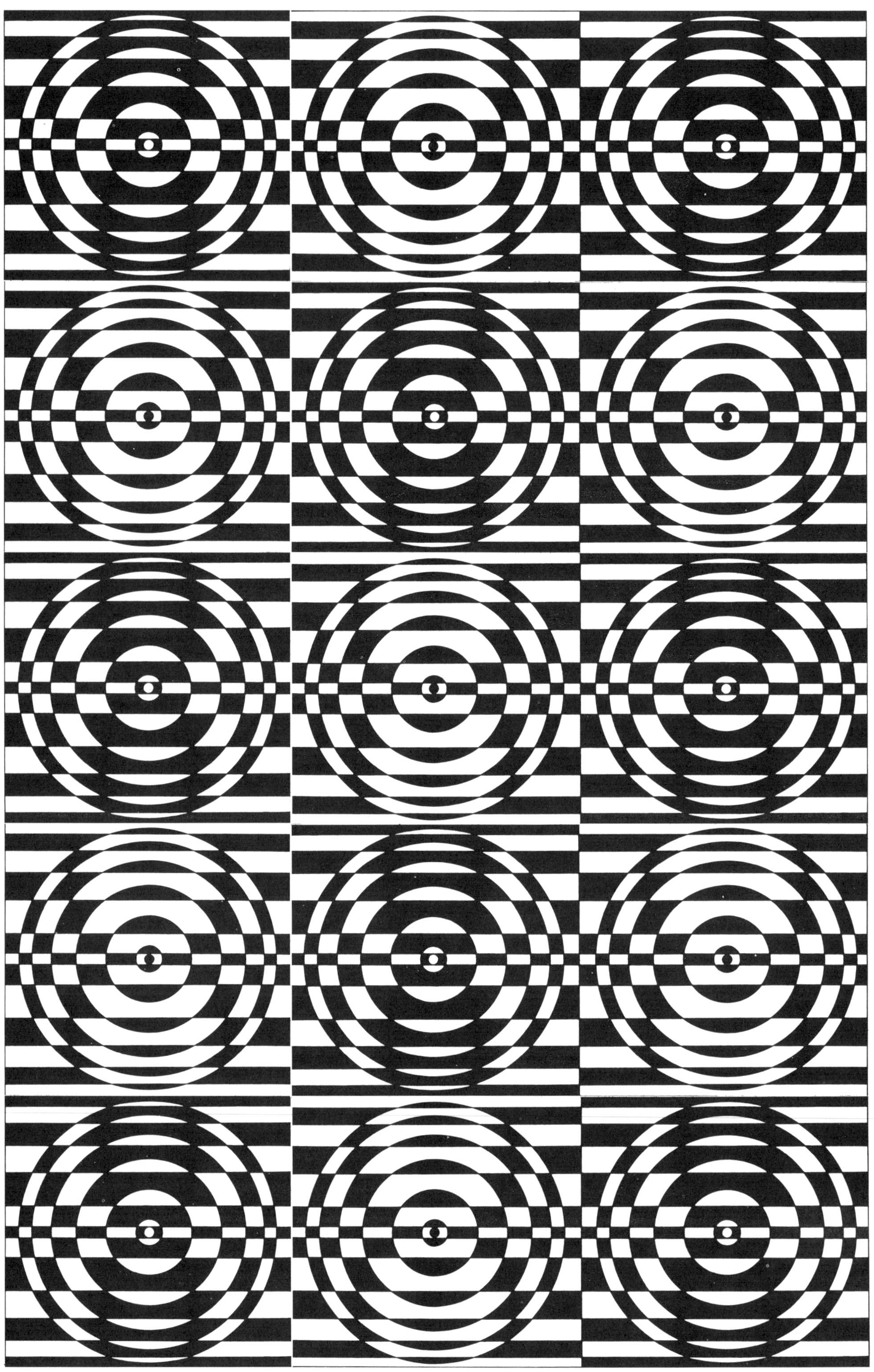

PLATE 6

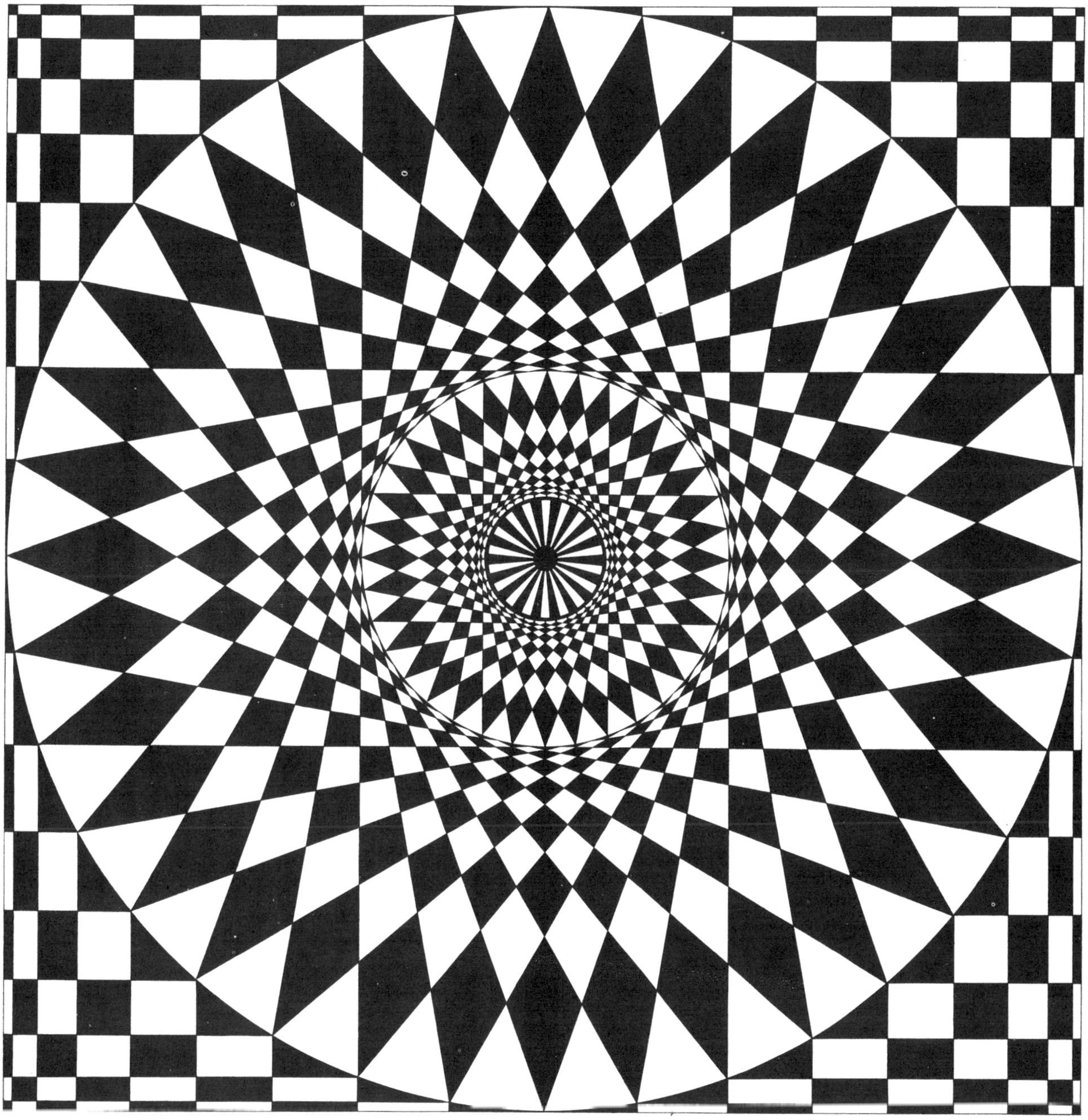

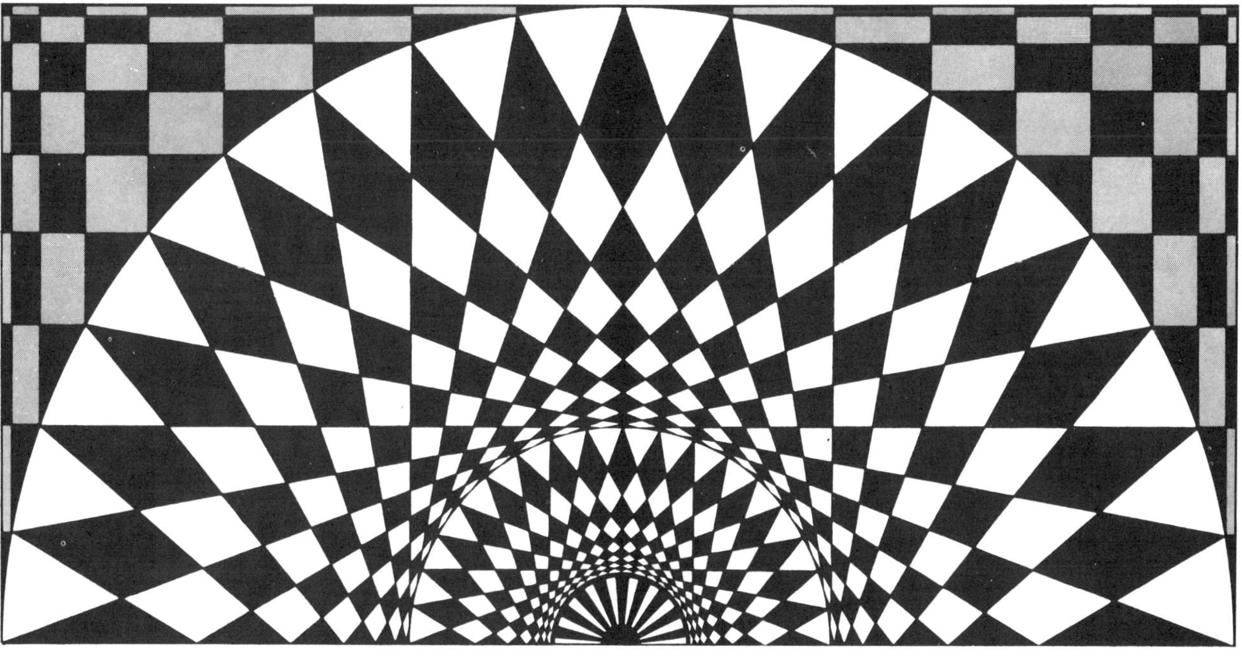

PLATE 7

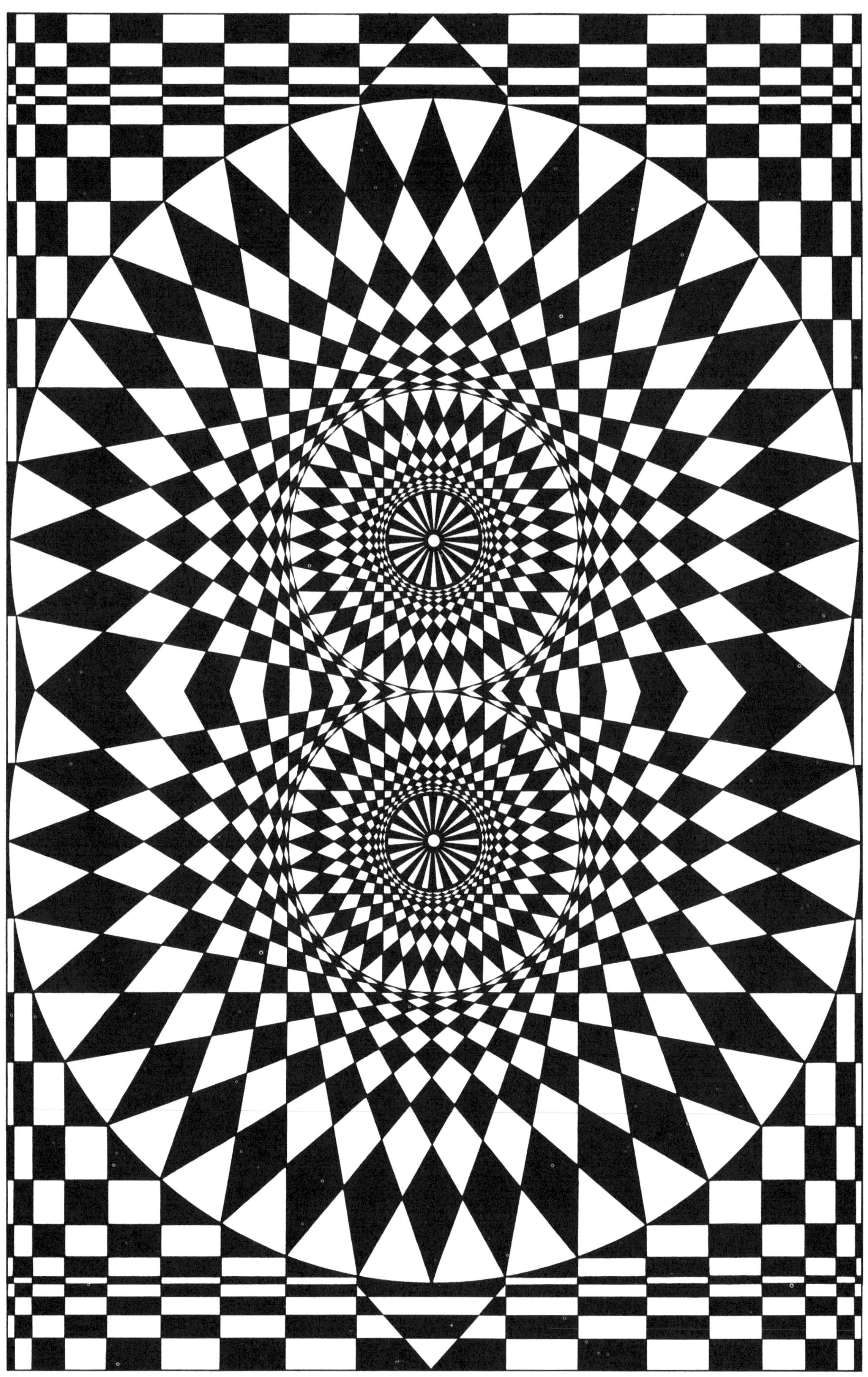

PLATE 8

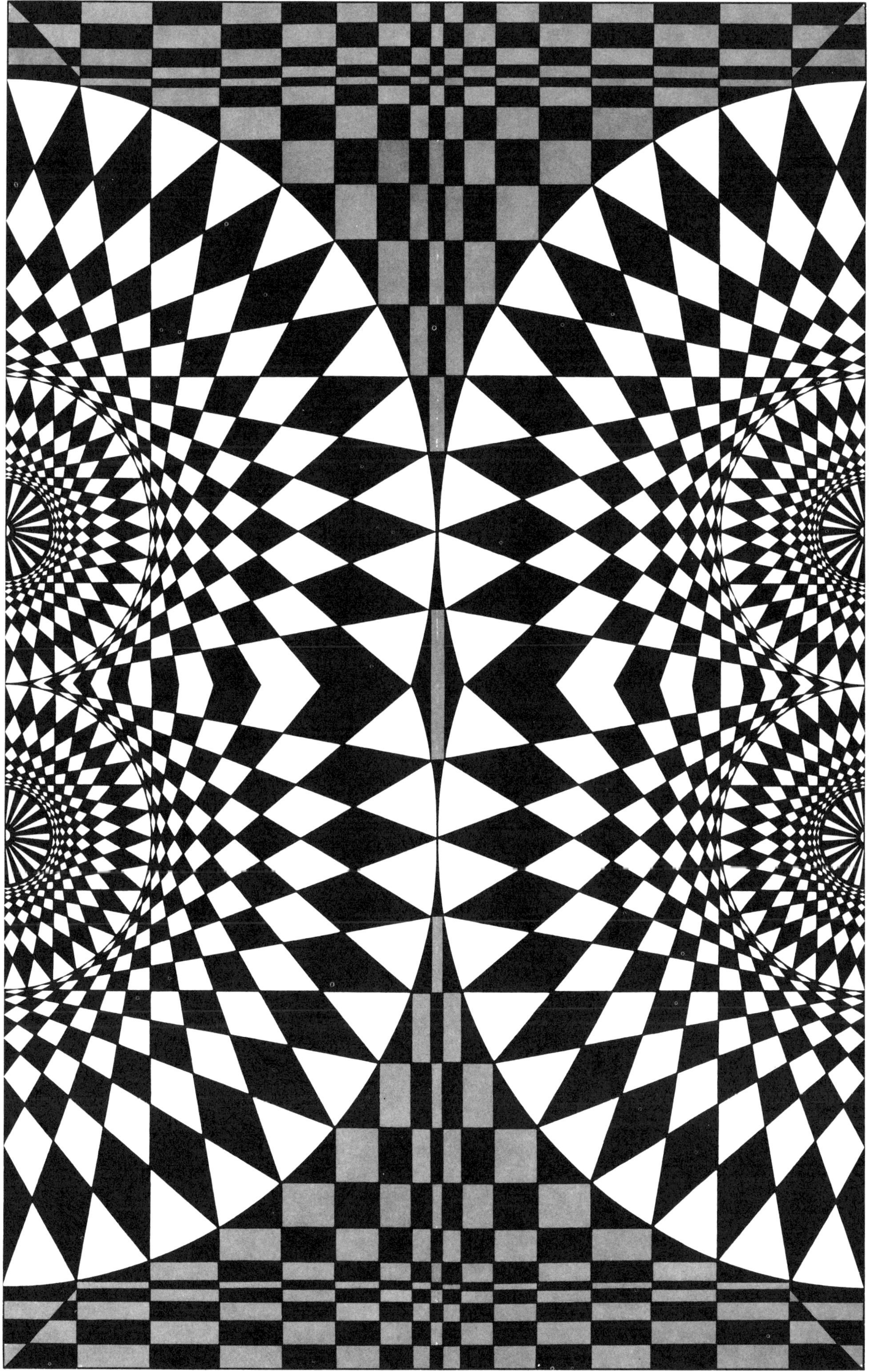

PLATE 9

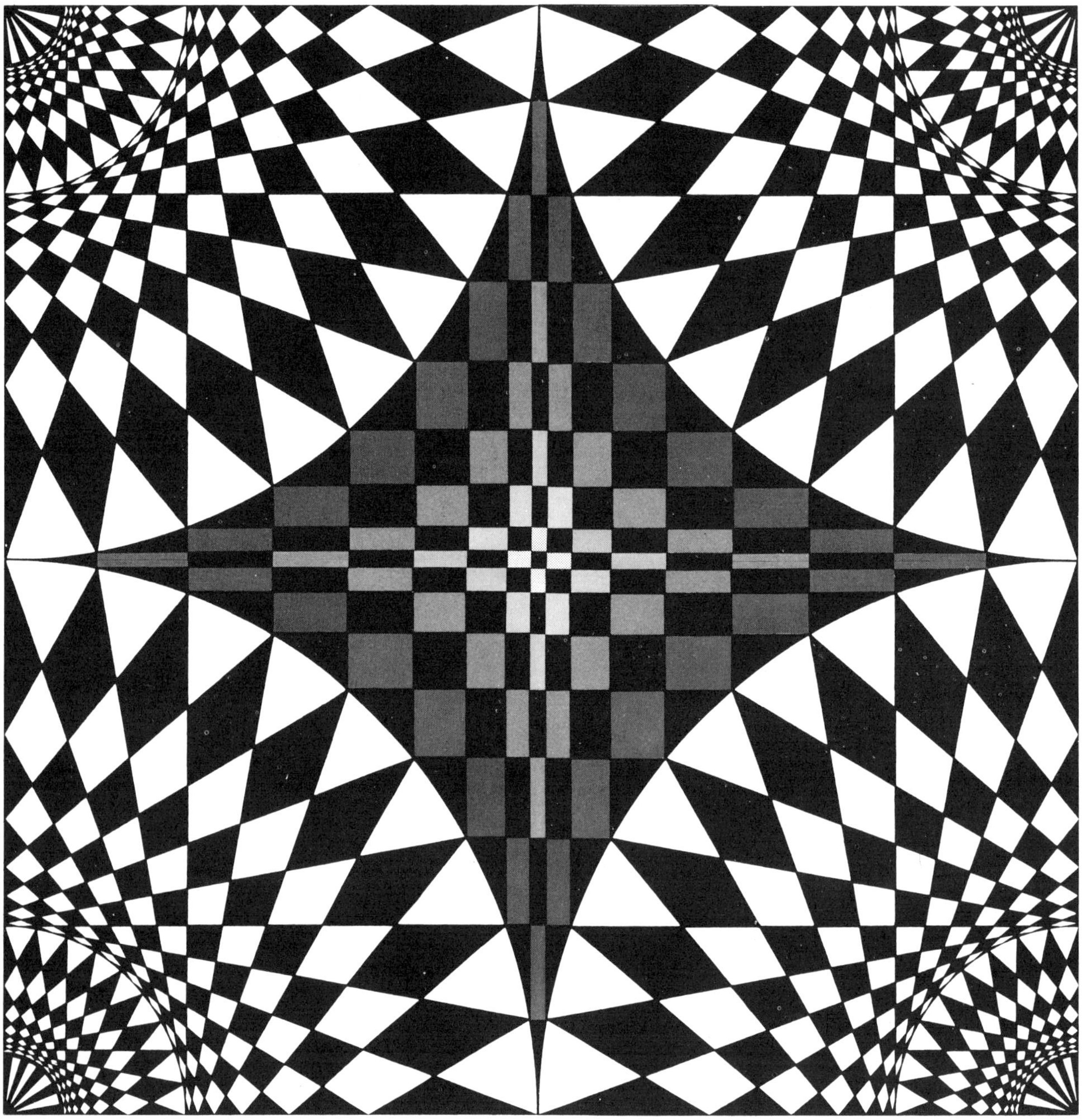

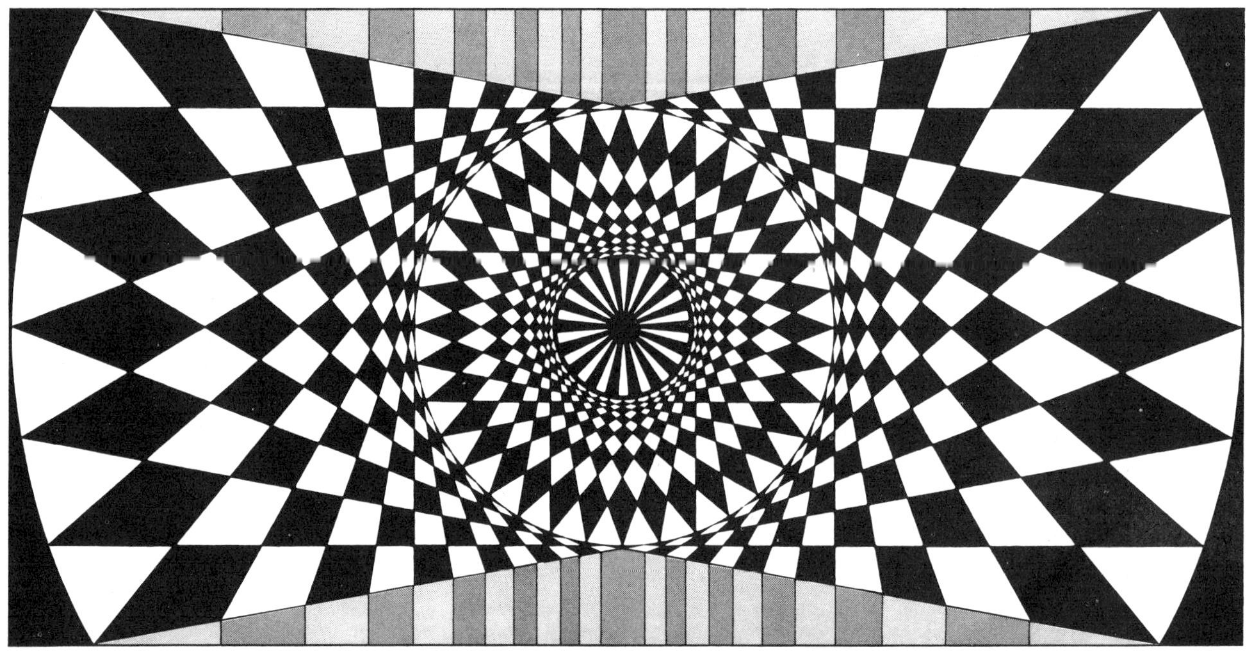

PLATE 10

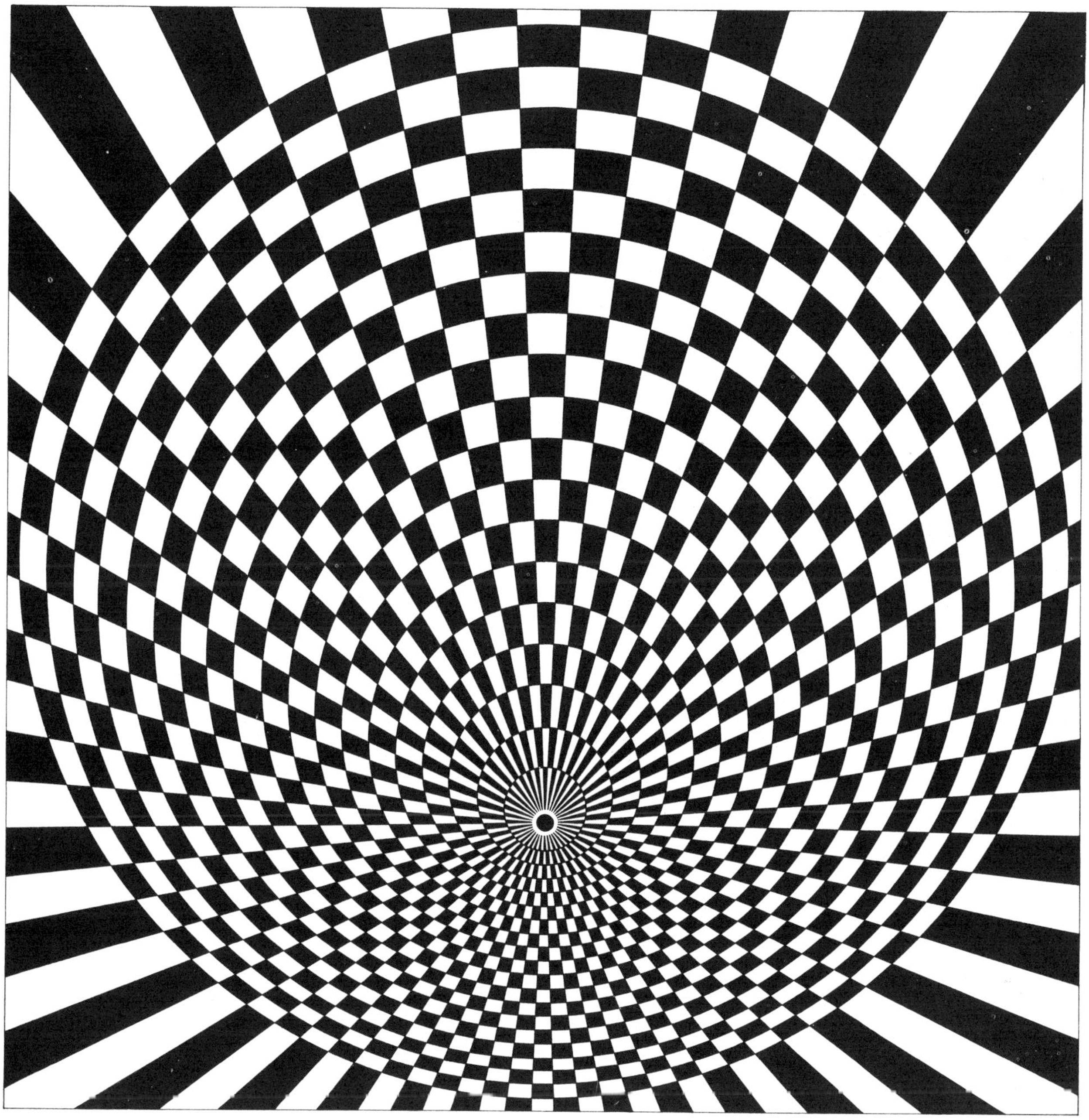

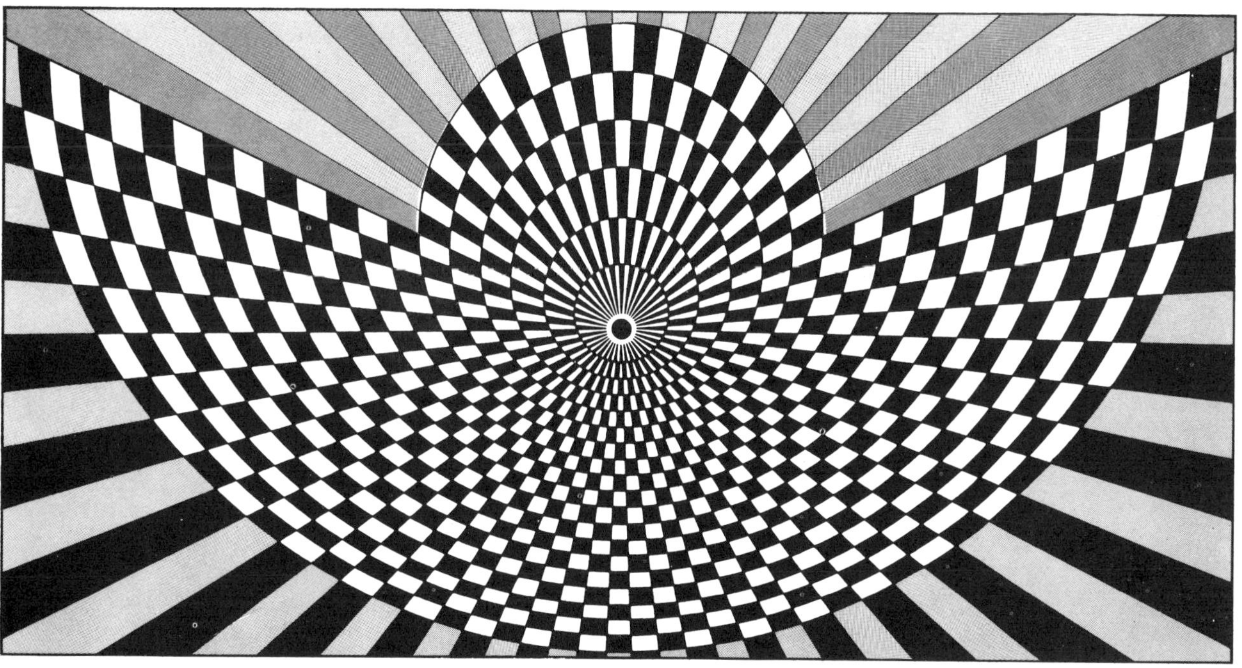

PLATE 11

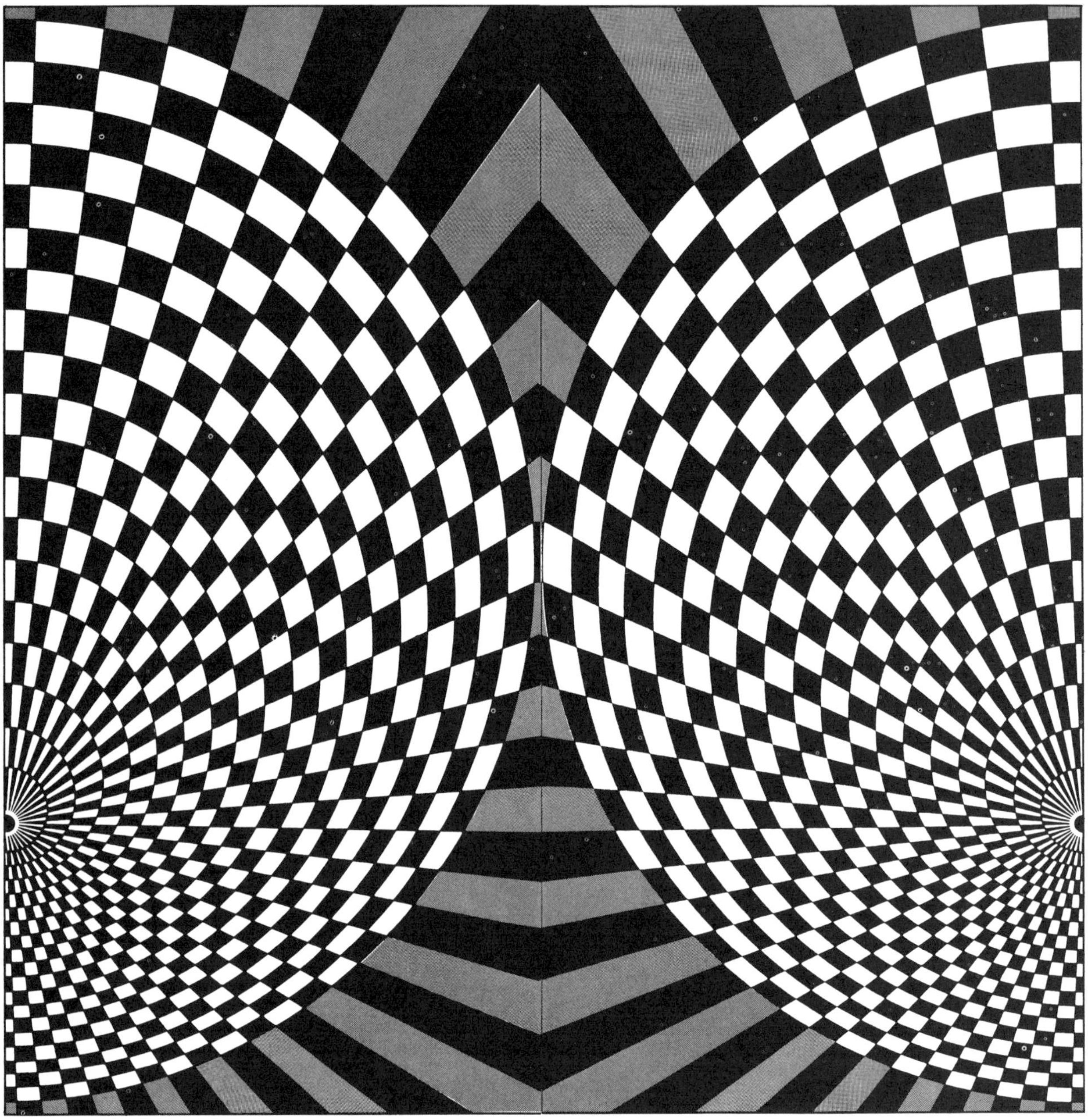

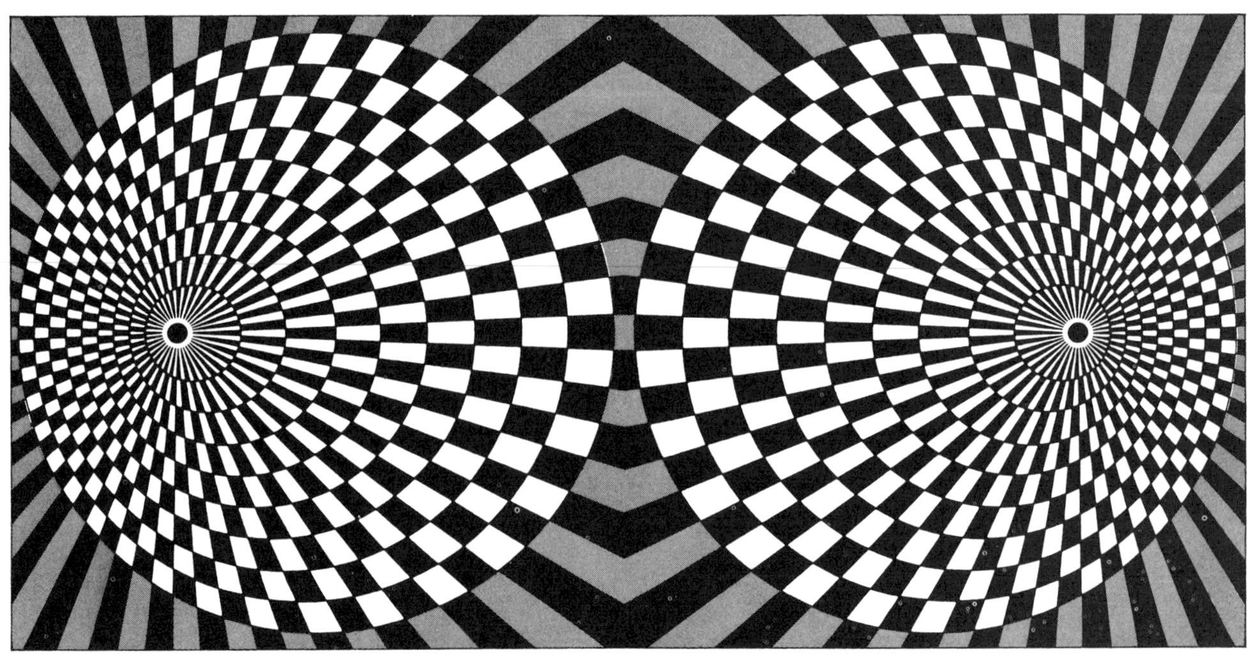

PLATE 12

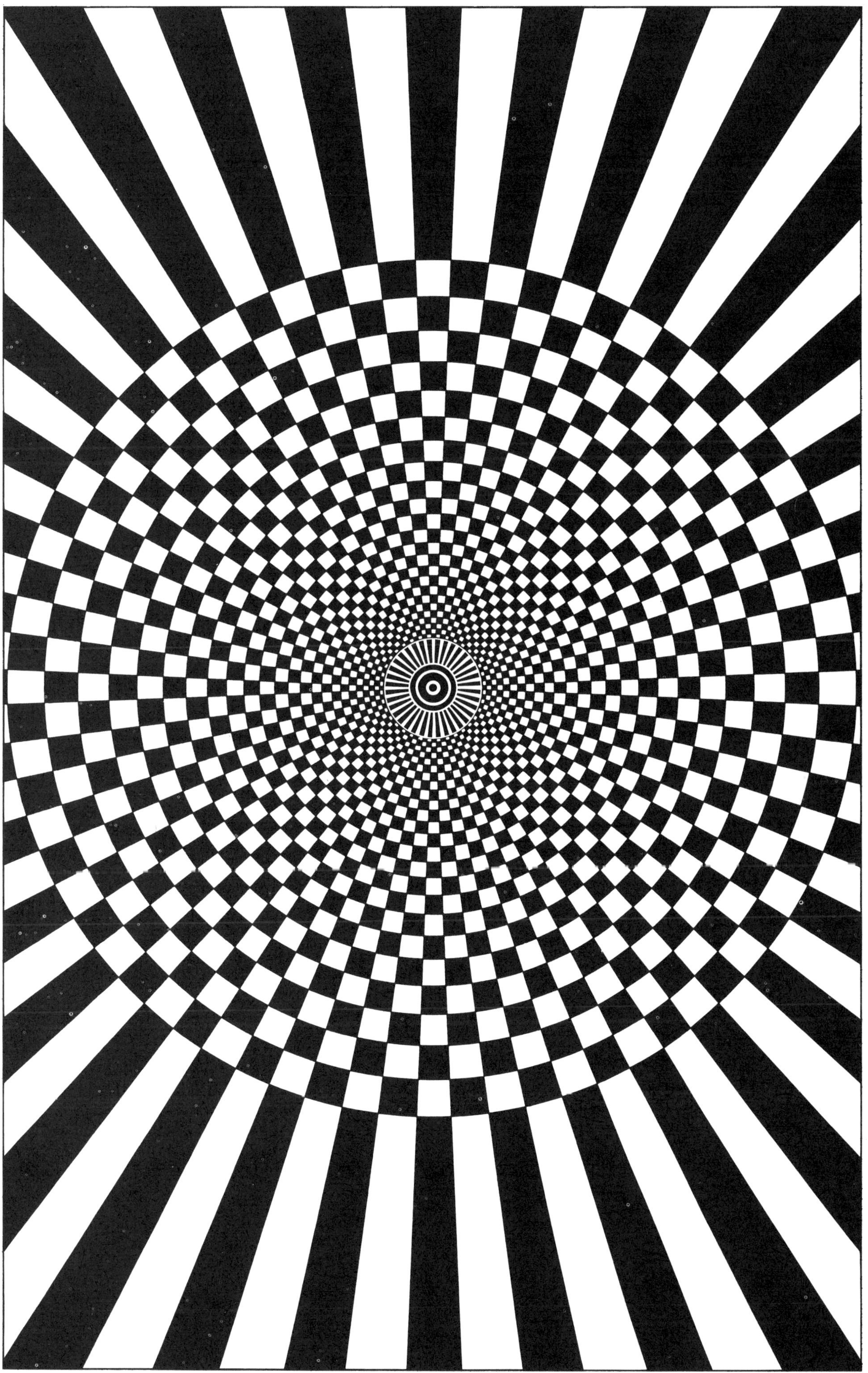

PLATE 13

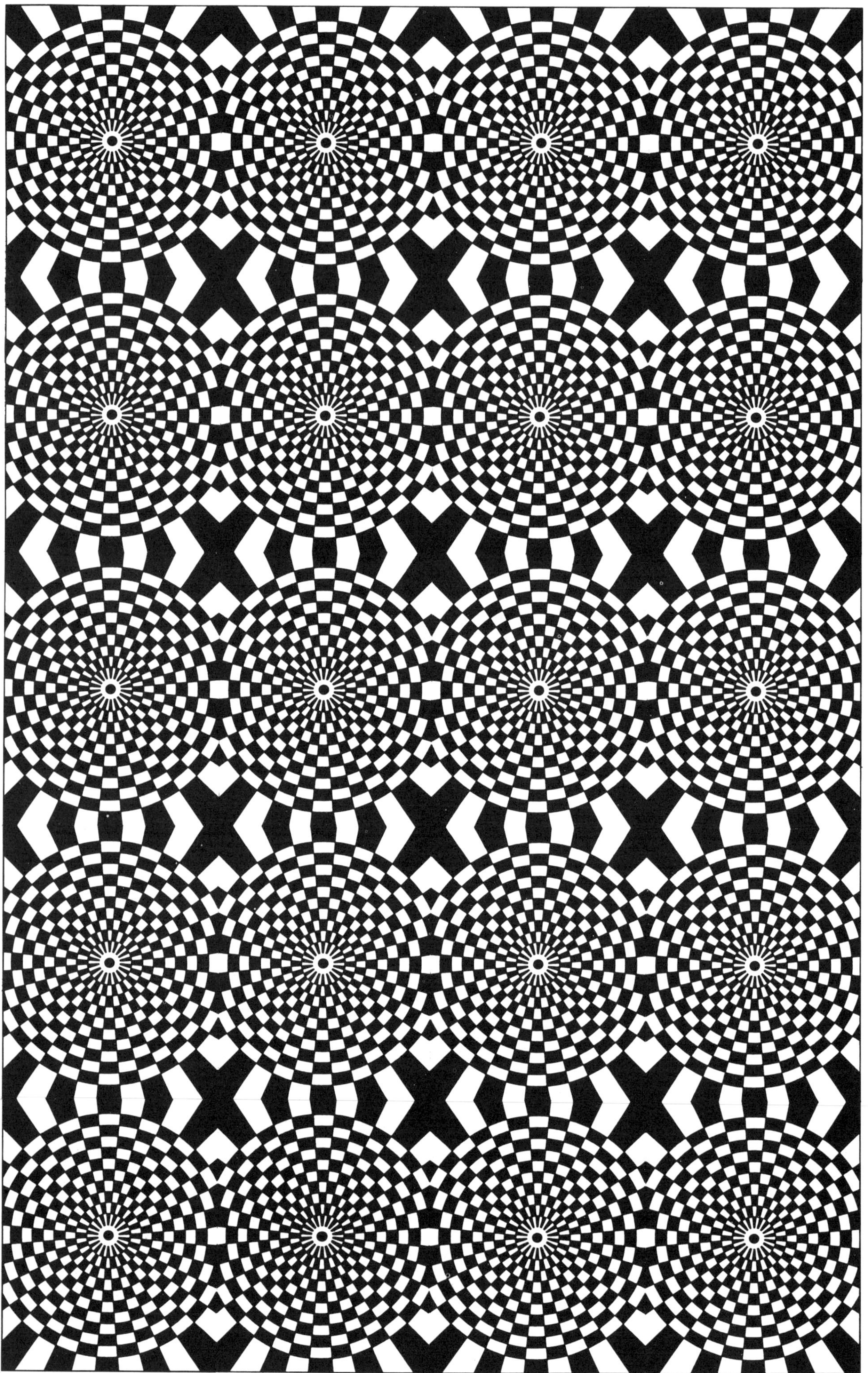

PLATE 14

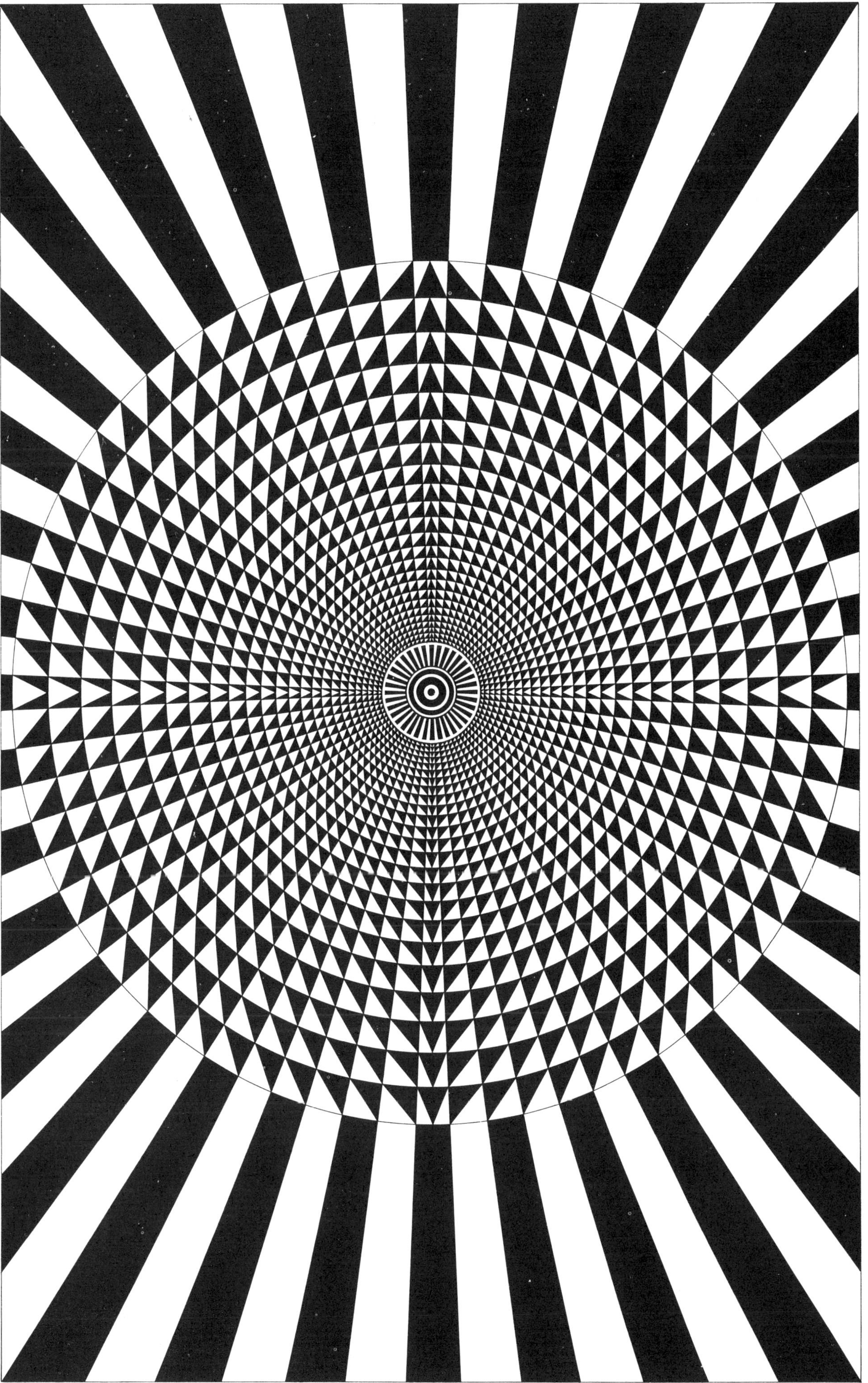

PLATE 15

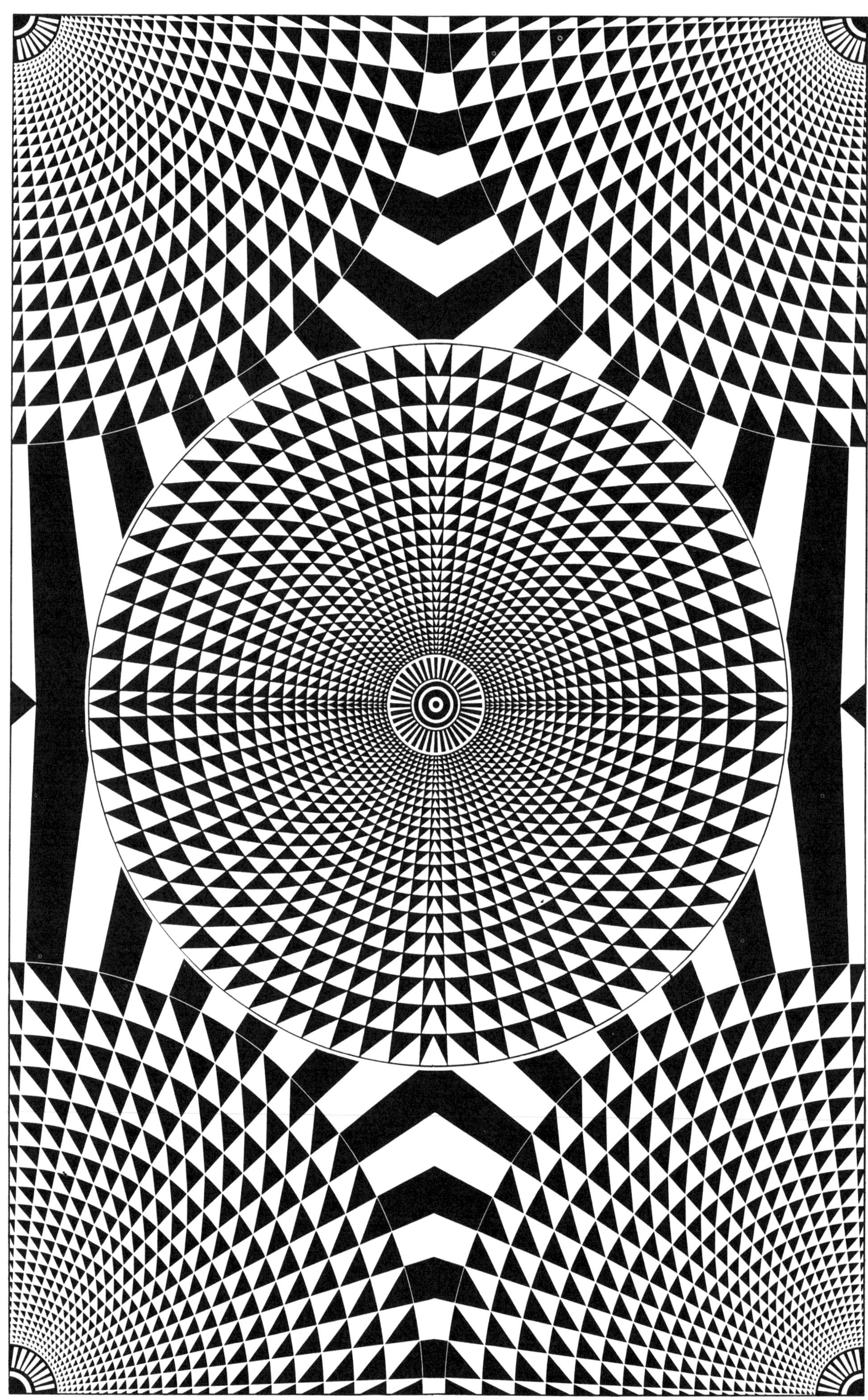

PLATE 16

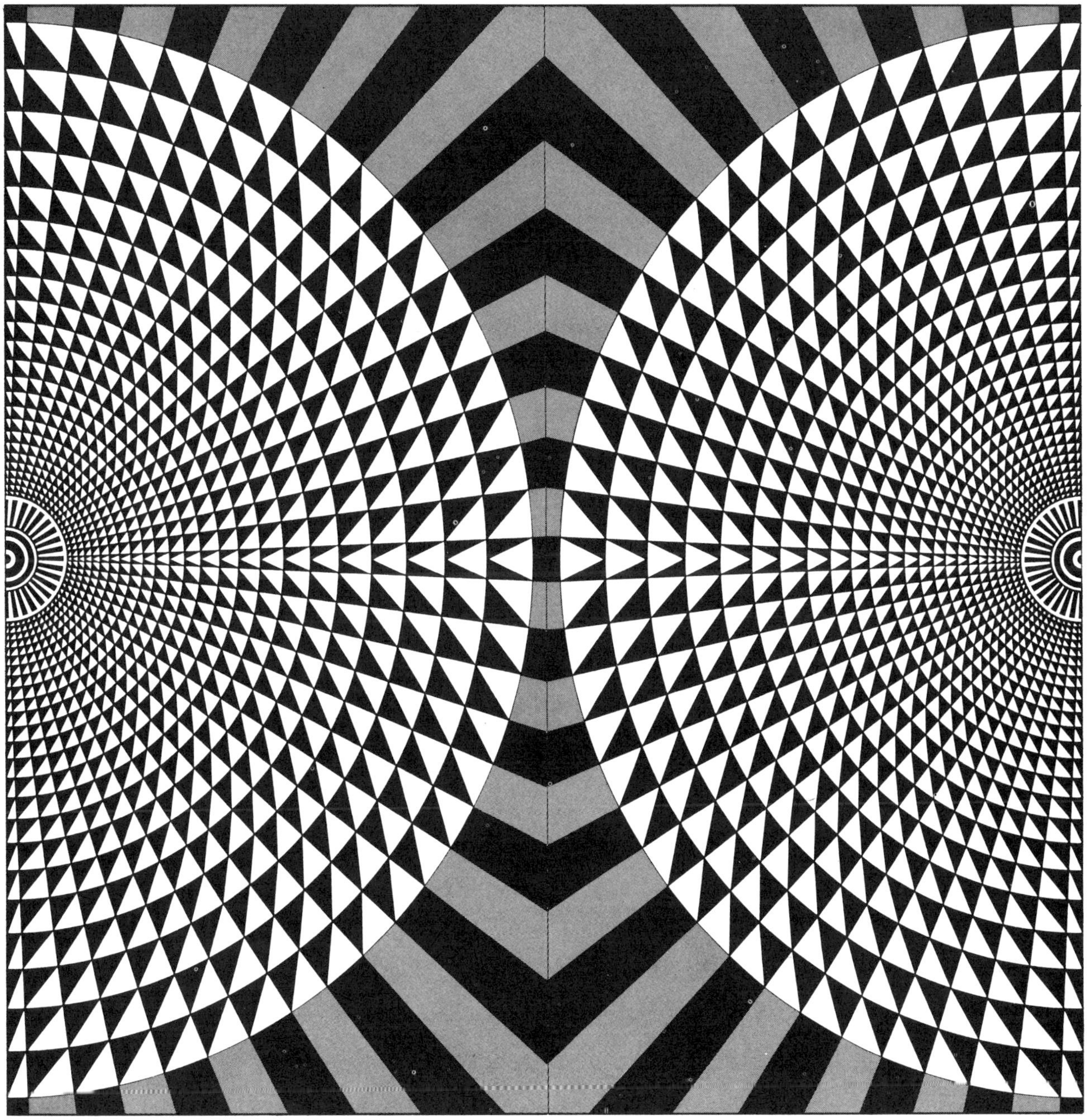

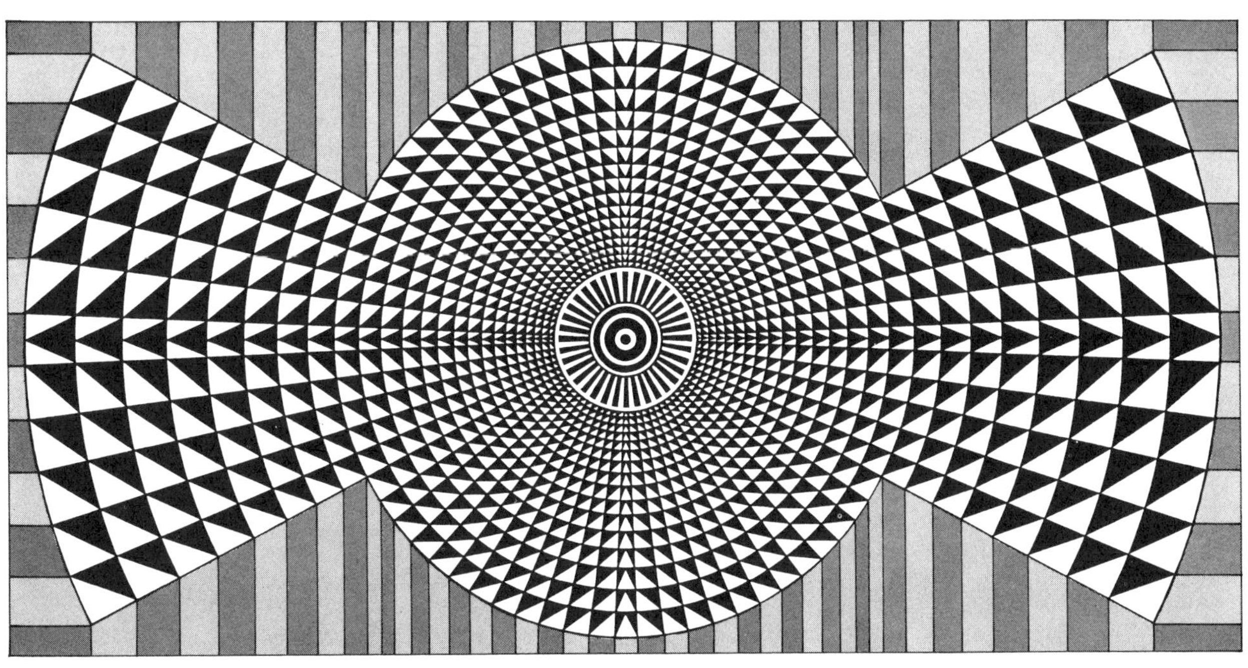

PLATE 17

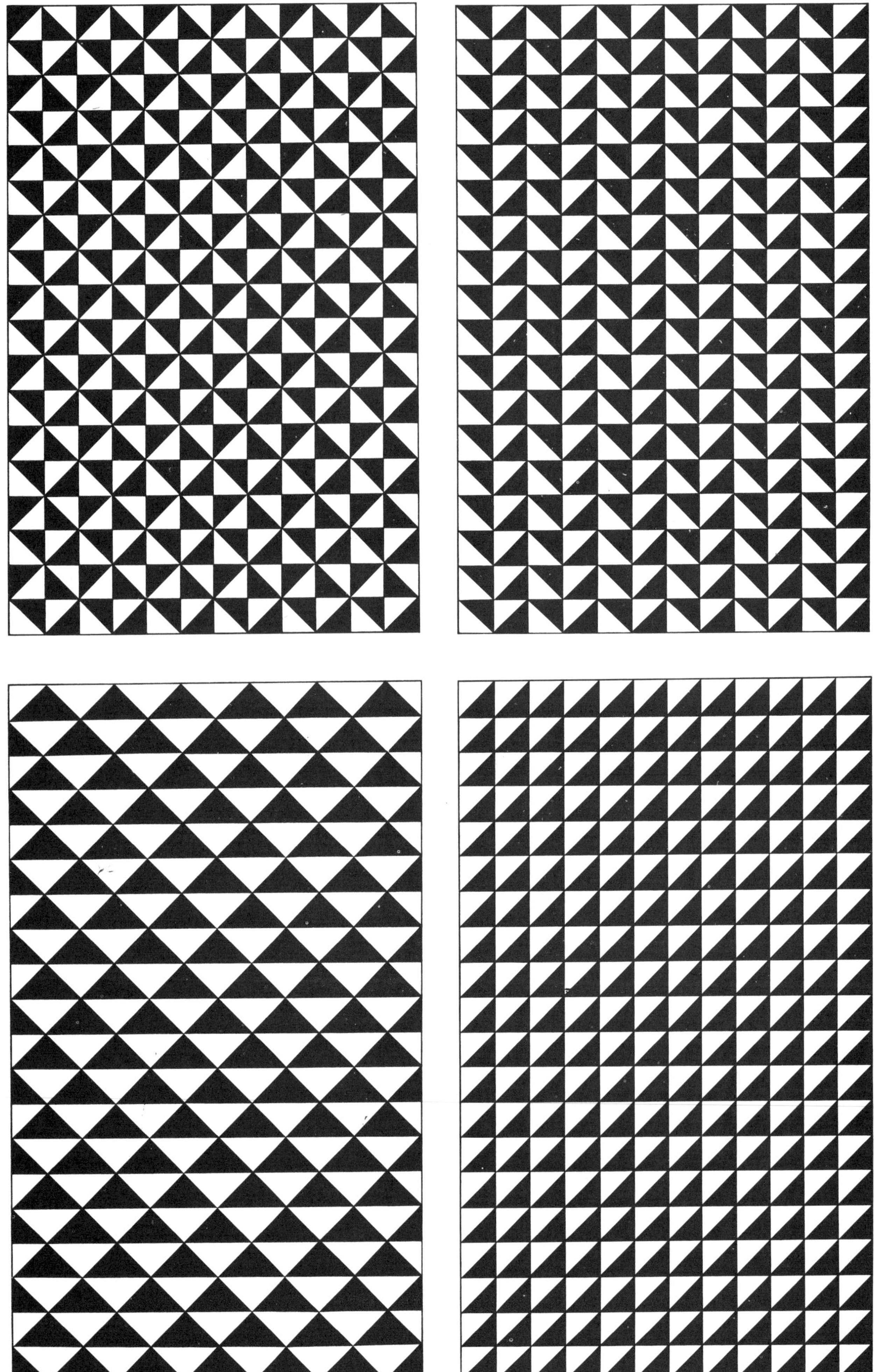

PLATE 18

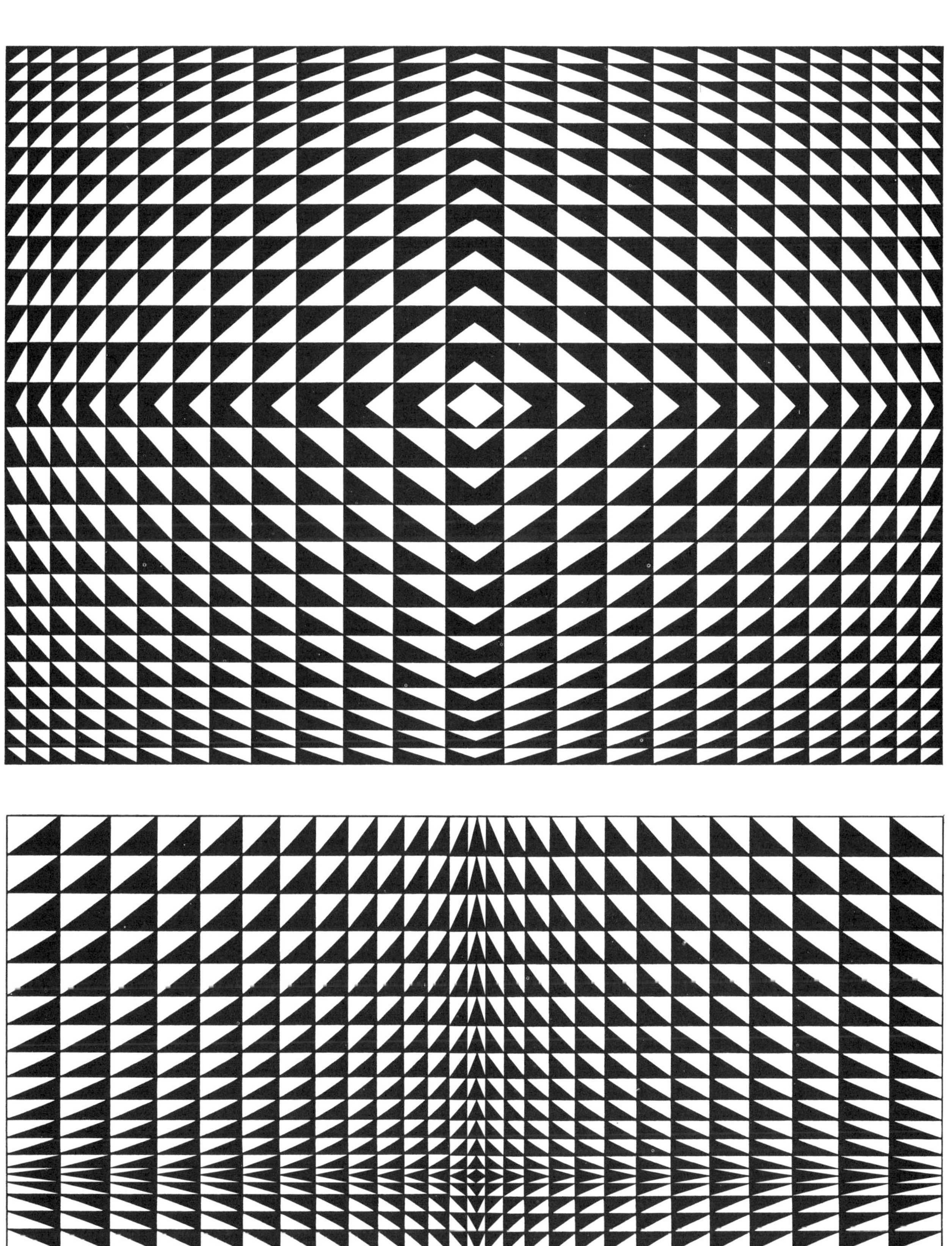

PLATE 19

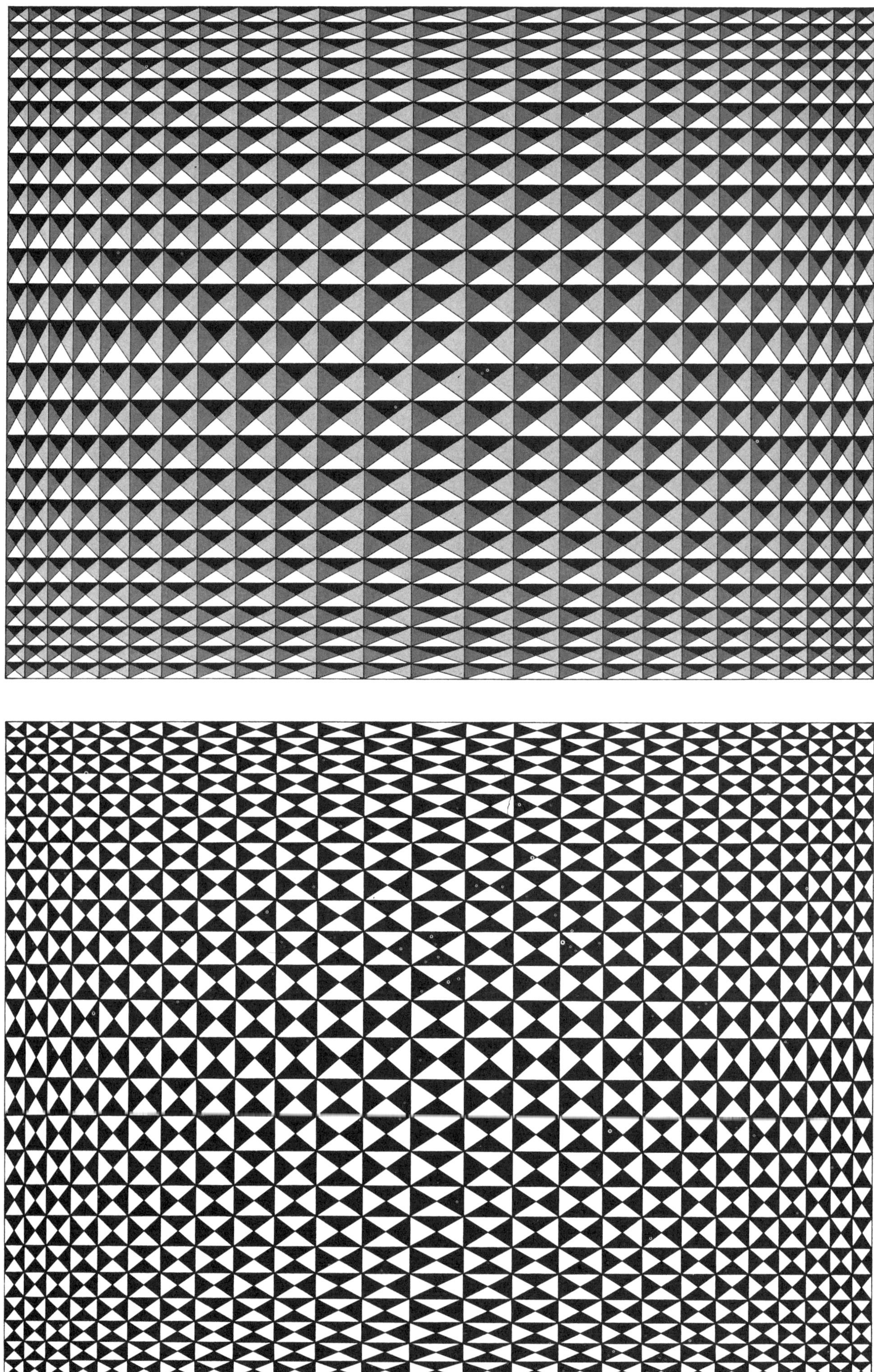

PLATE 20

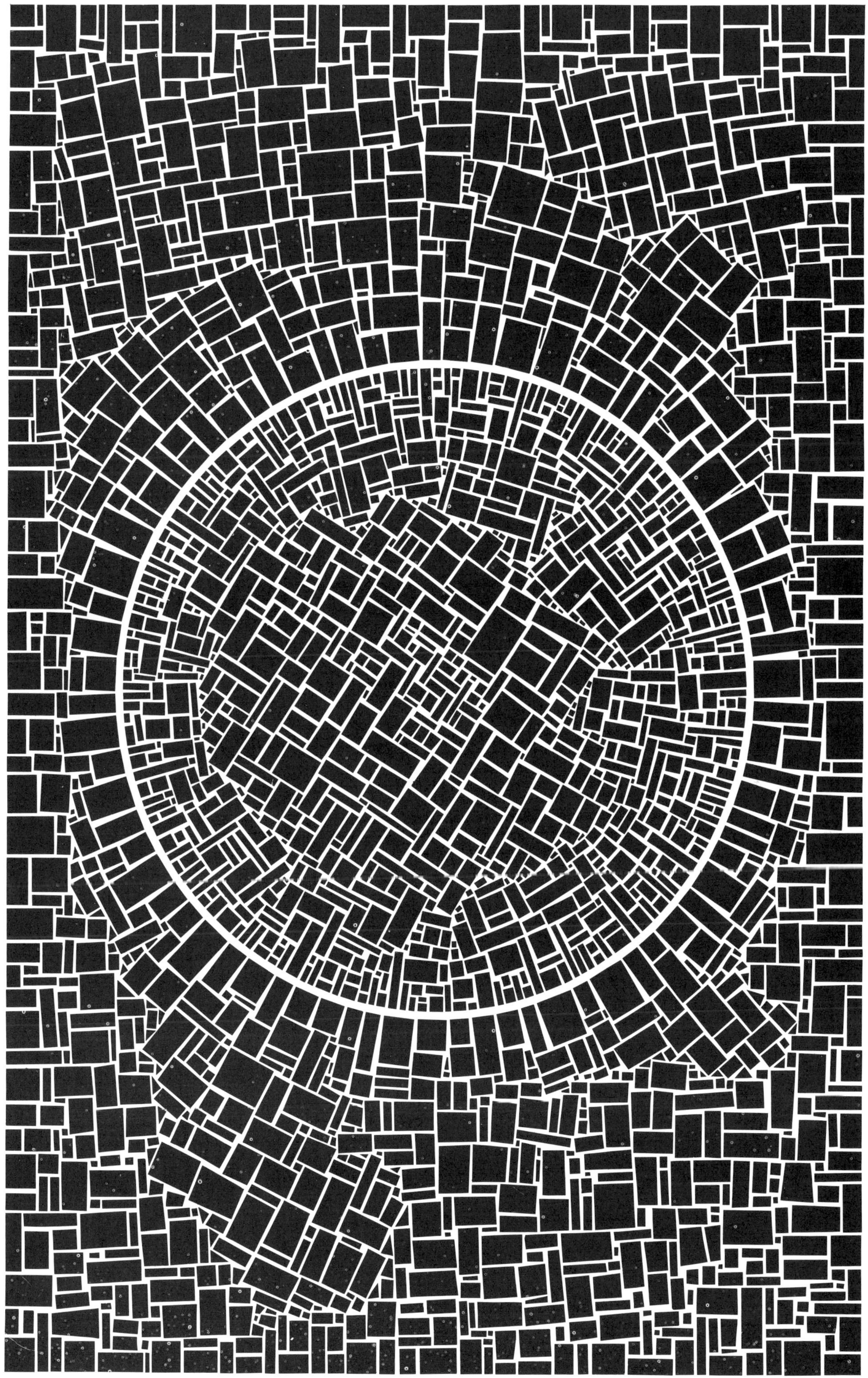

PLATE 21

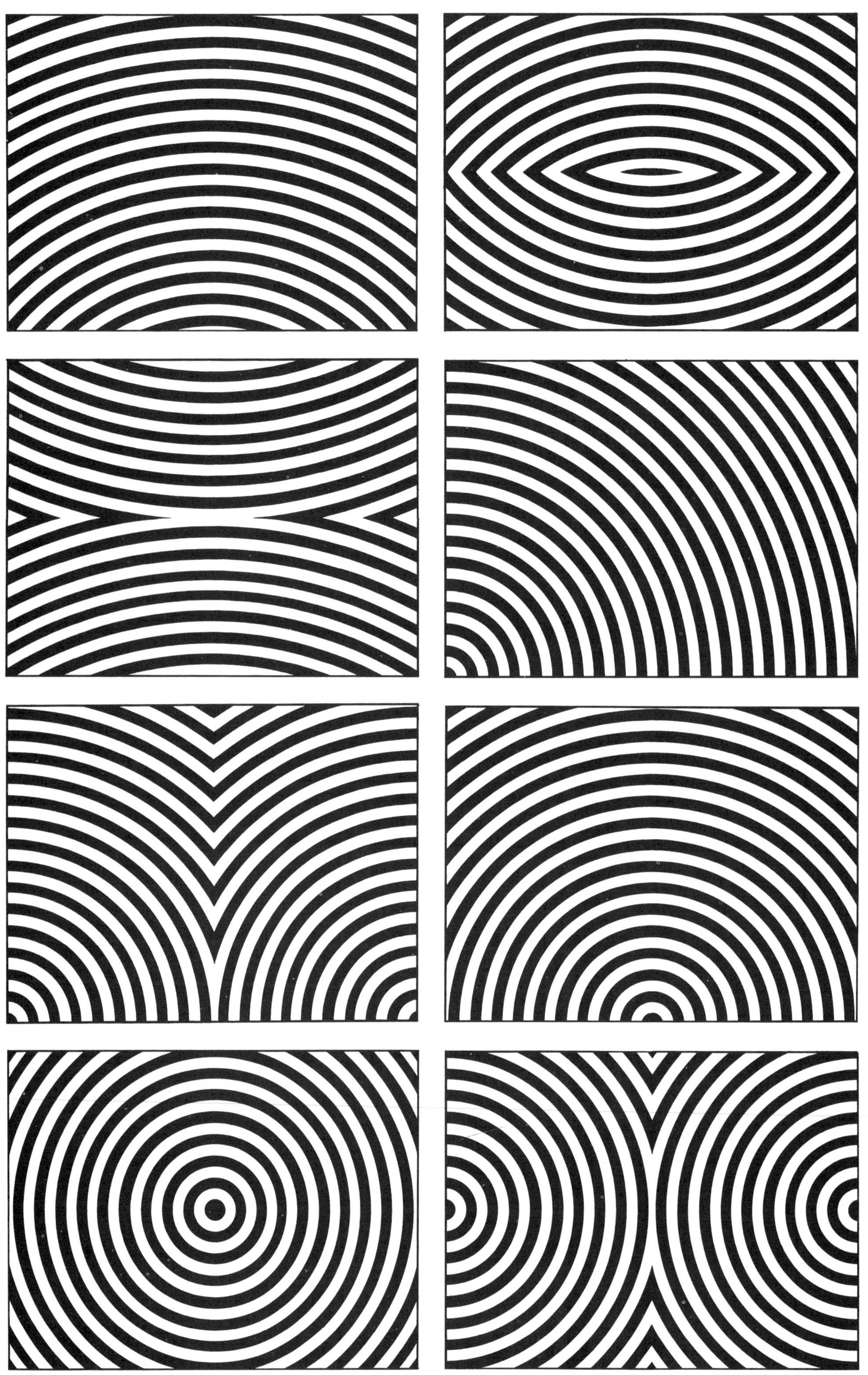

PLATE 22

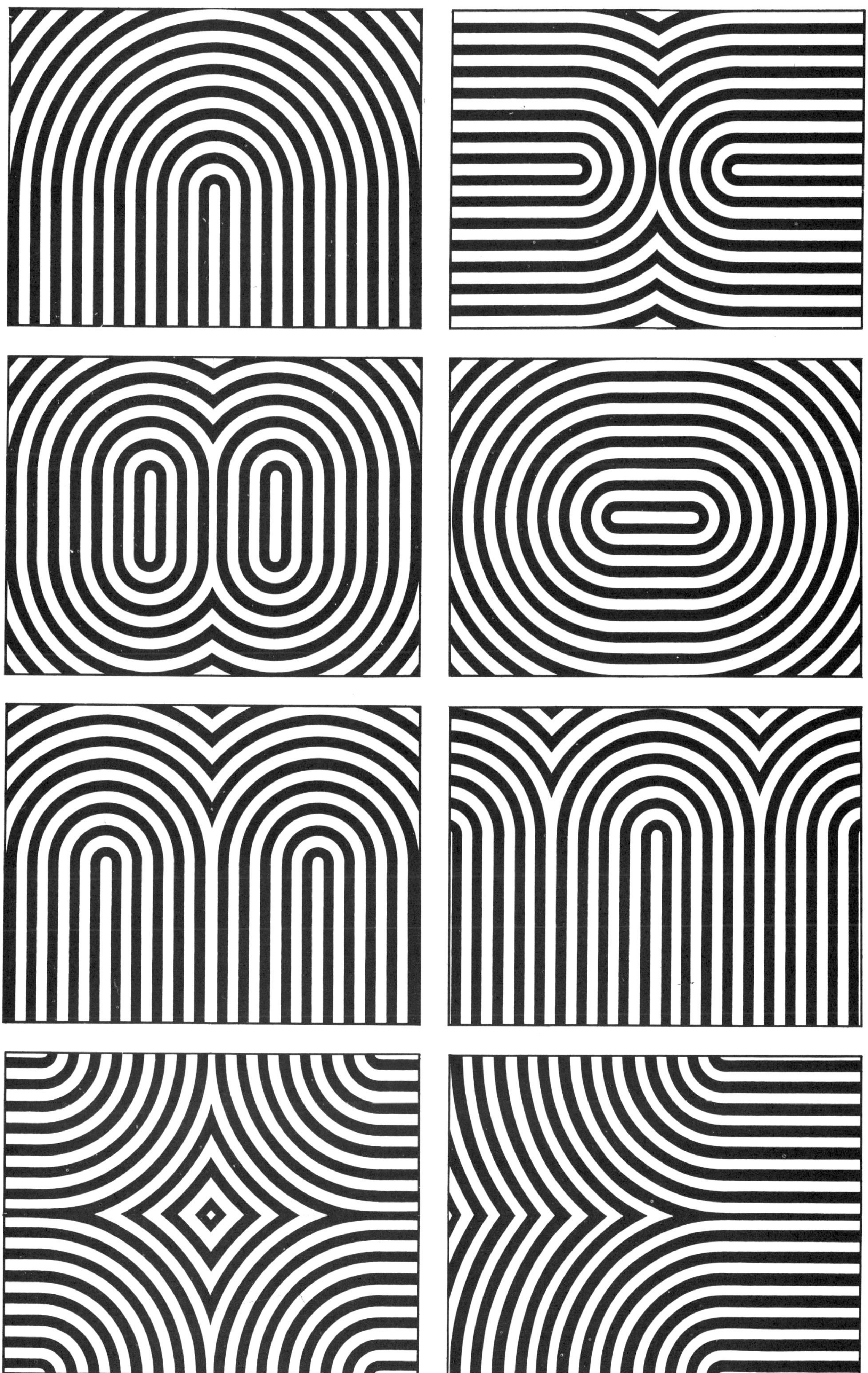

PLATE 23

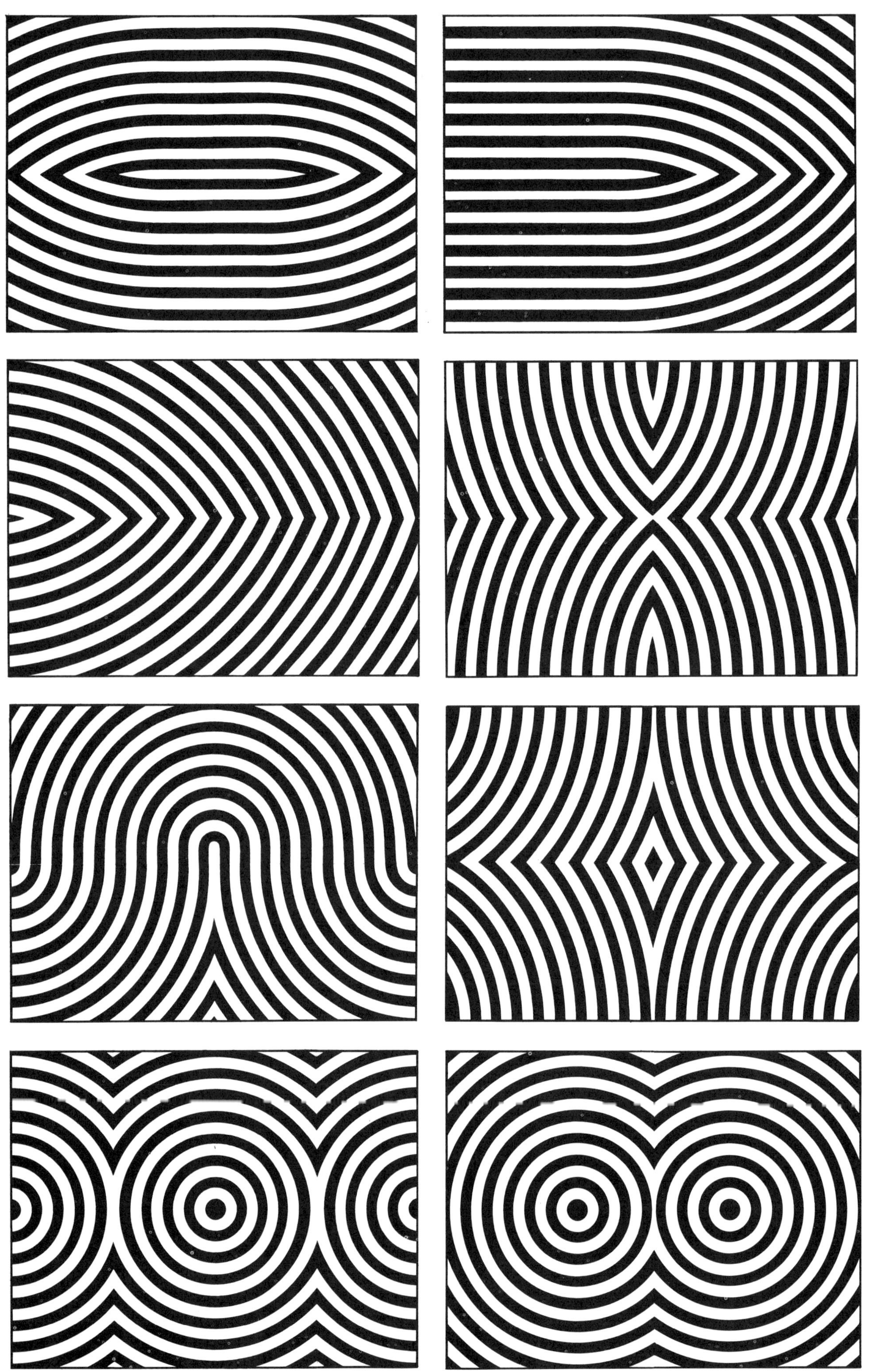

PLATE 24

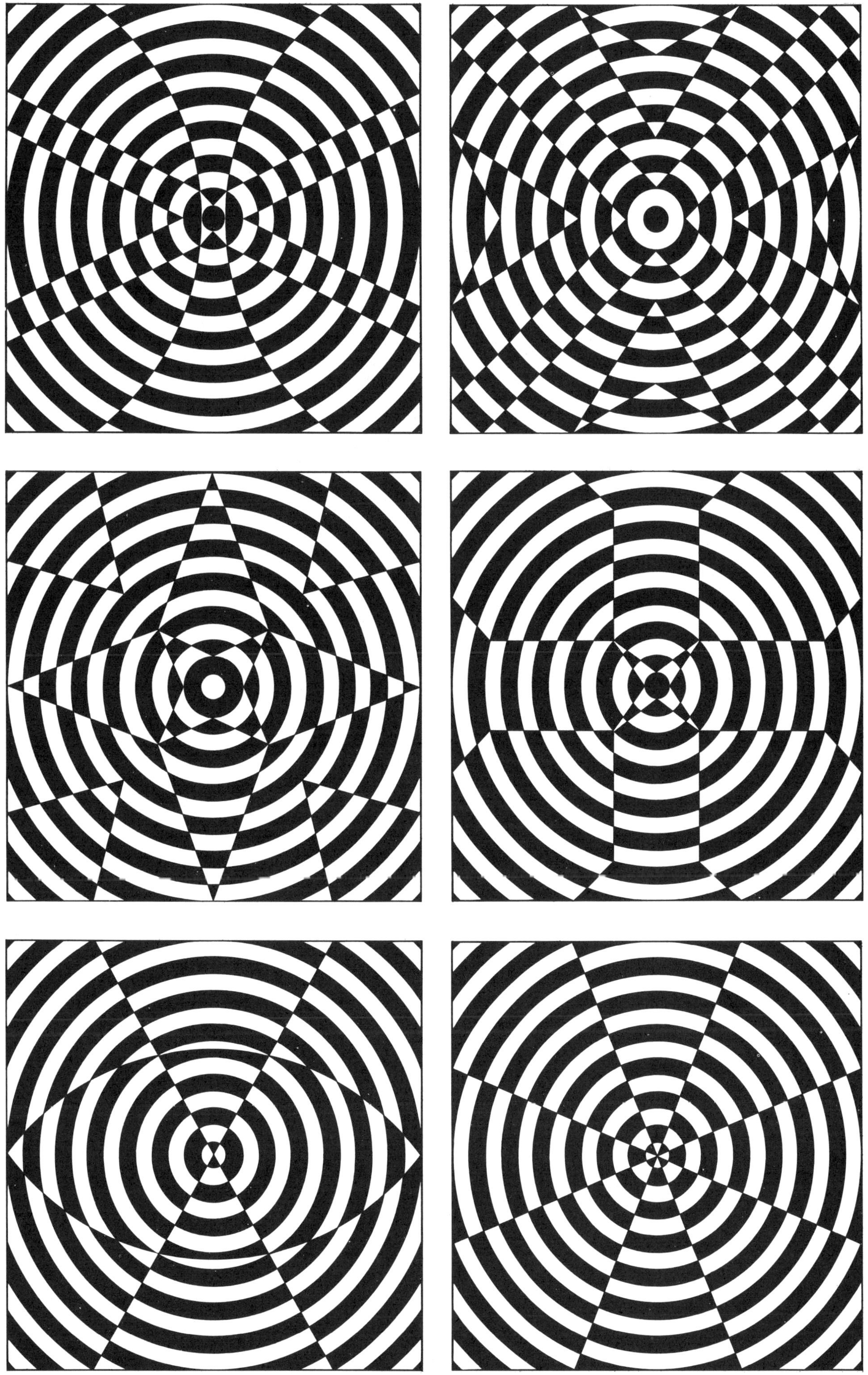

PLATE 25

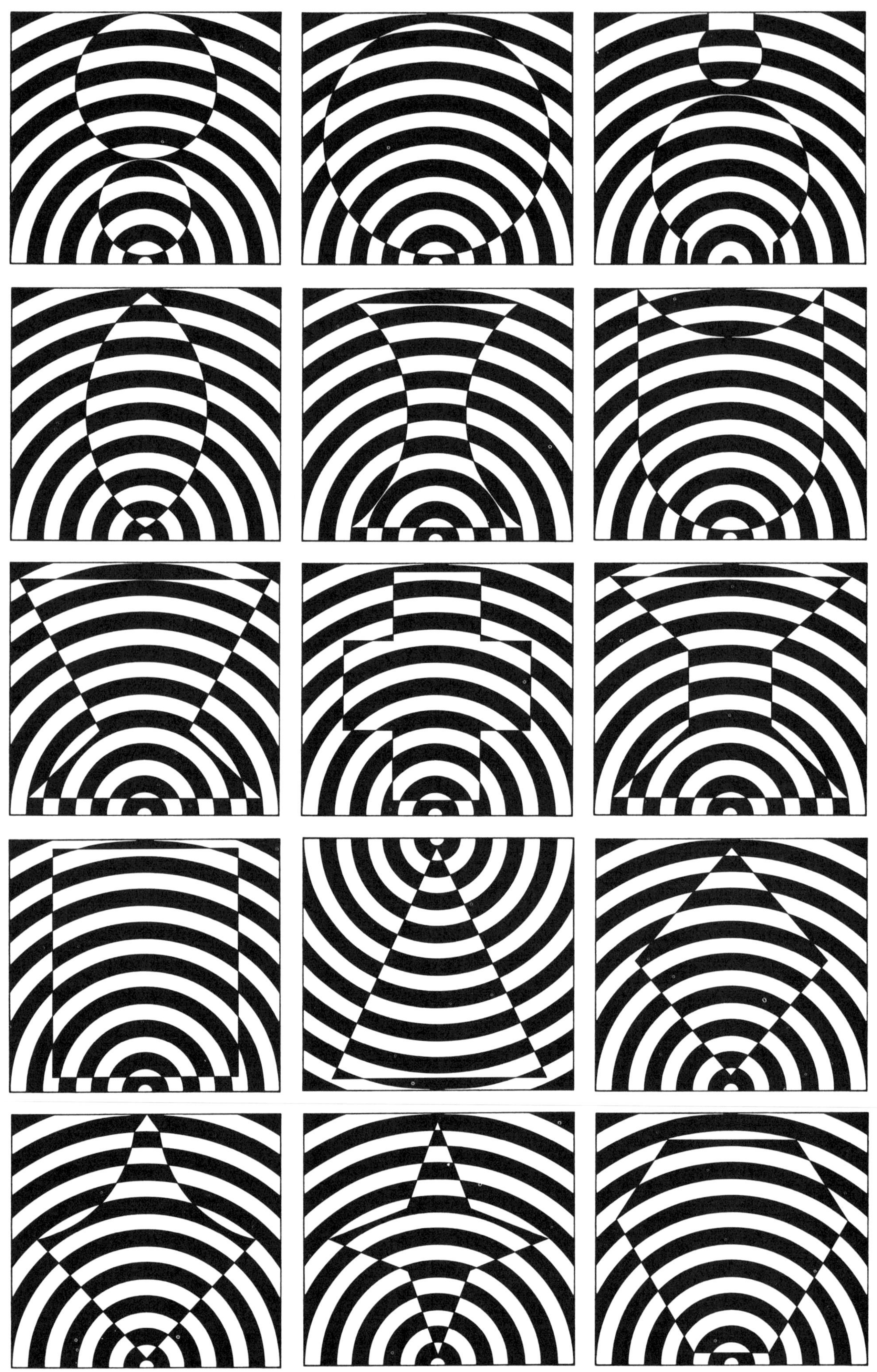

PLATE 26

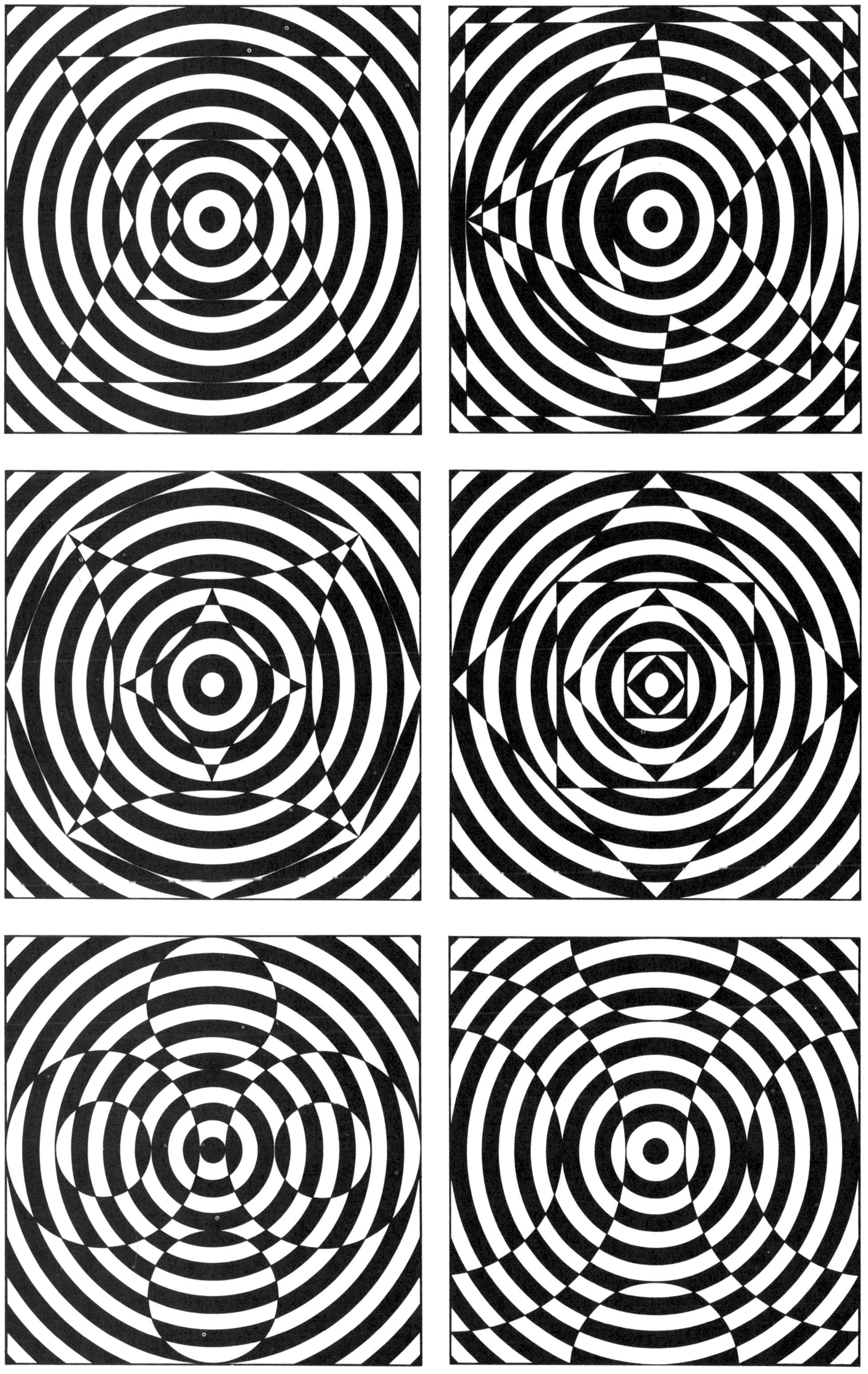

PLATE 27

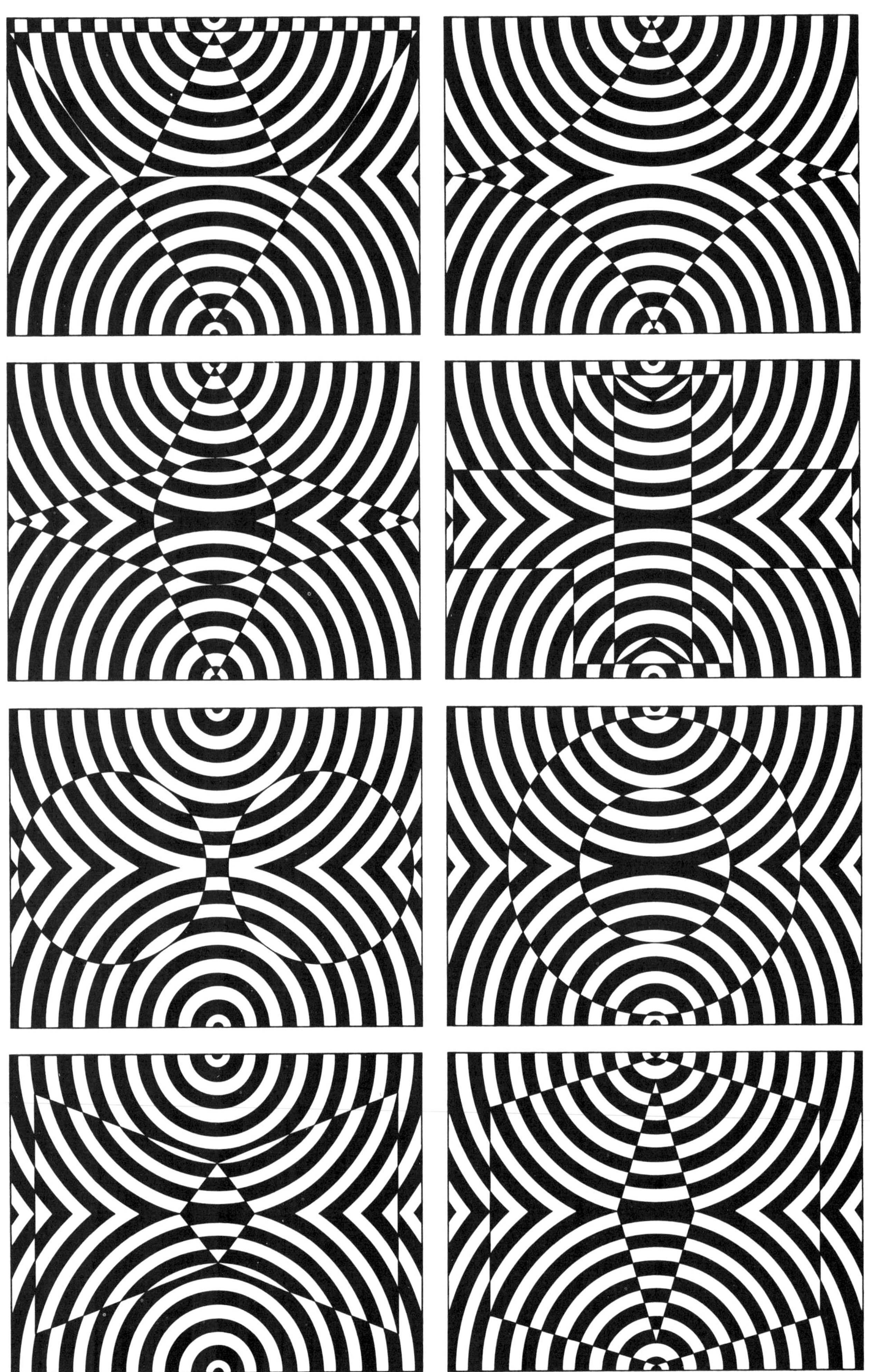

PLATE 28

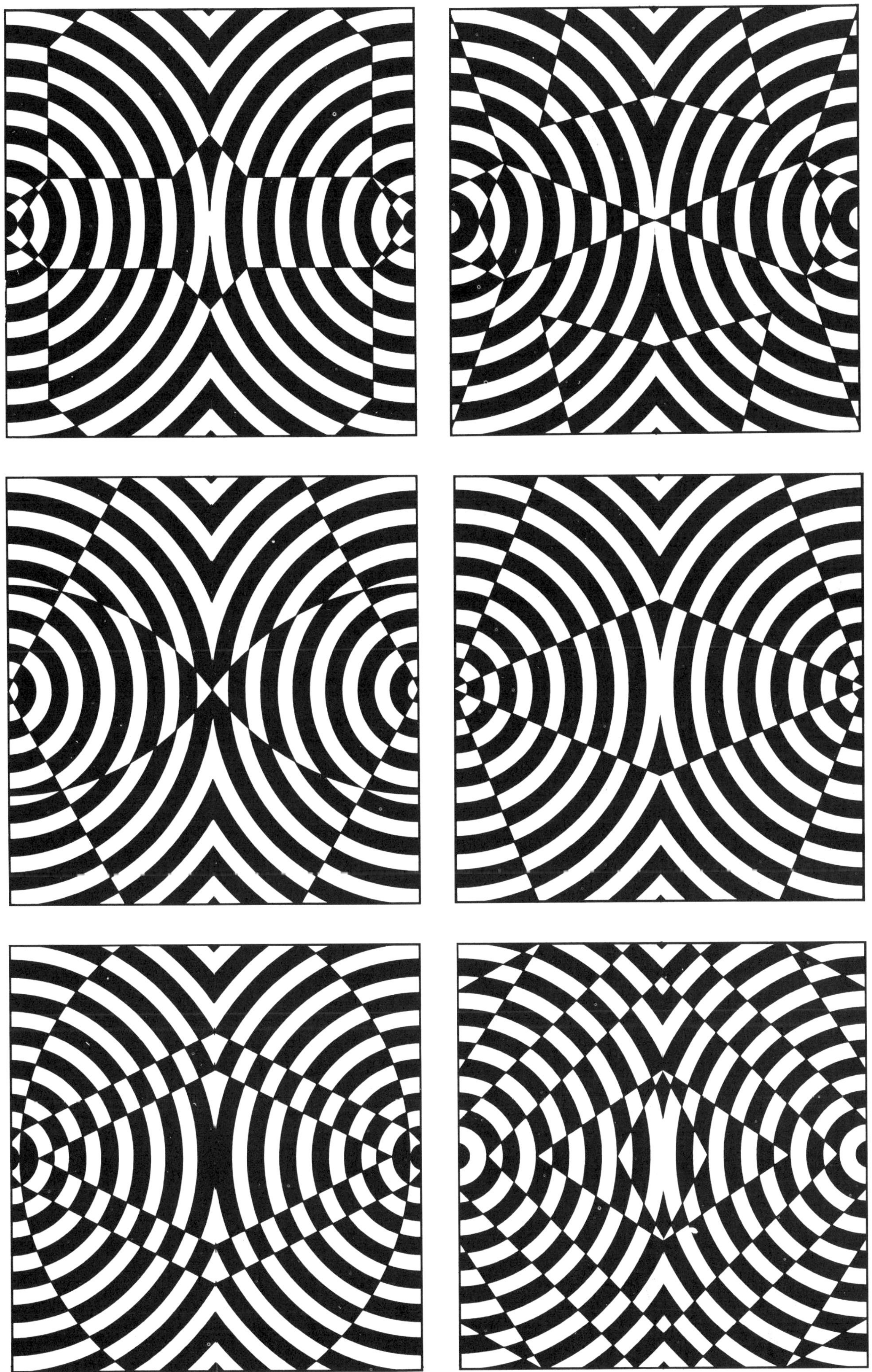

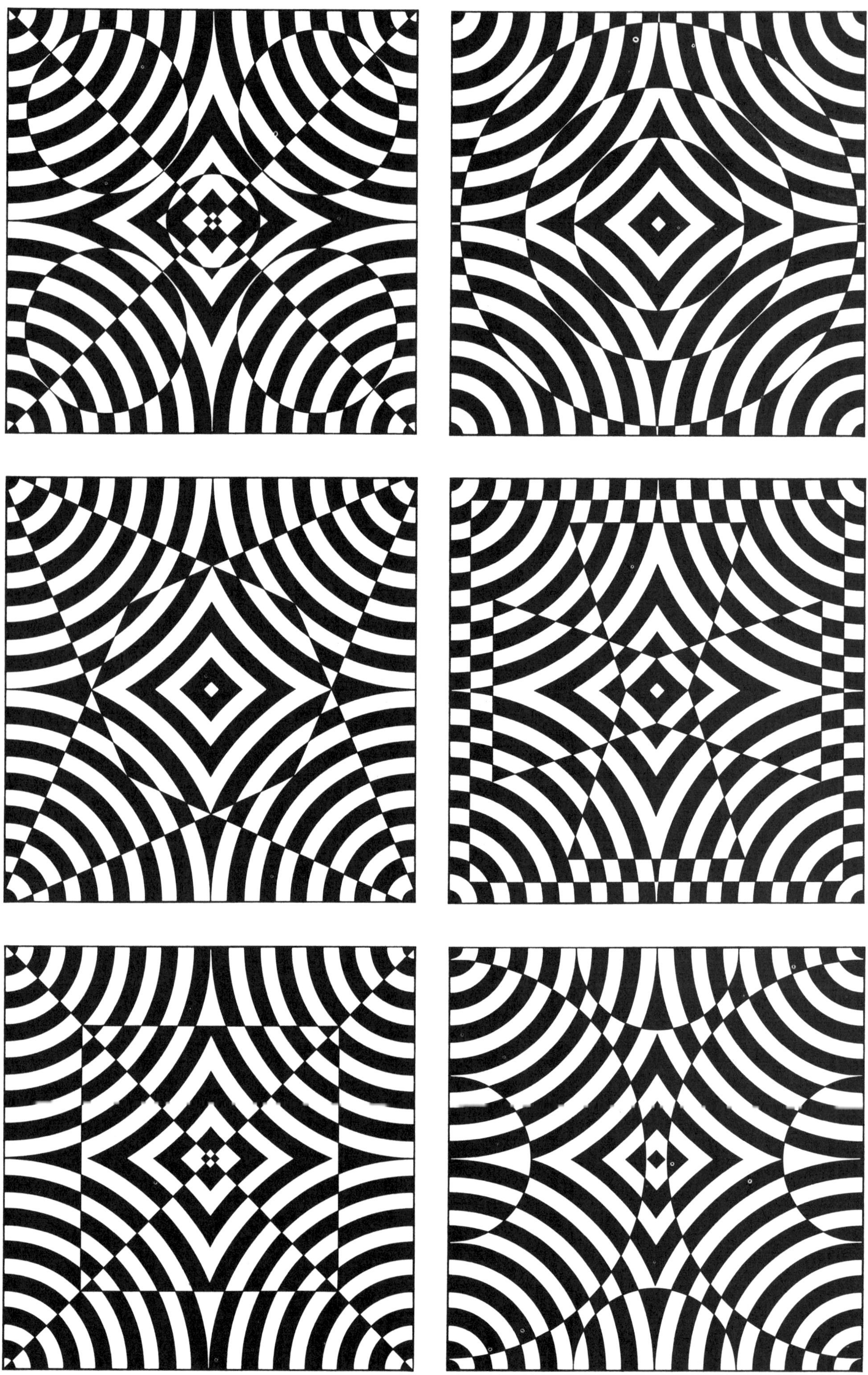

PLATE 30

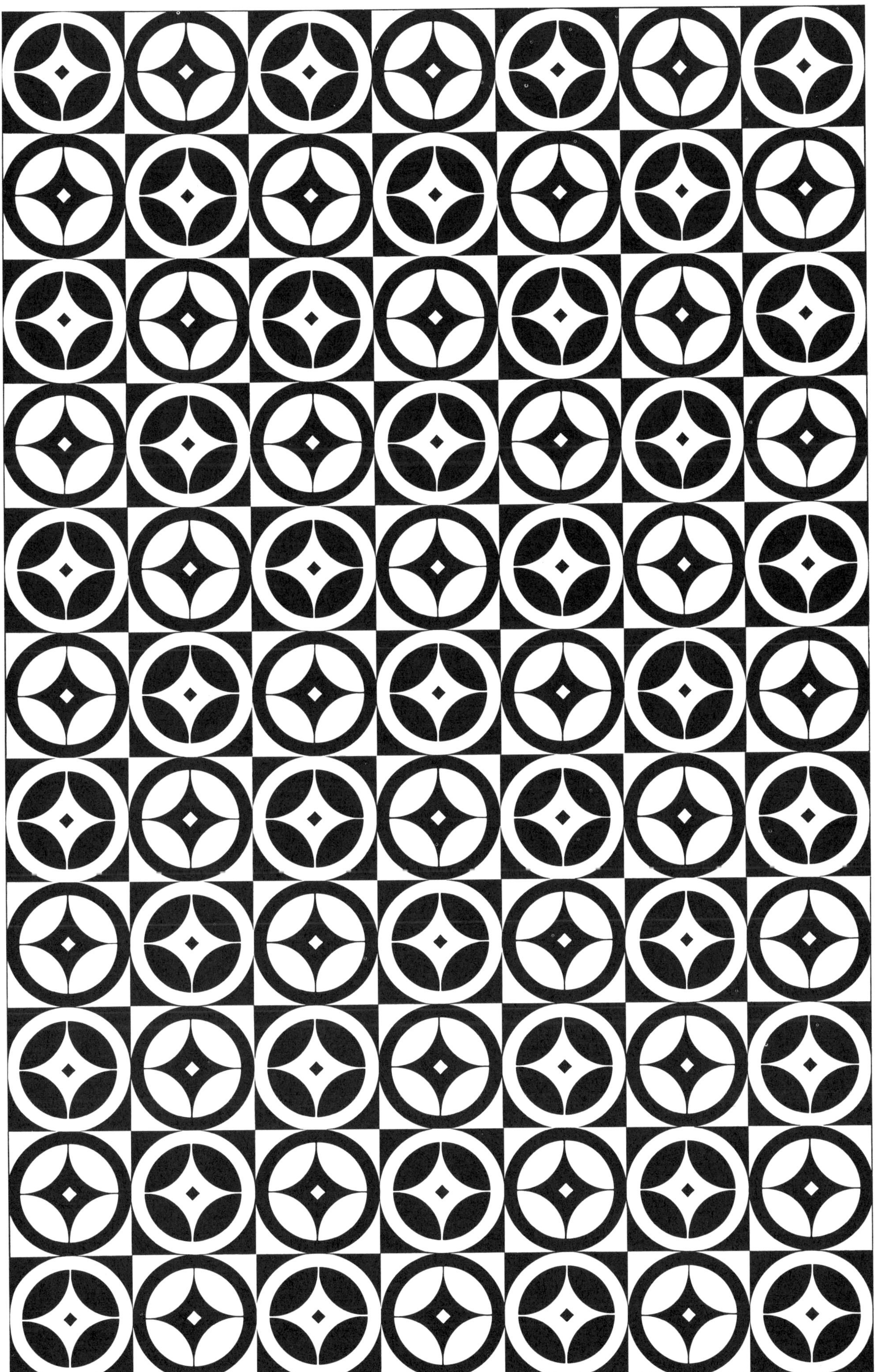

PLATE 31

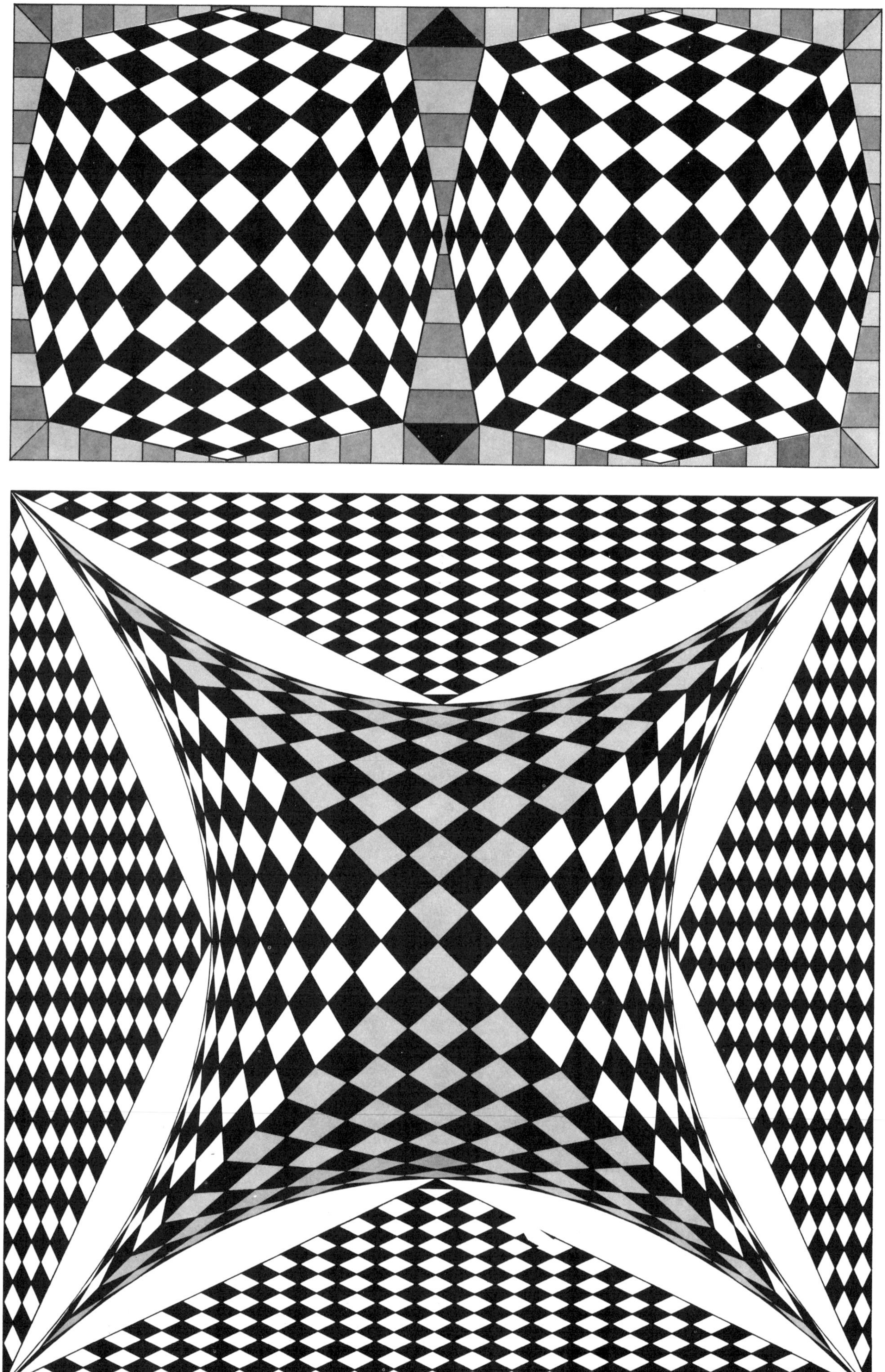

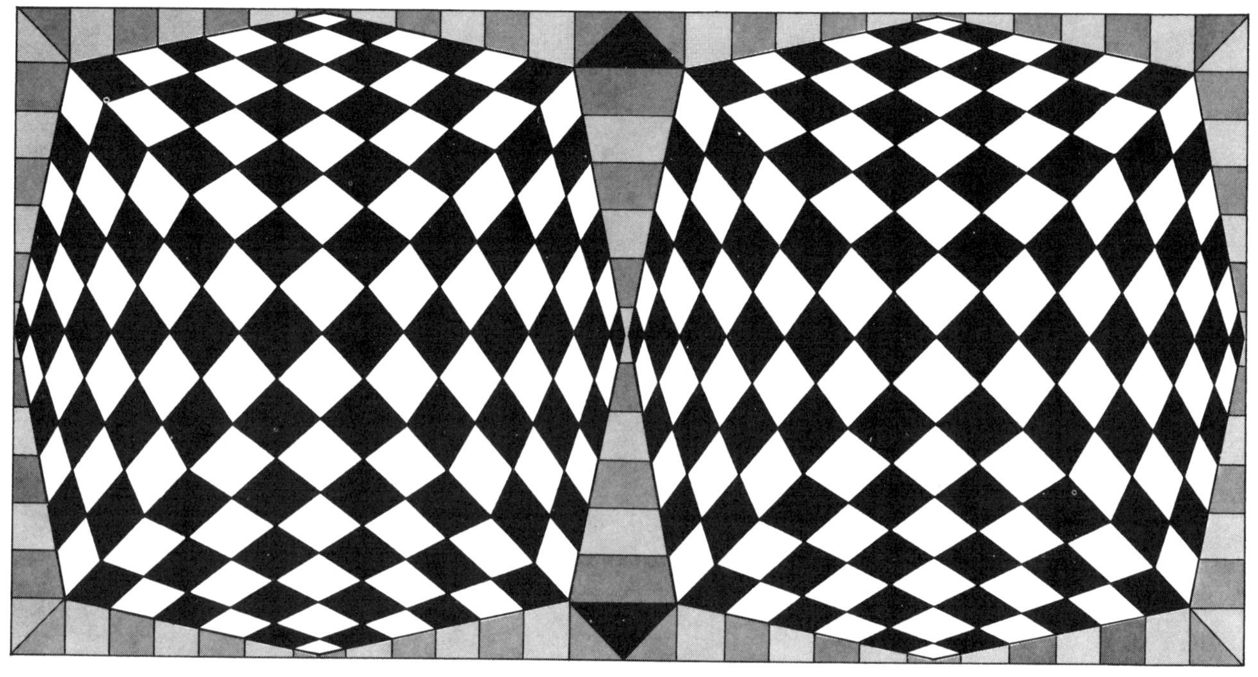

PLATE 32

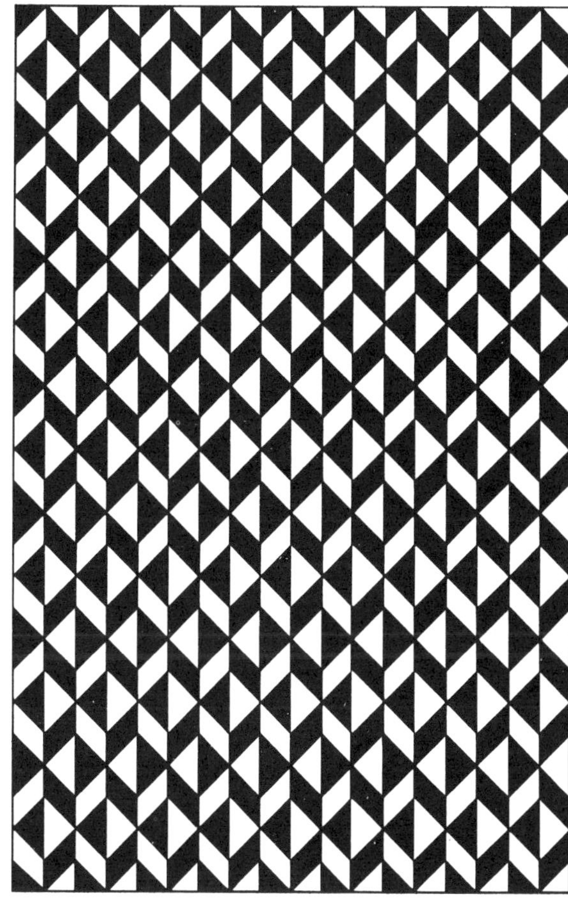

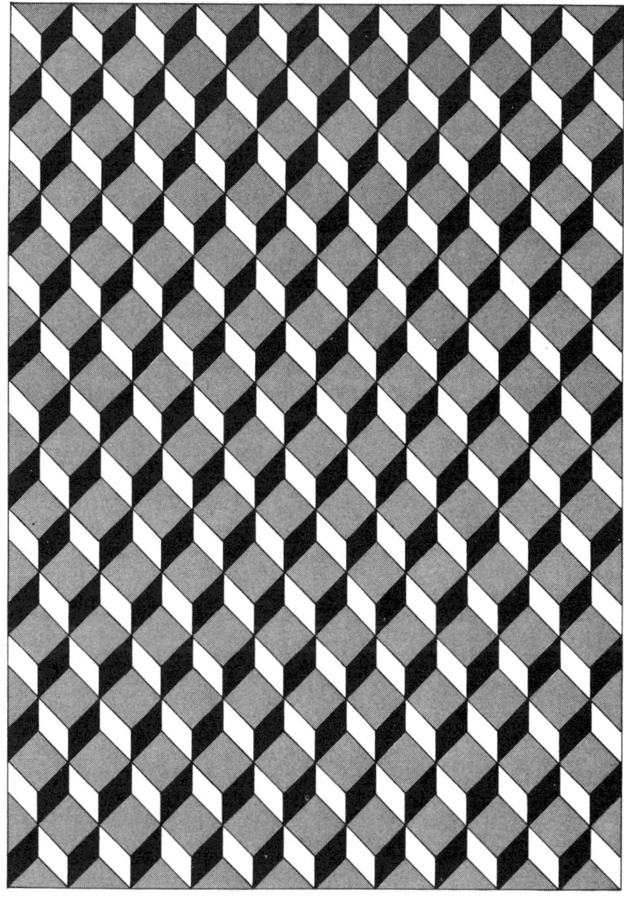

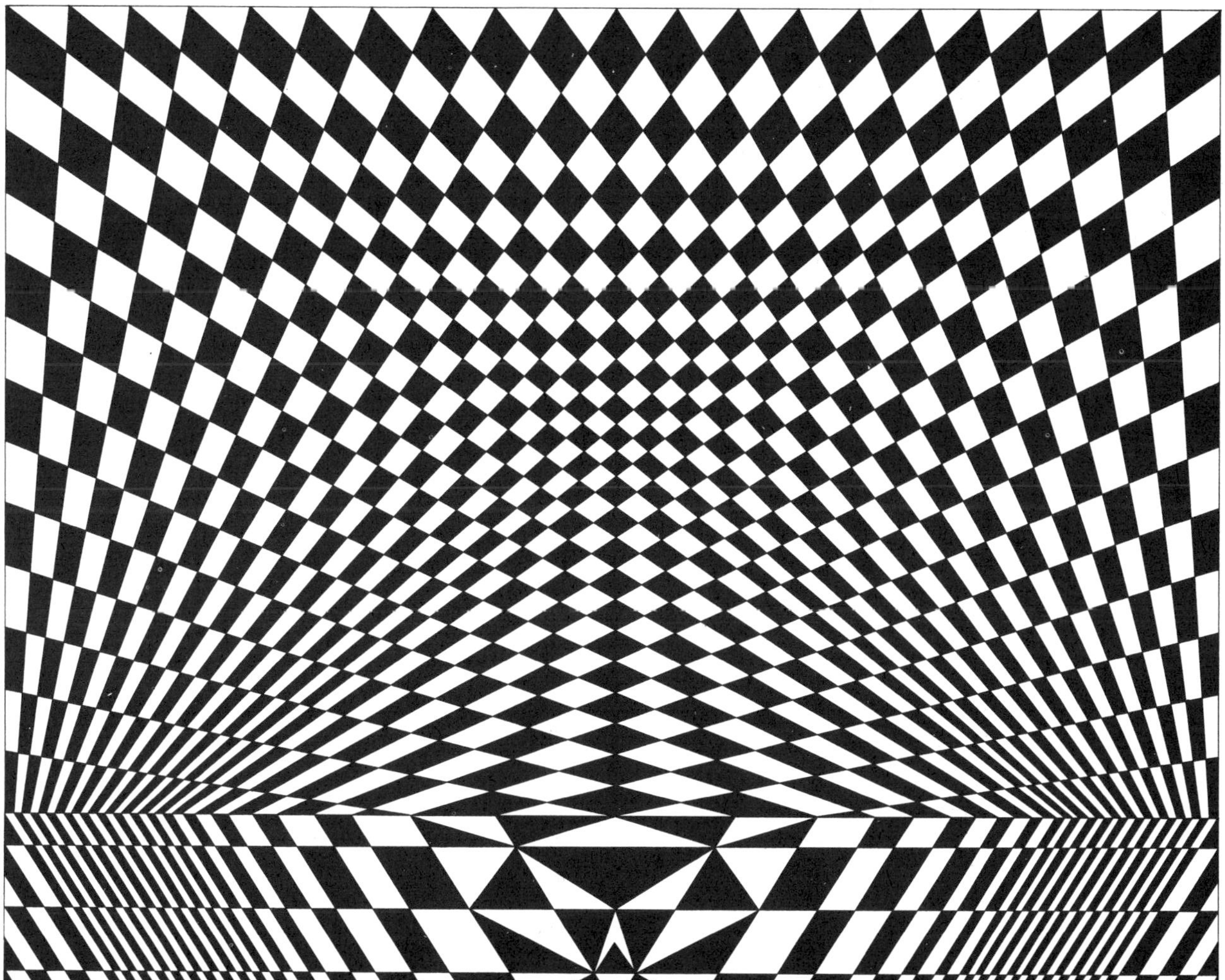

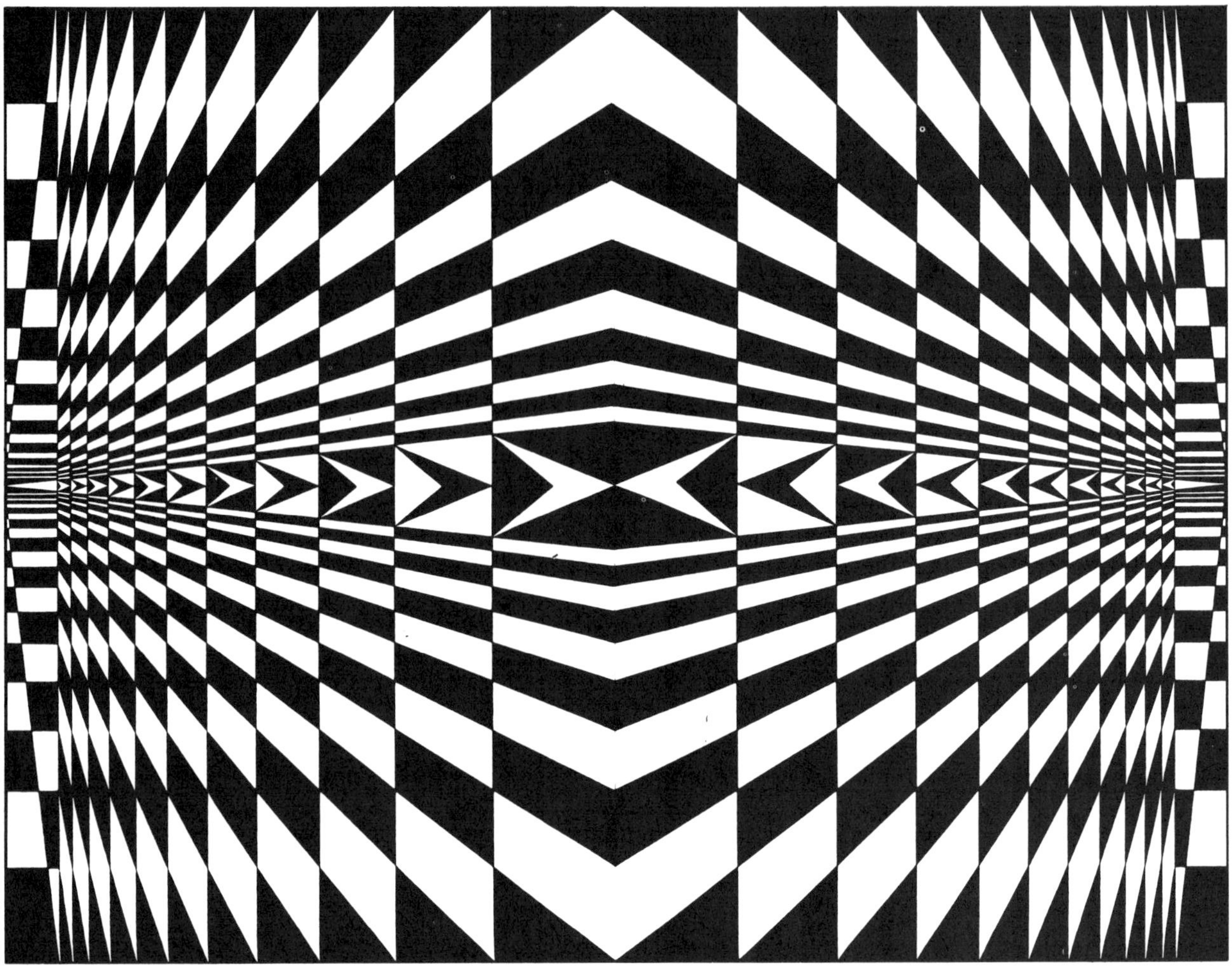

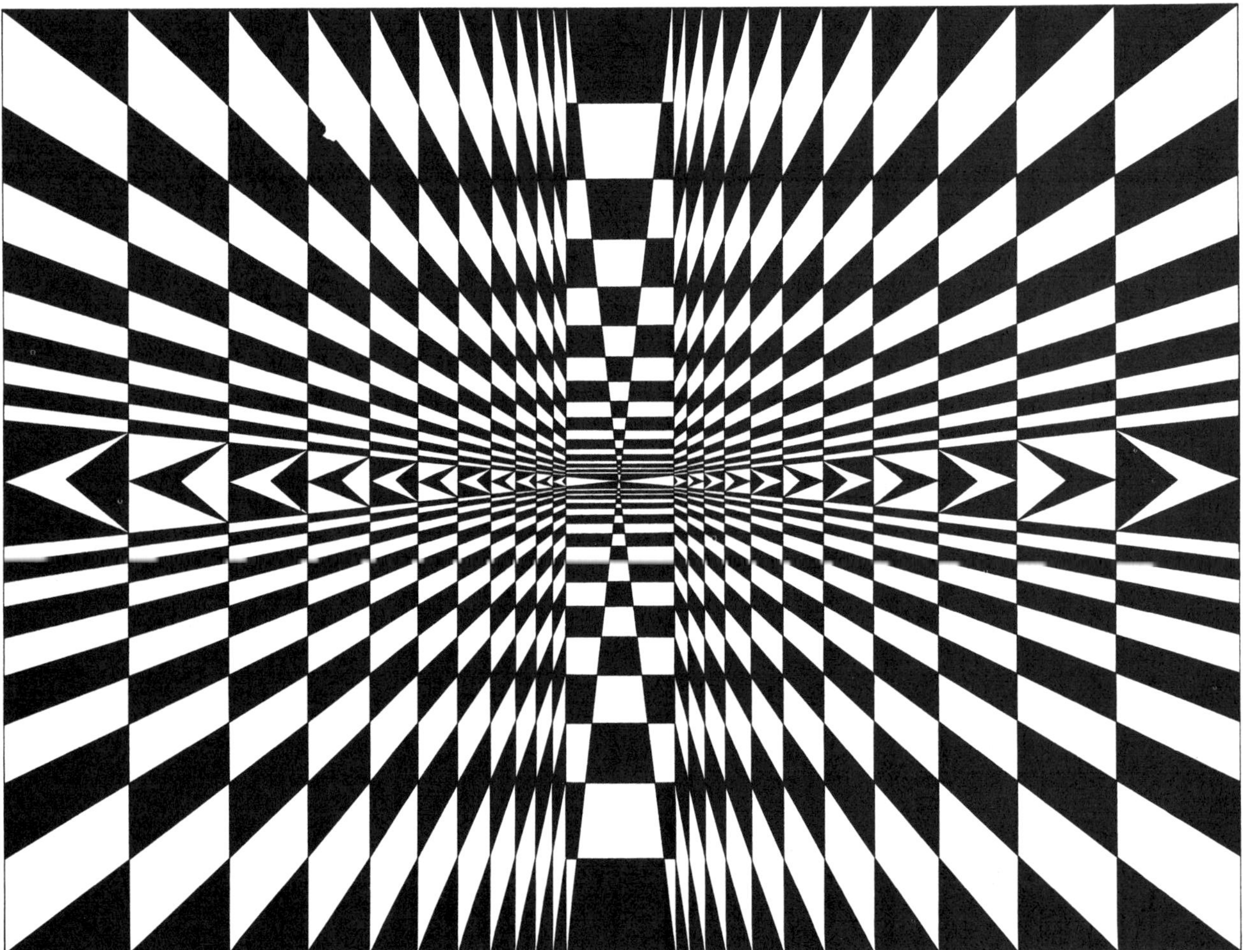

PLATE 34

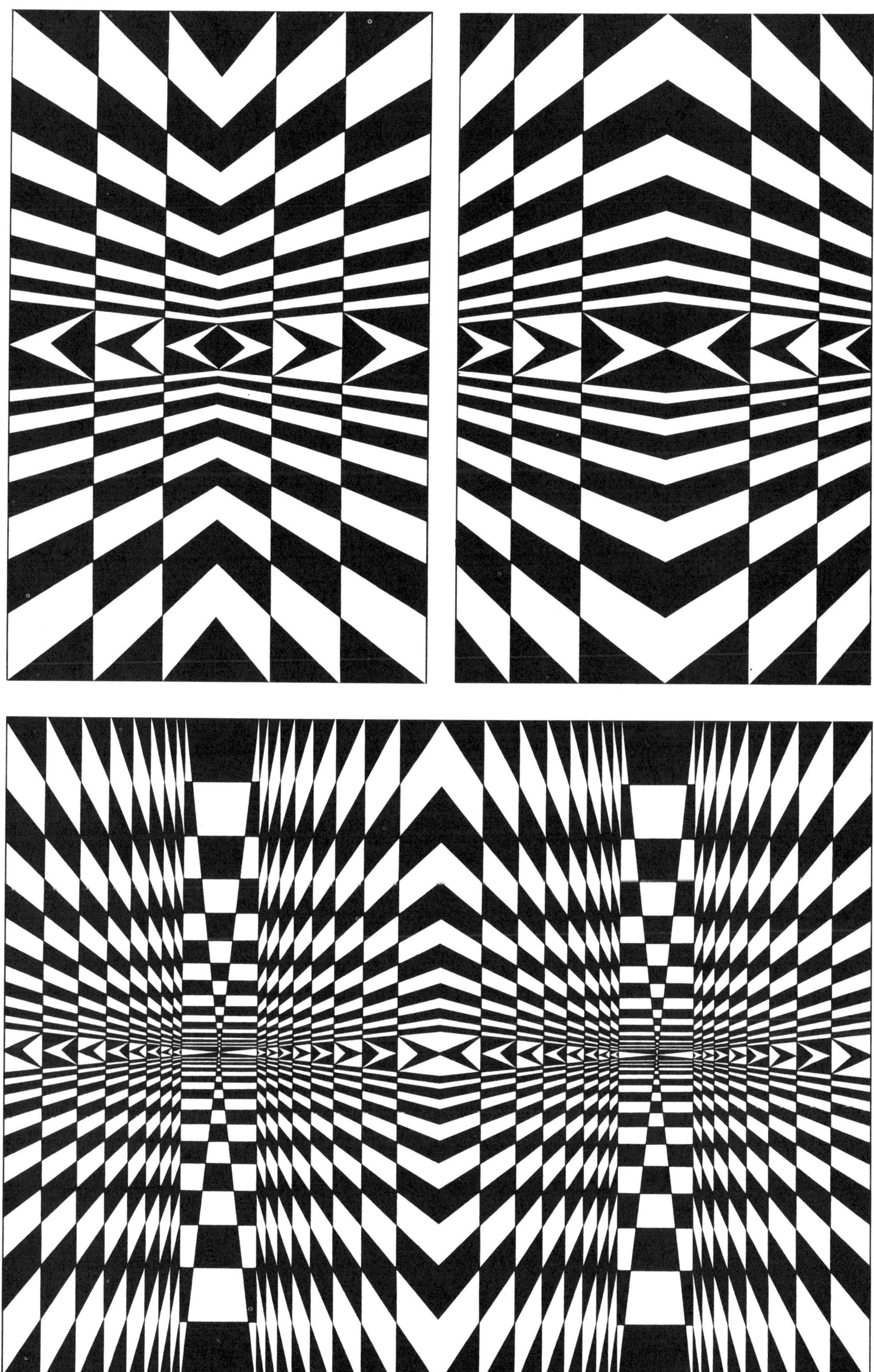

PLATE 35

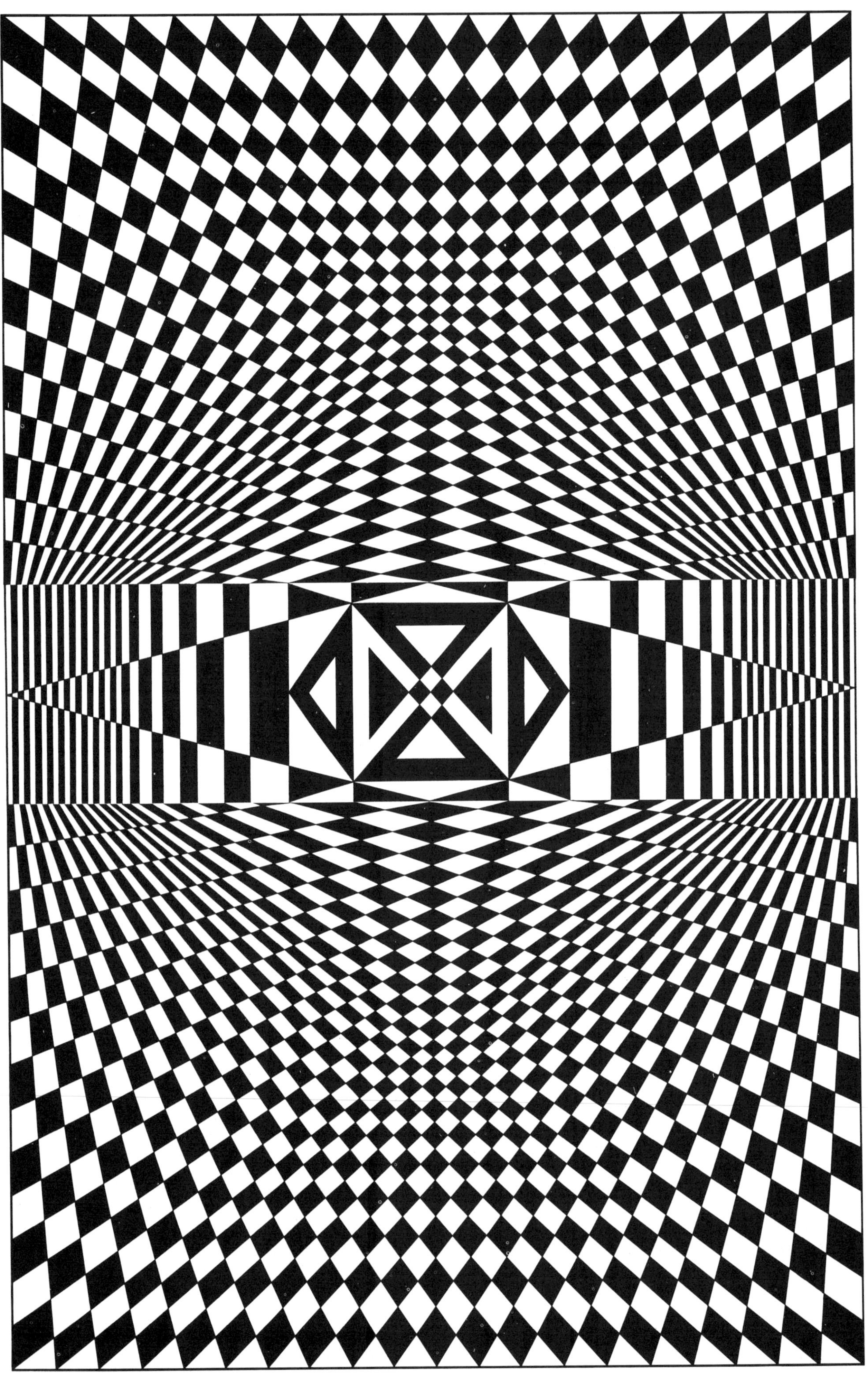

PLATE 36

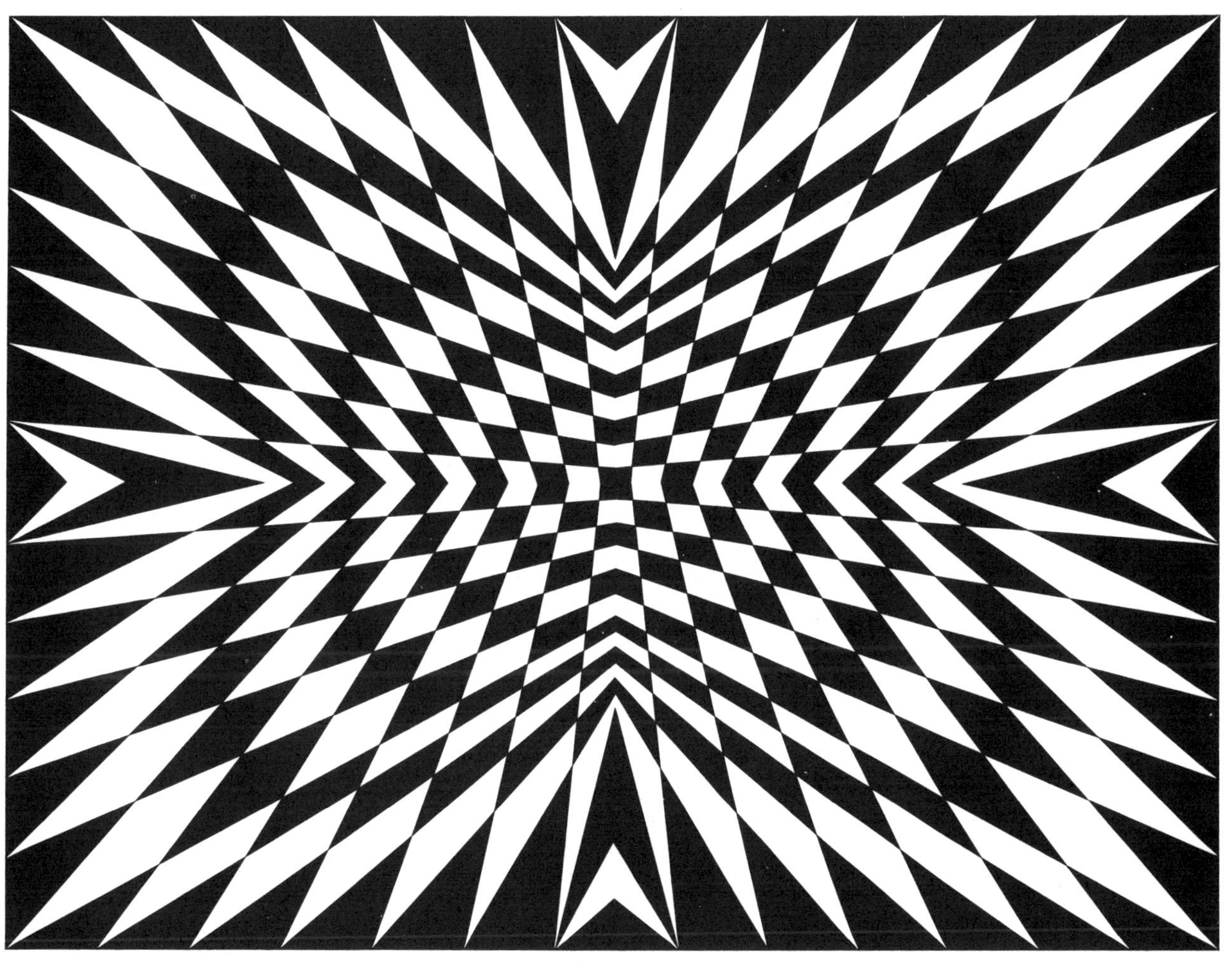

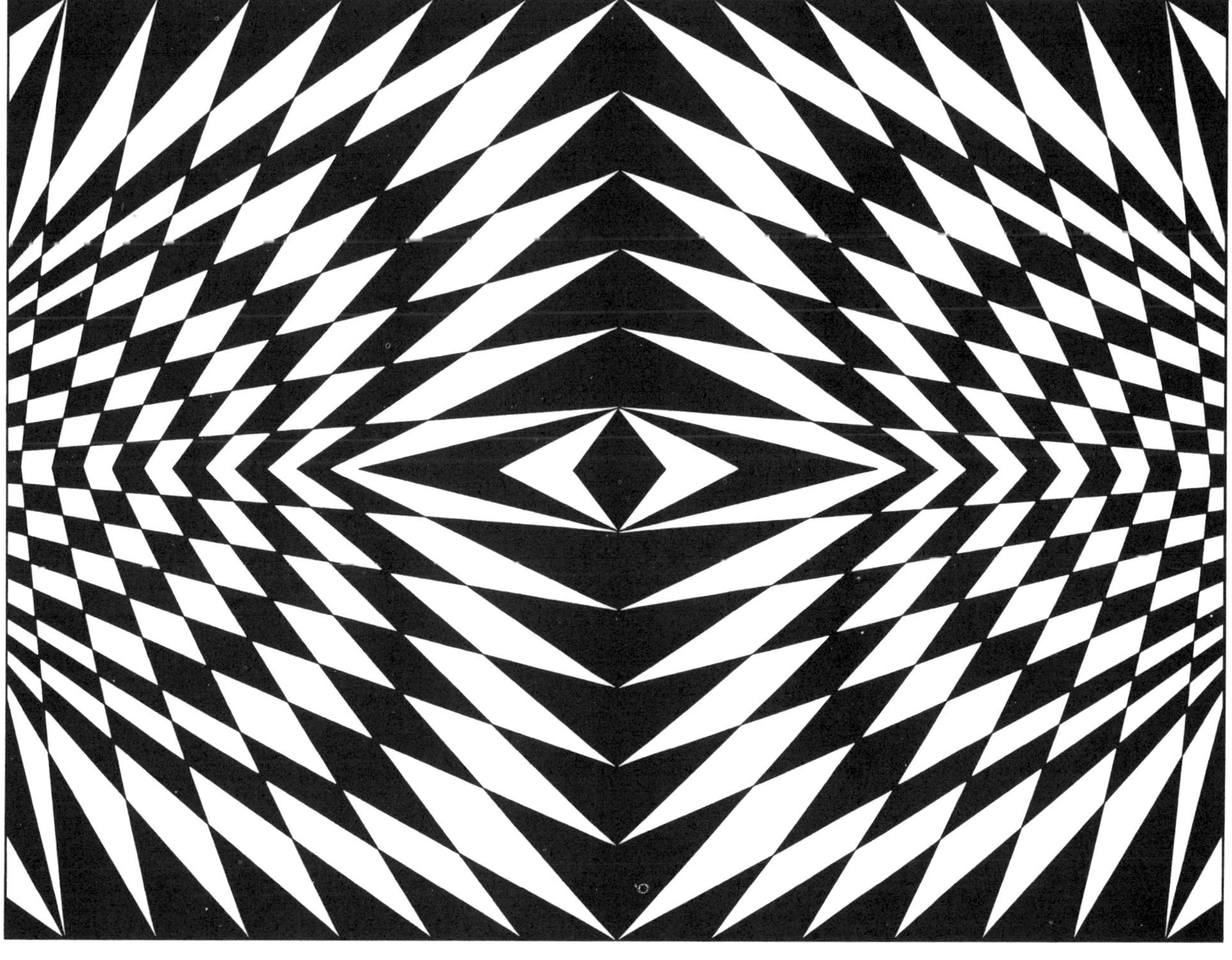

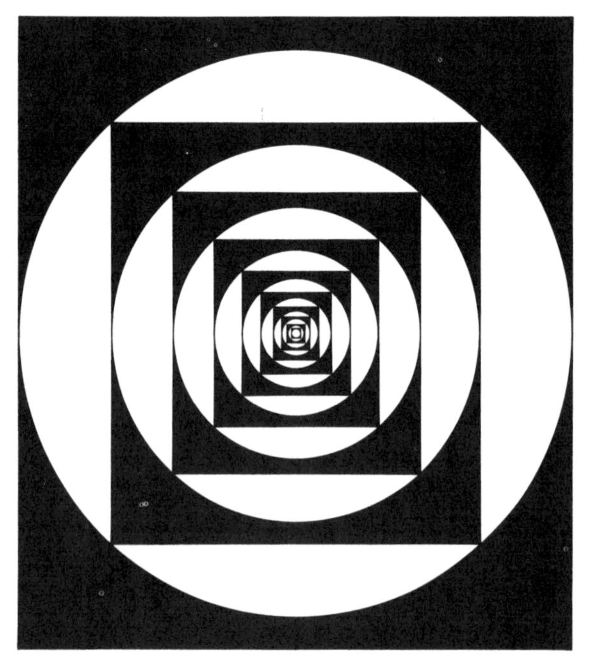

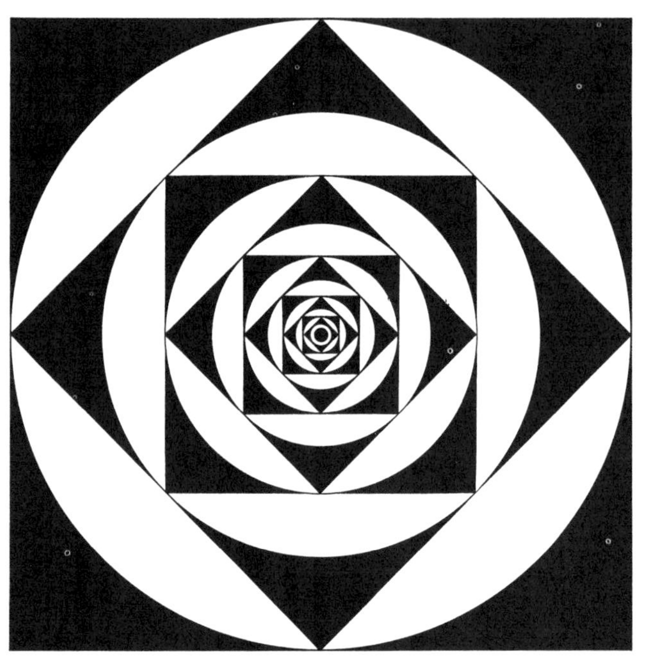

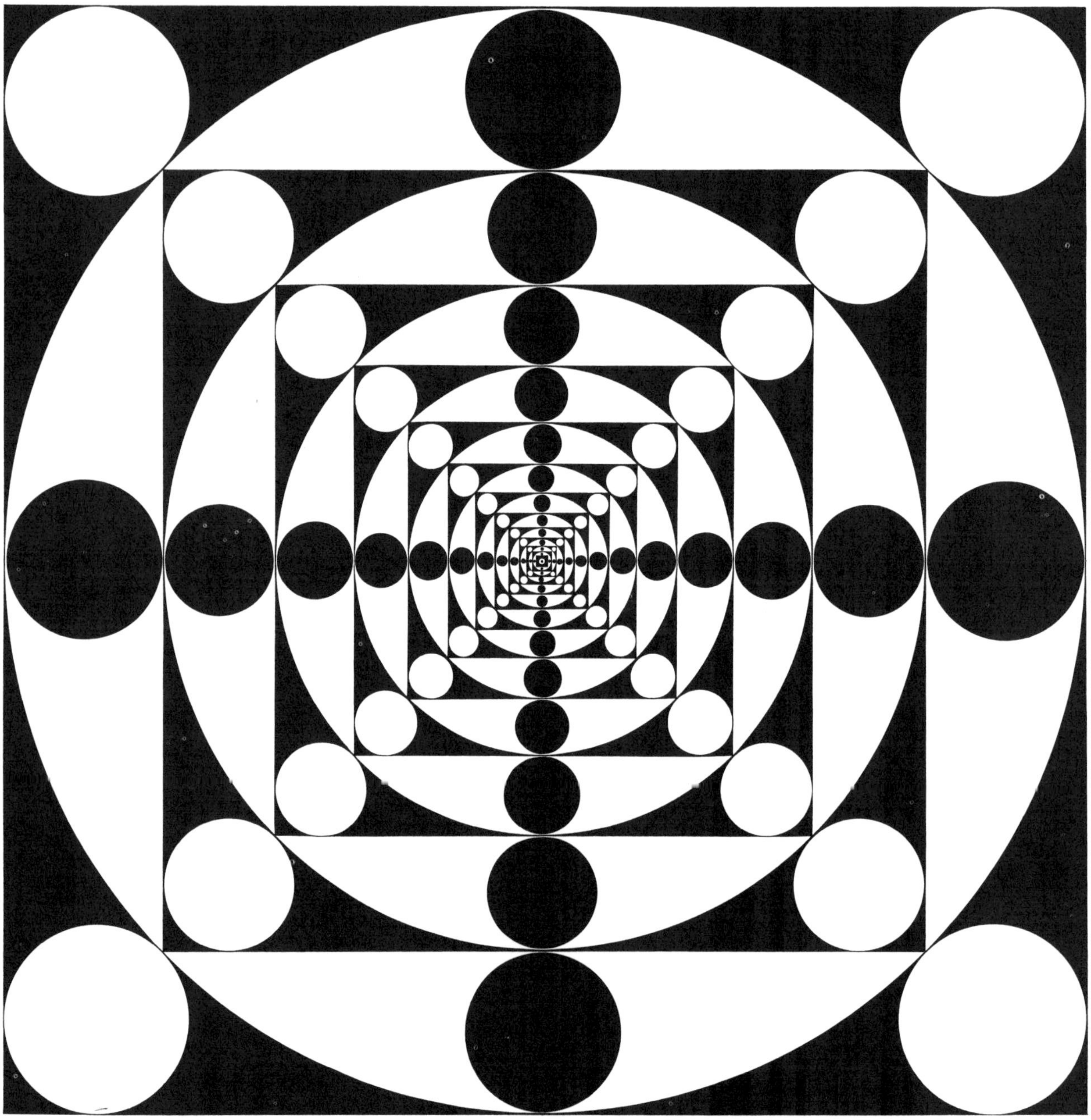

PLATE 38

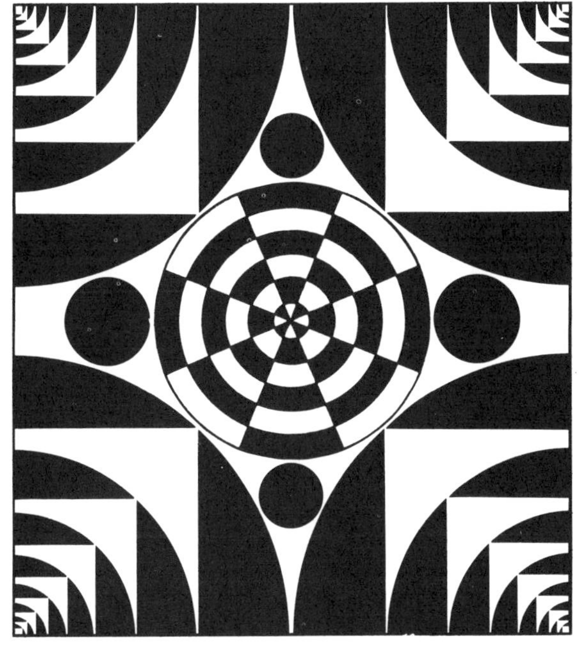

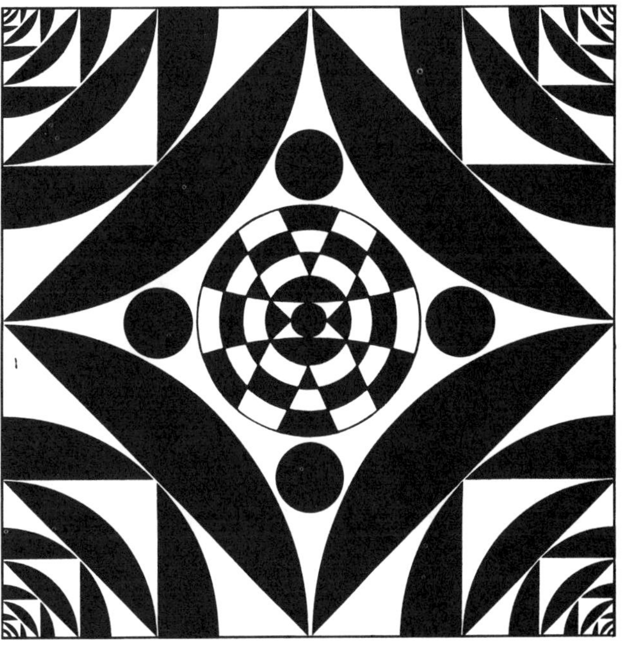

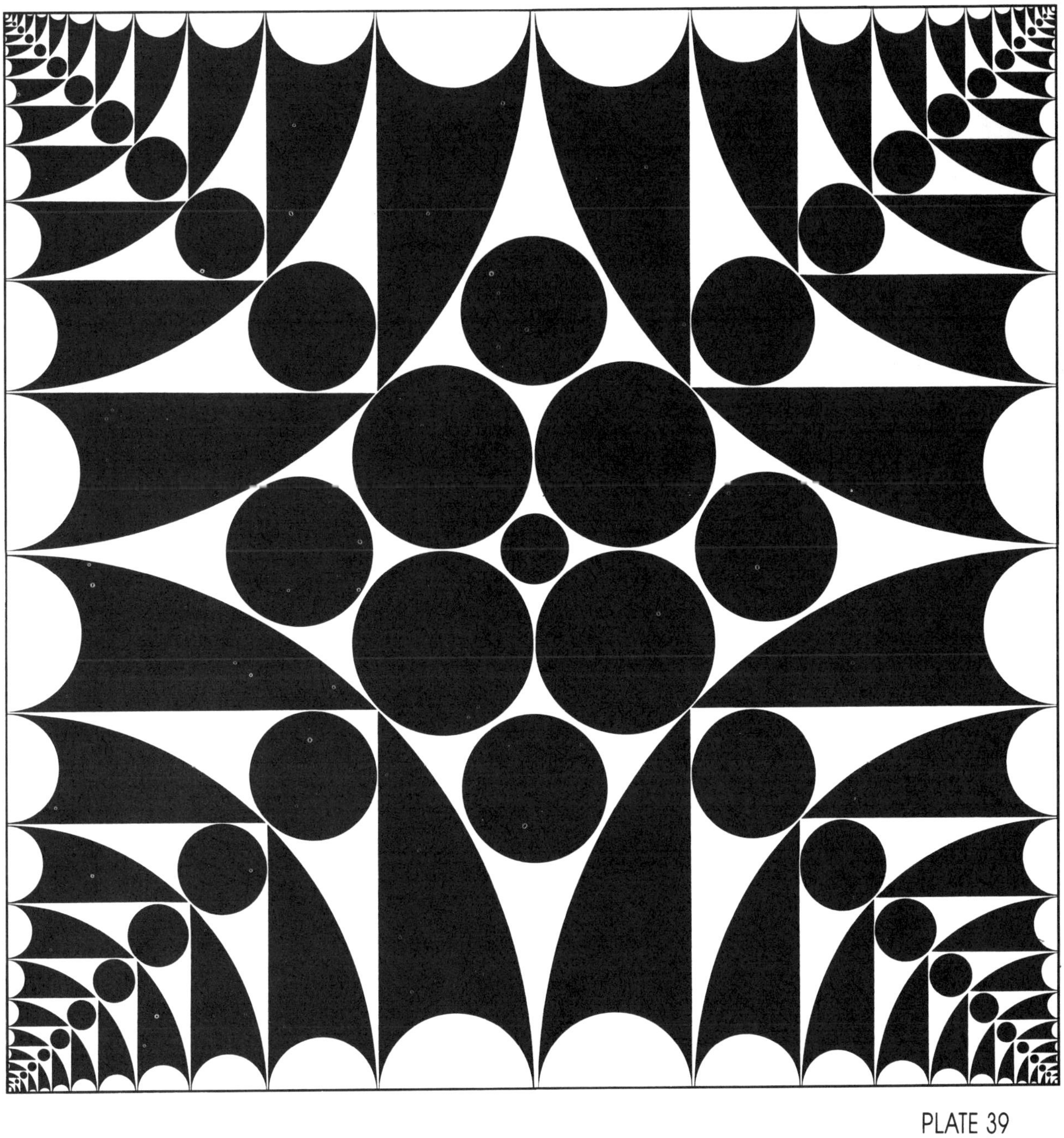

PLATE 39

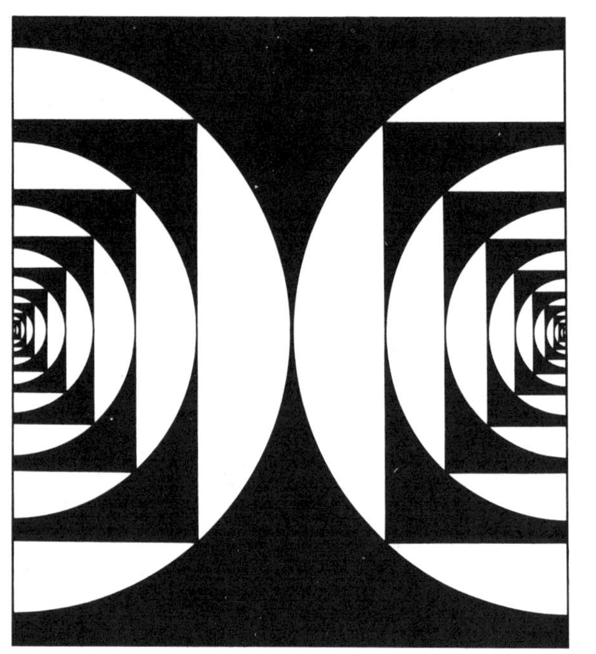

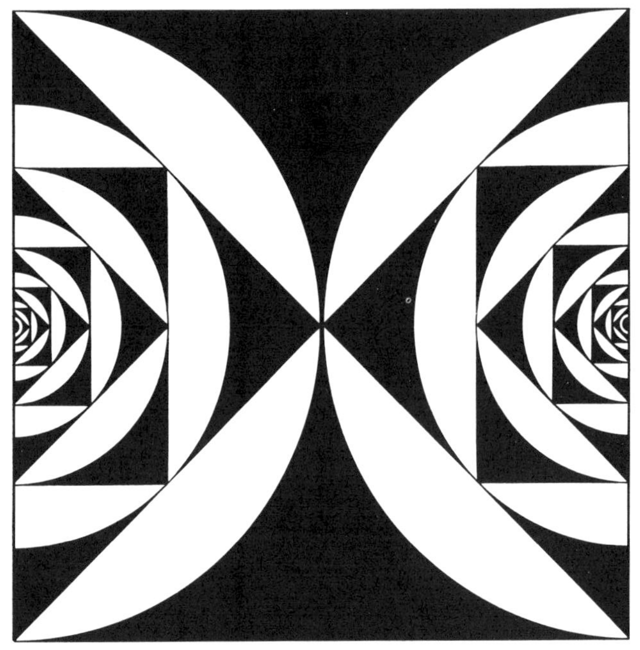

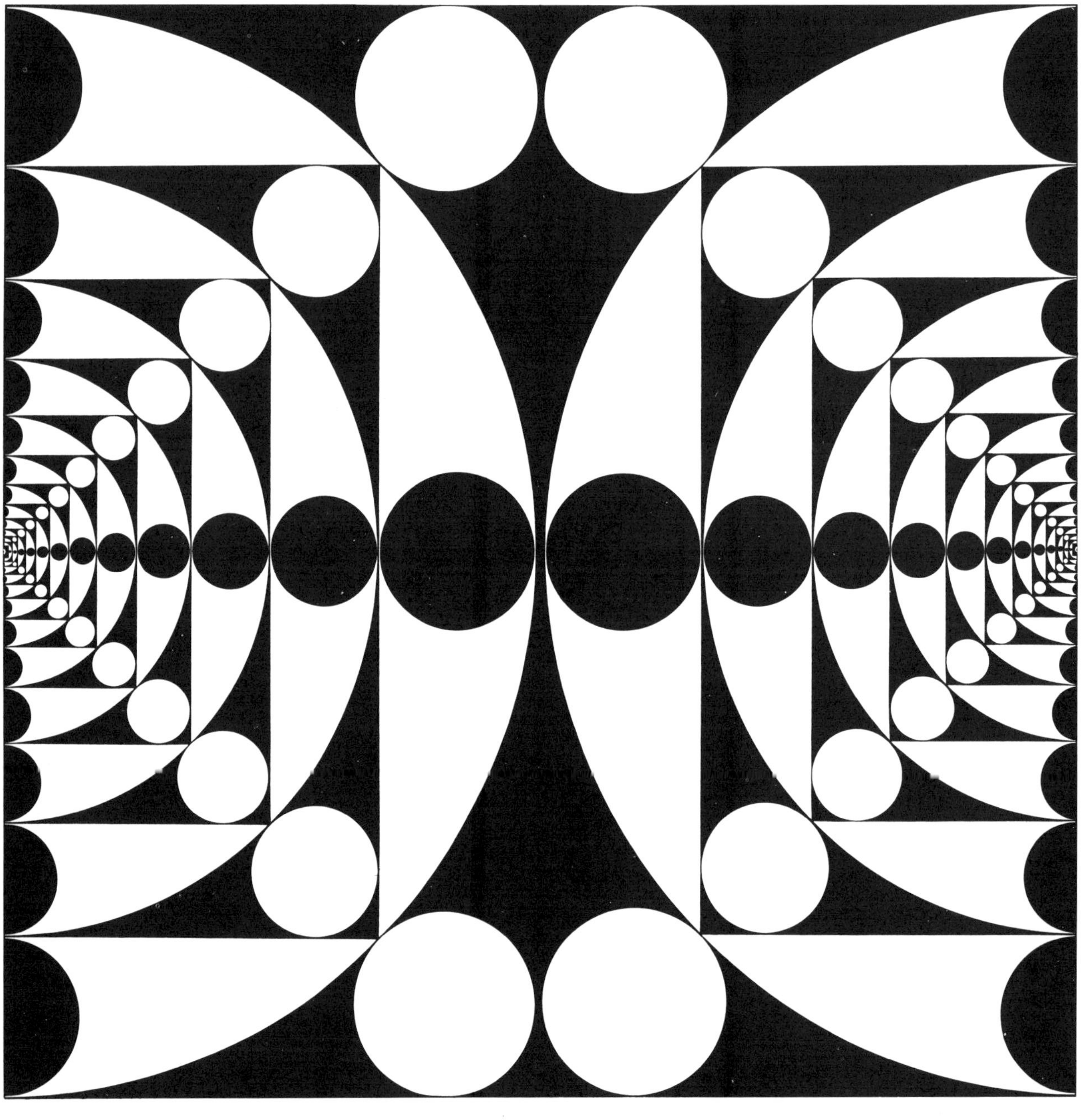

PLATE 40

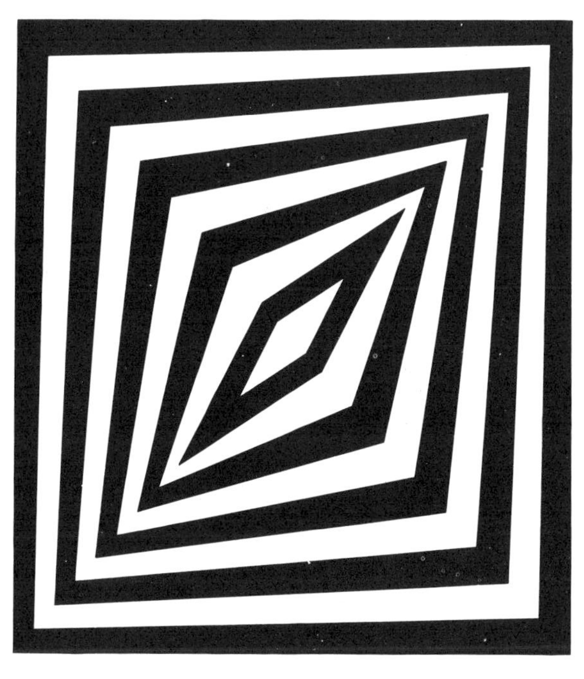

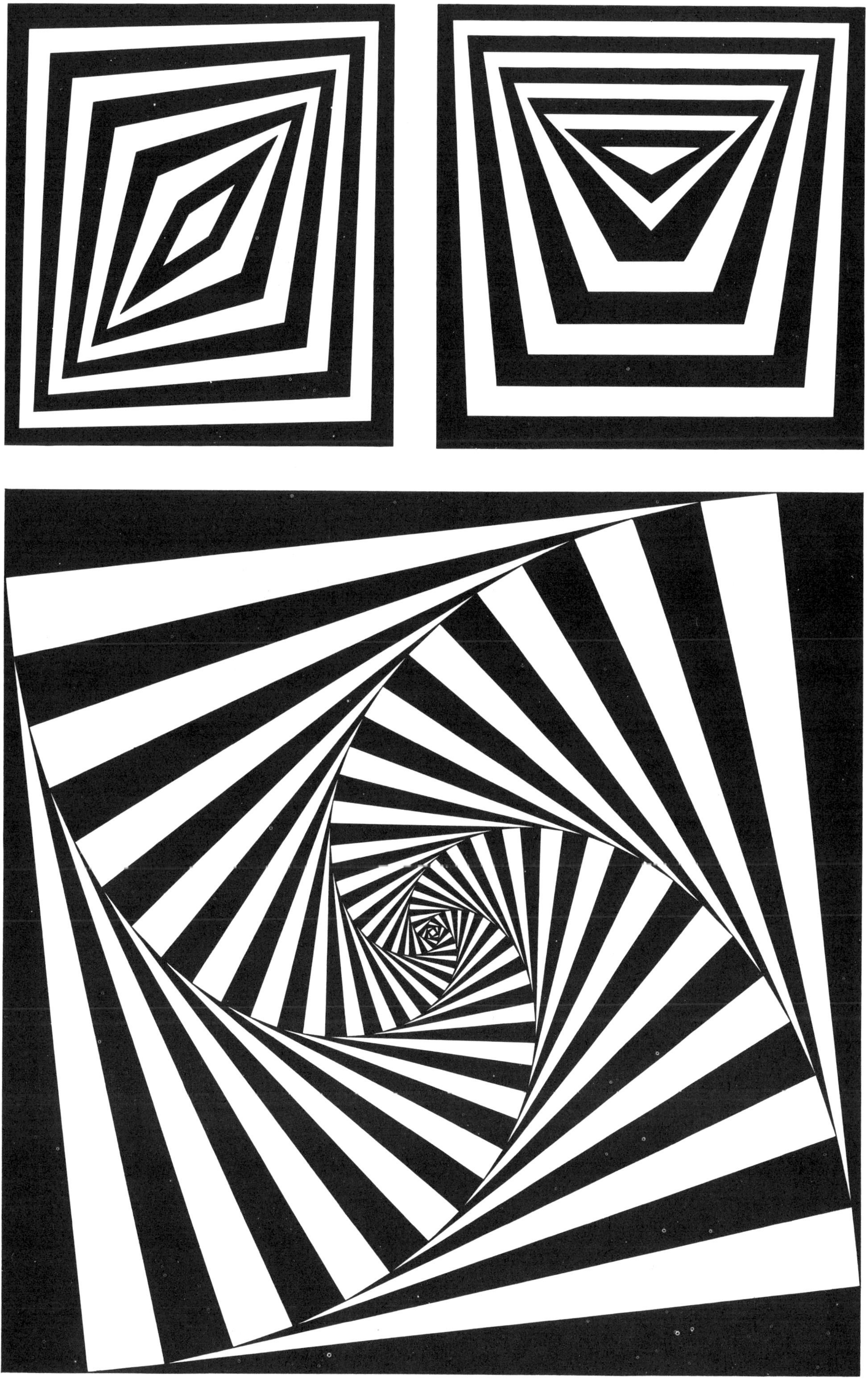

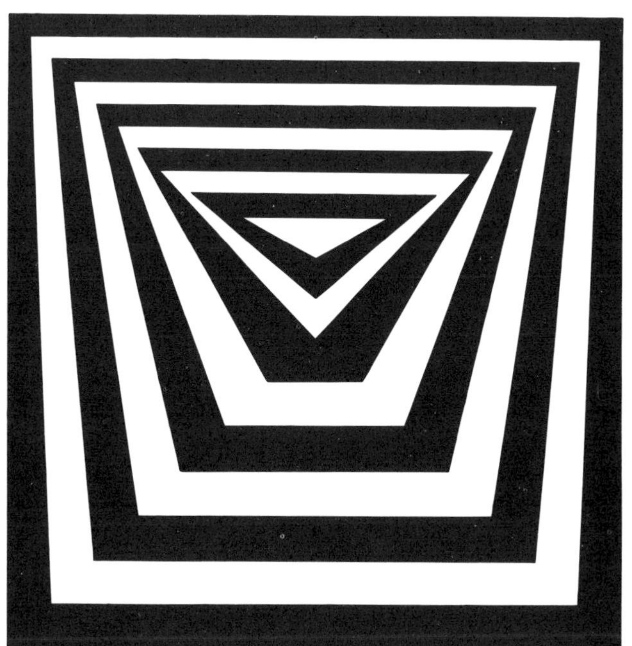

PLATE 41

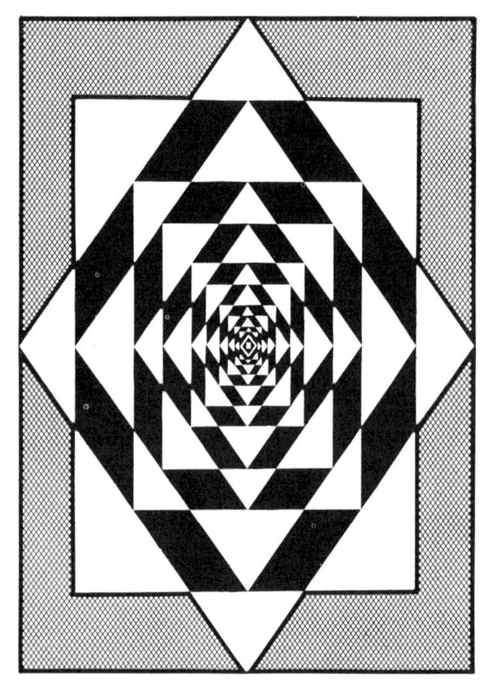

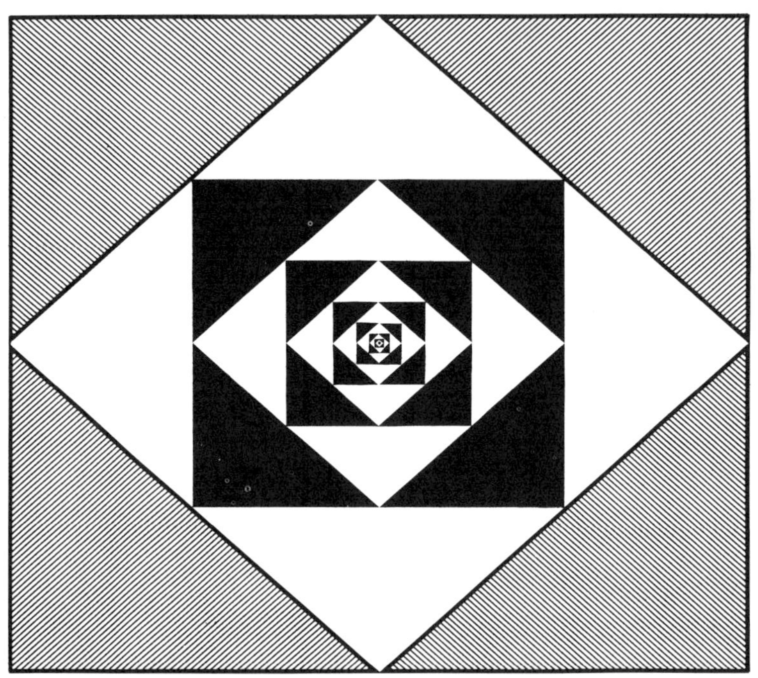

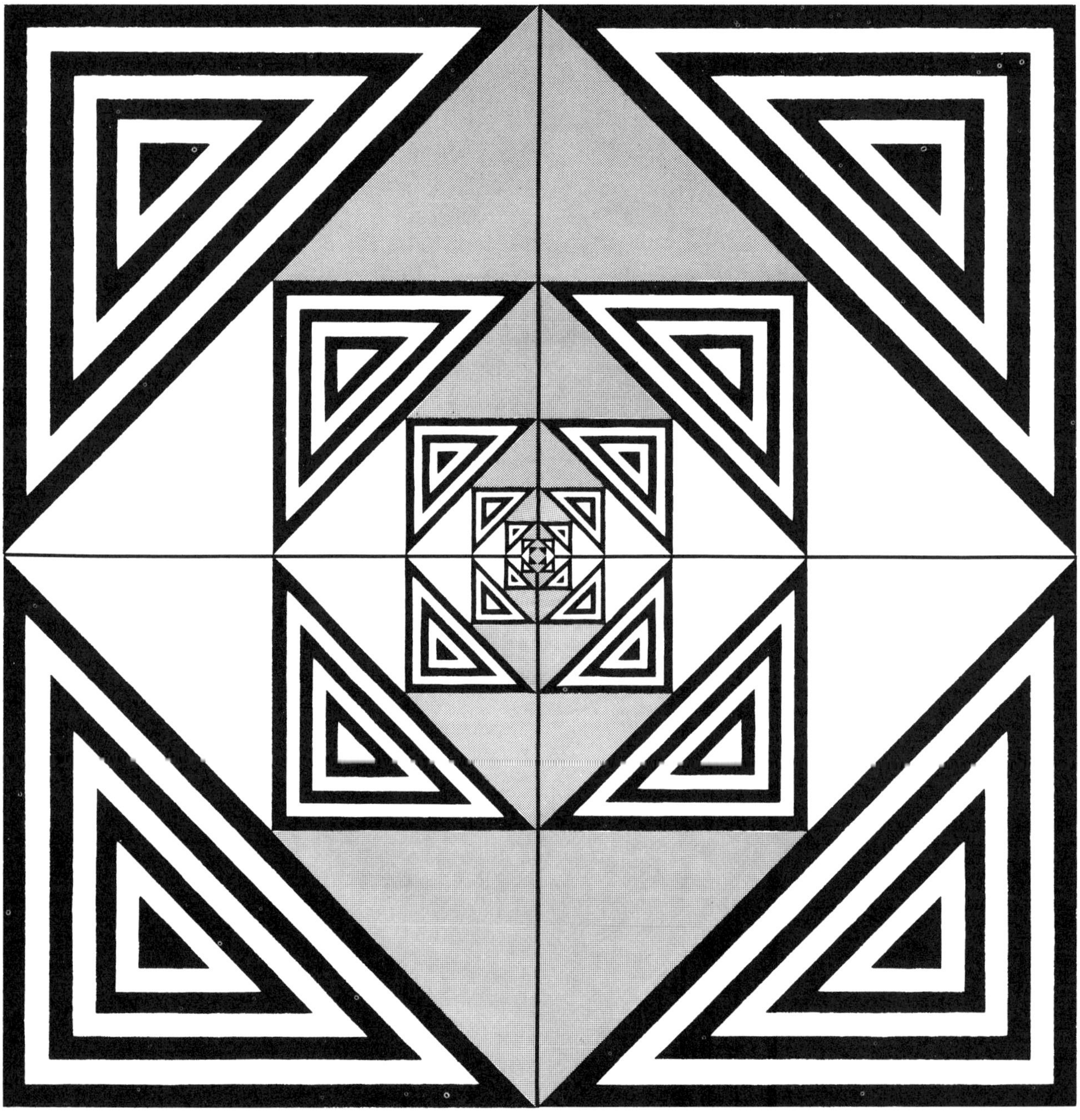

PLATE 42

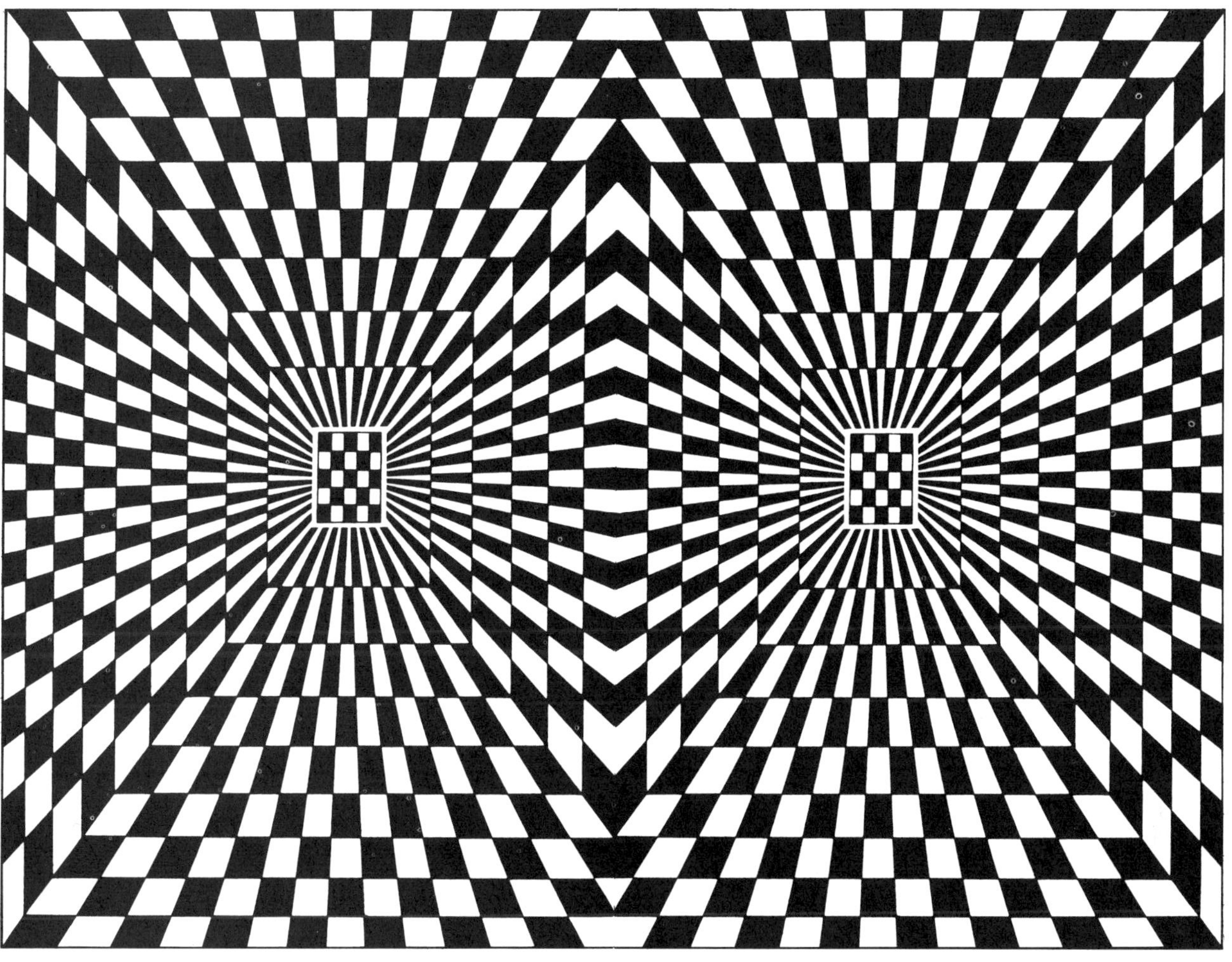

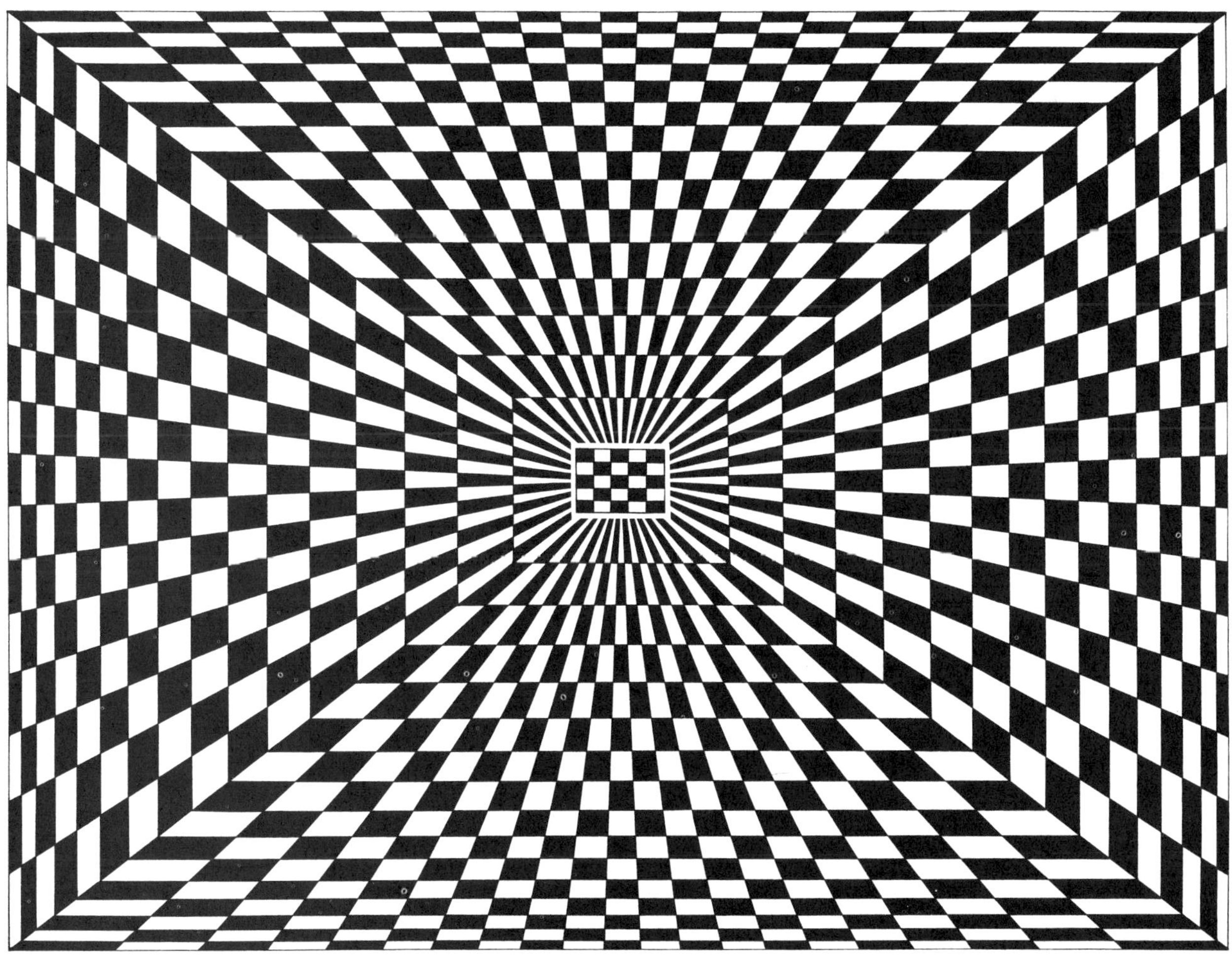

PLATE 43

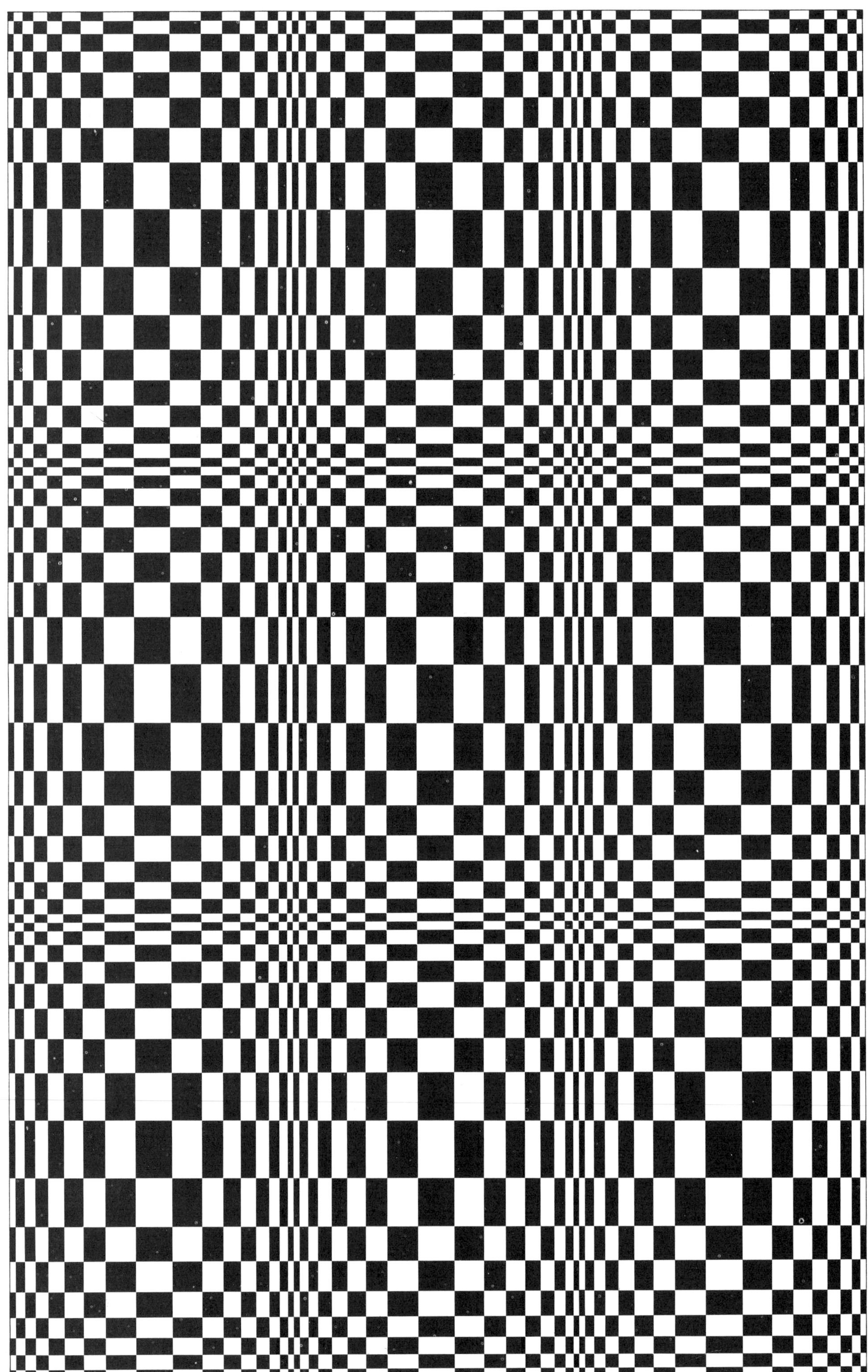

PLATE 44

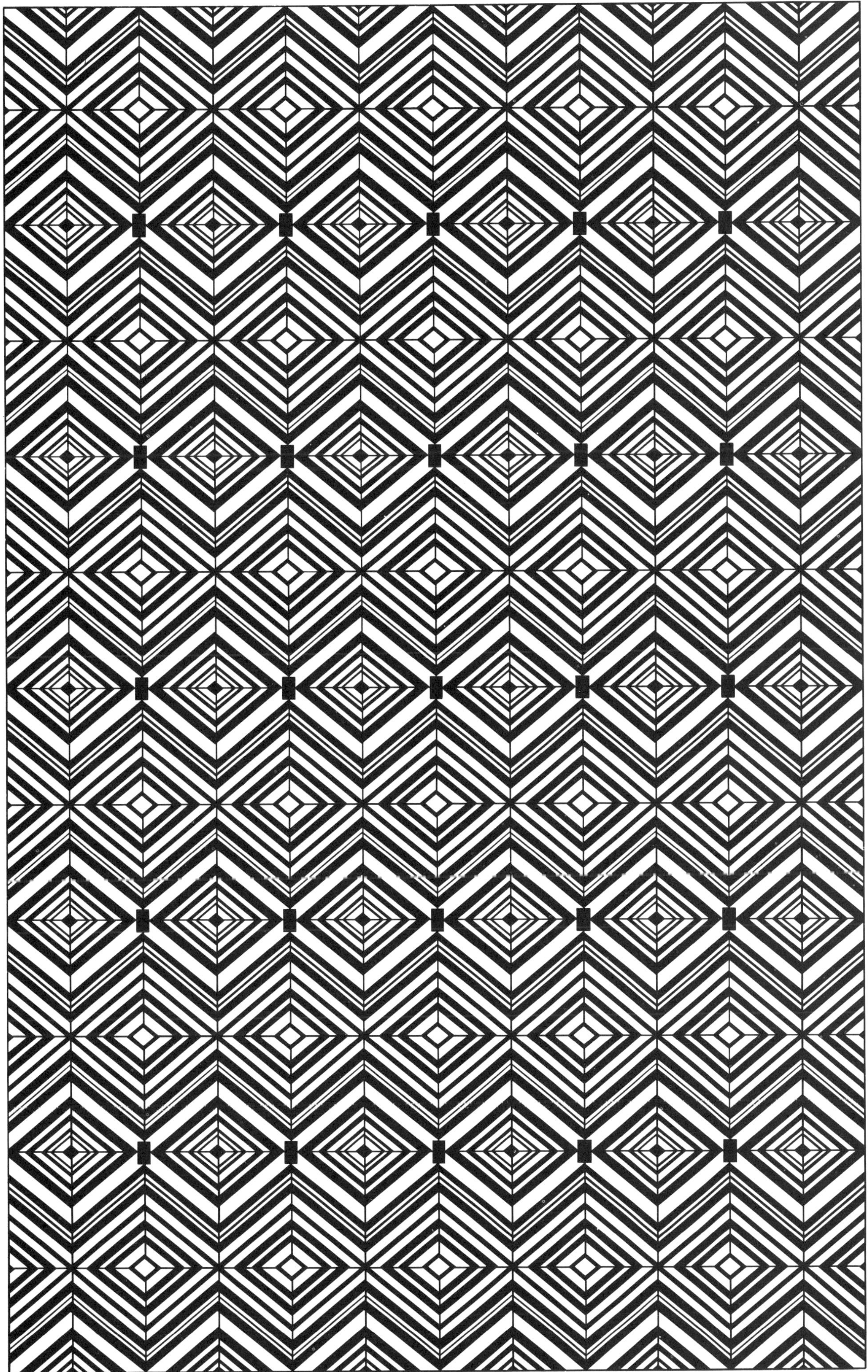

PLATE 45

PLATE 46

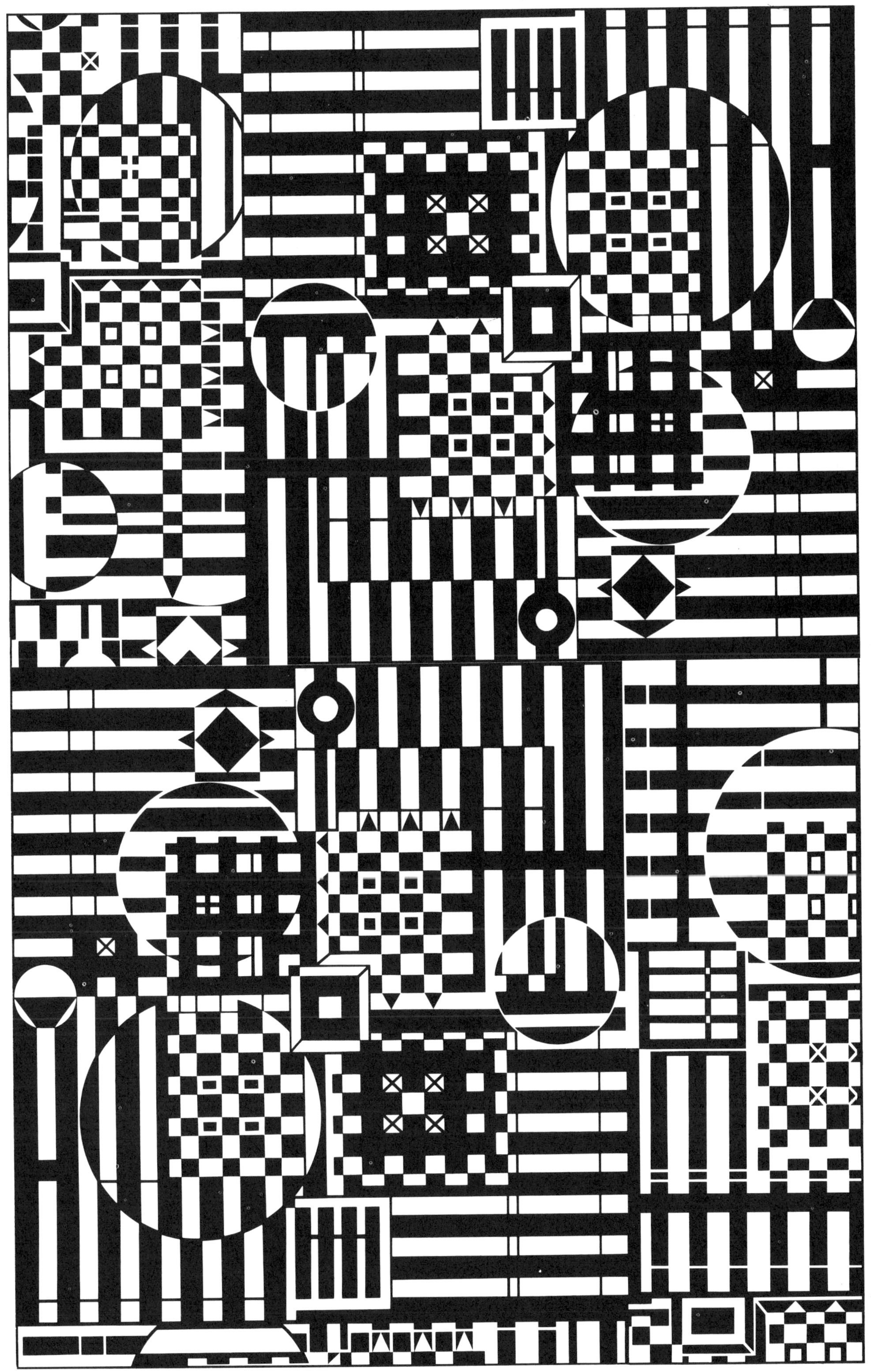

PLATE 47

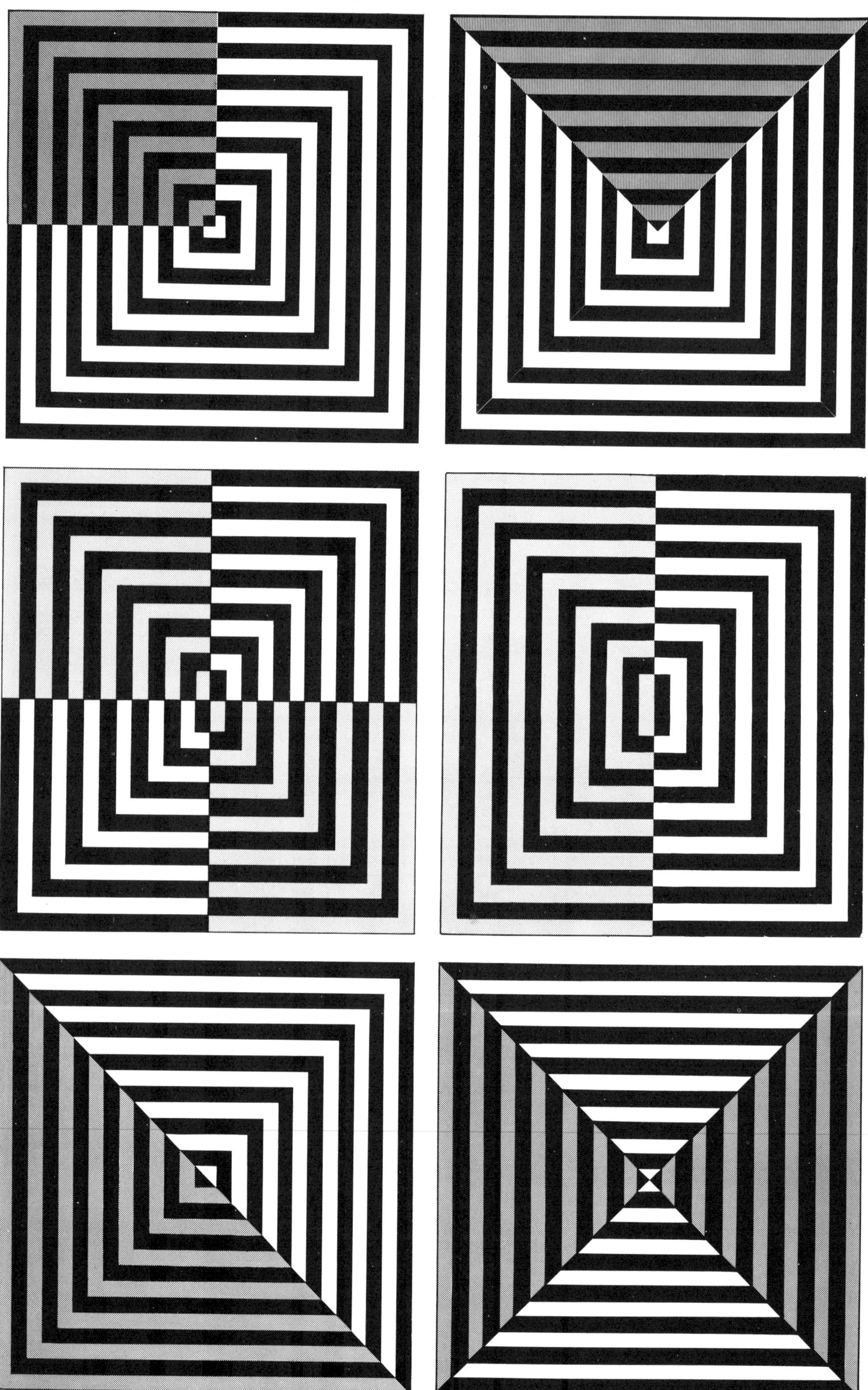

PLATE 48

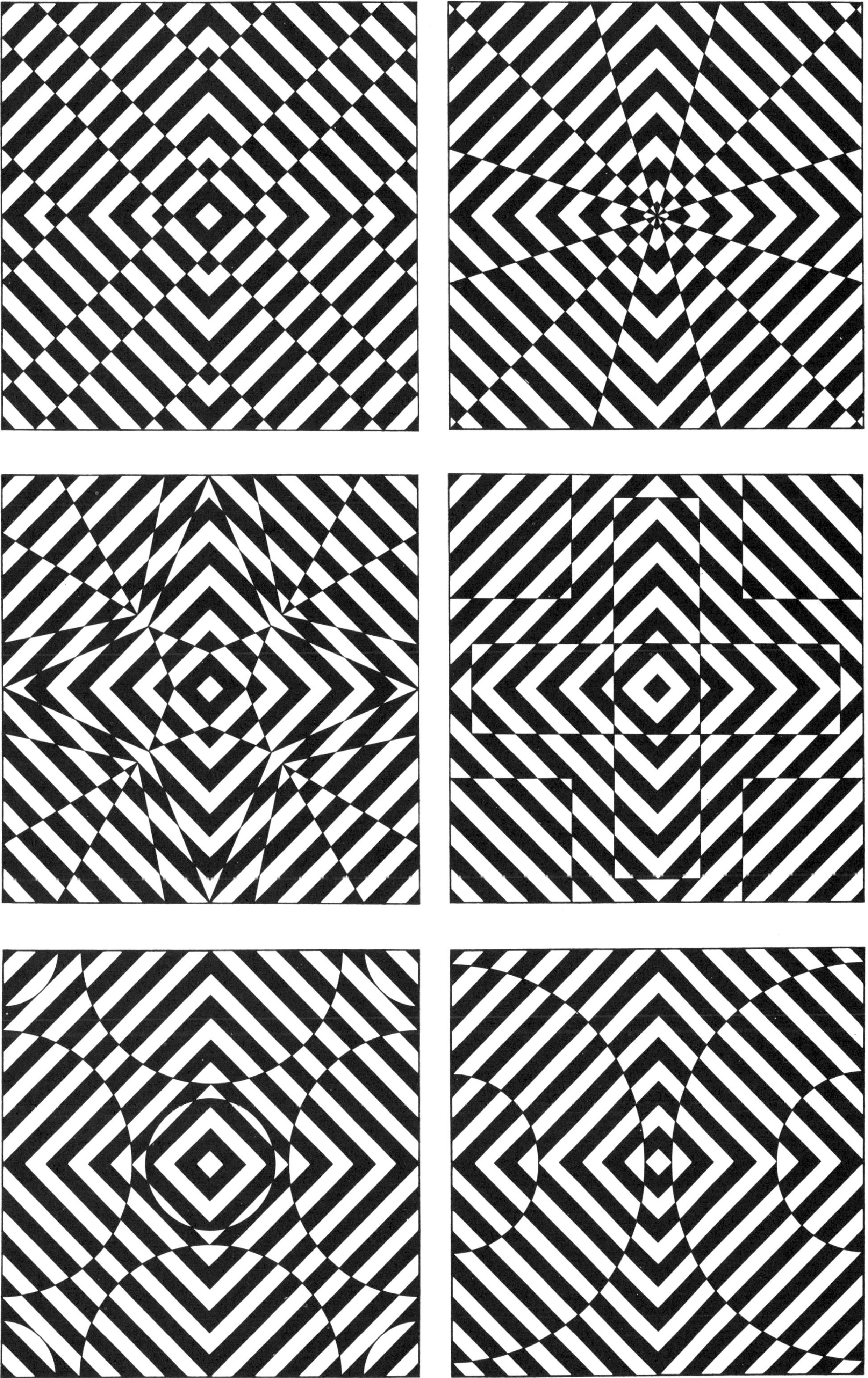

PLATE 49

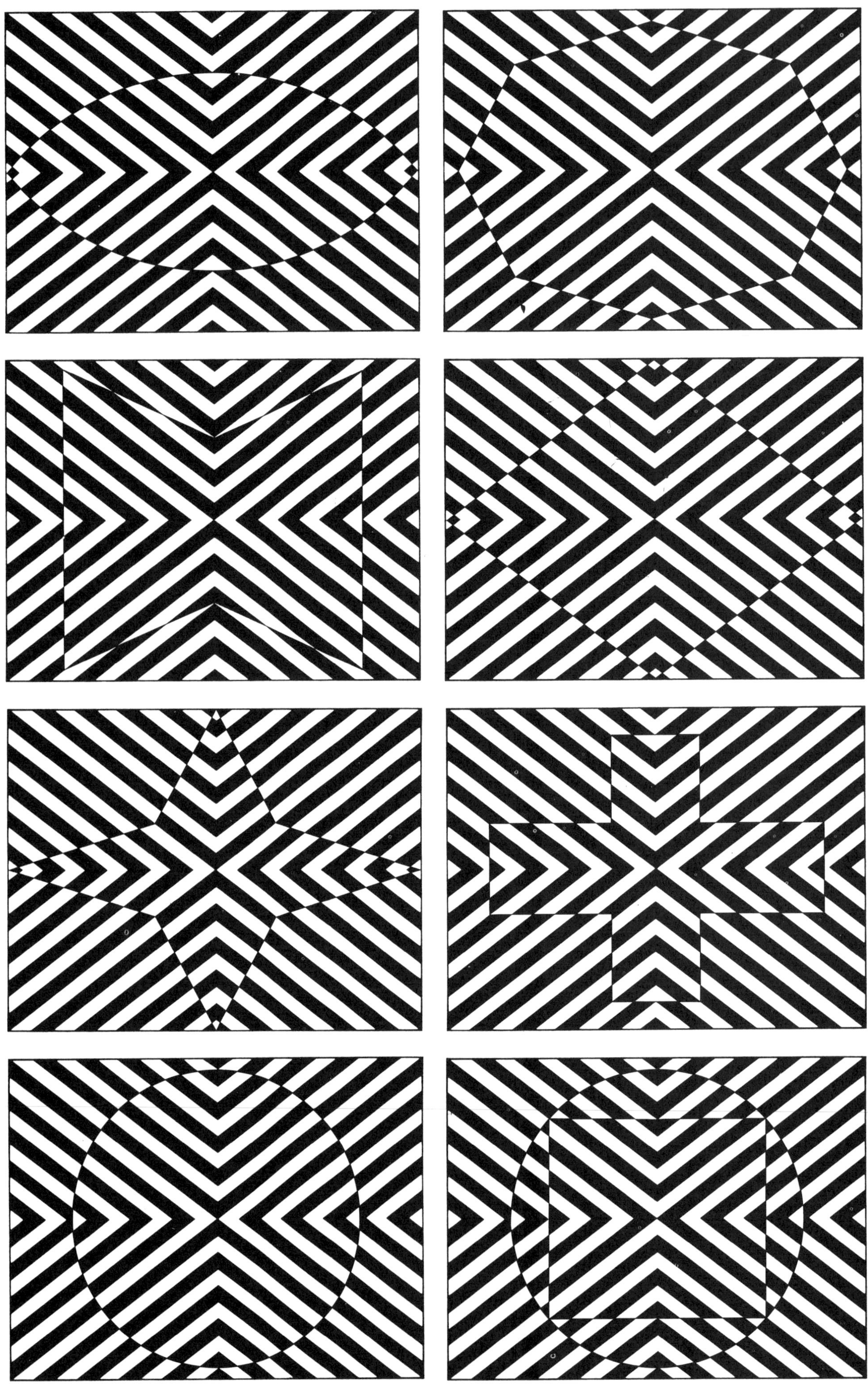

PLATE 50

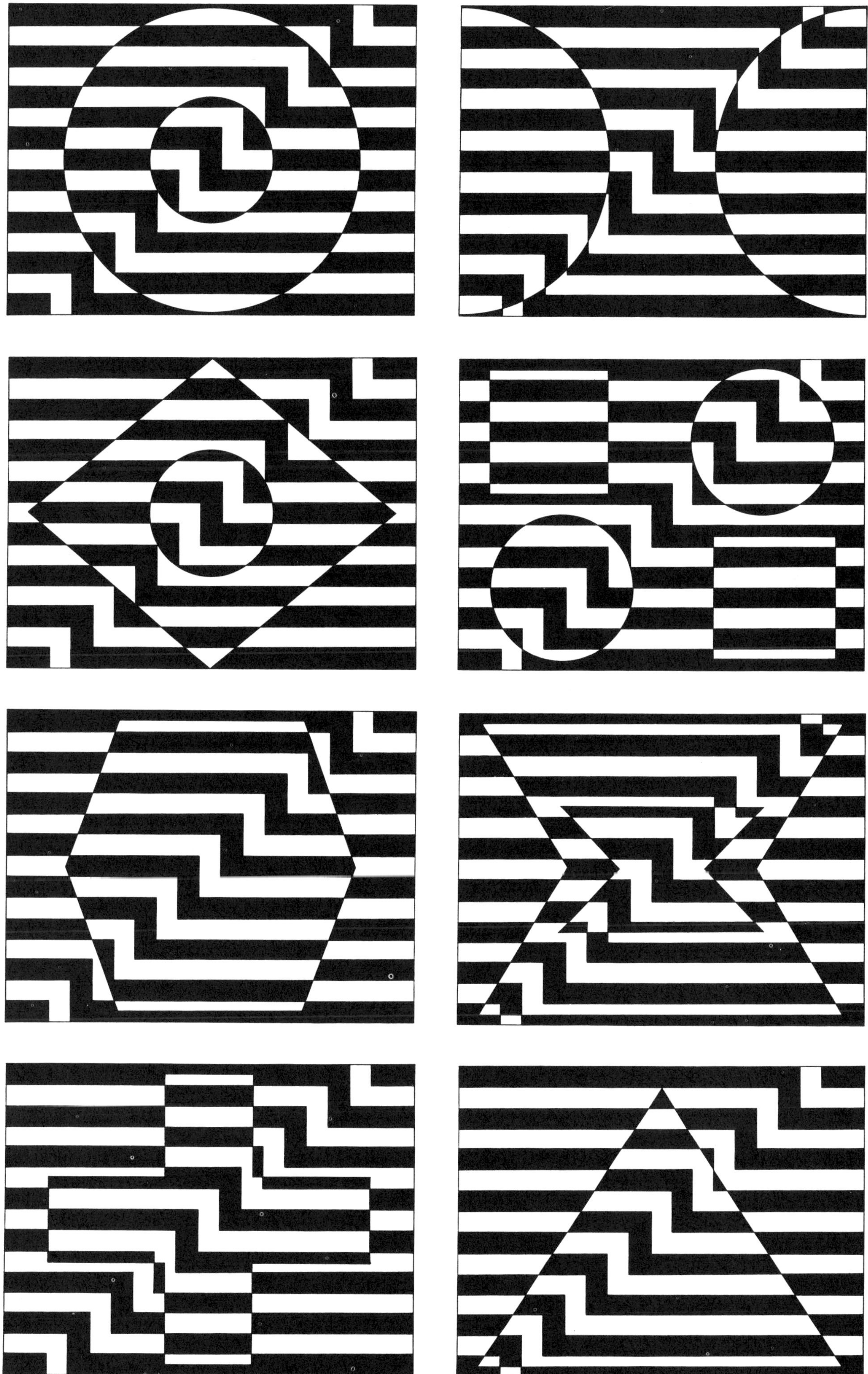

PLATE 51

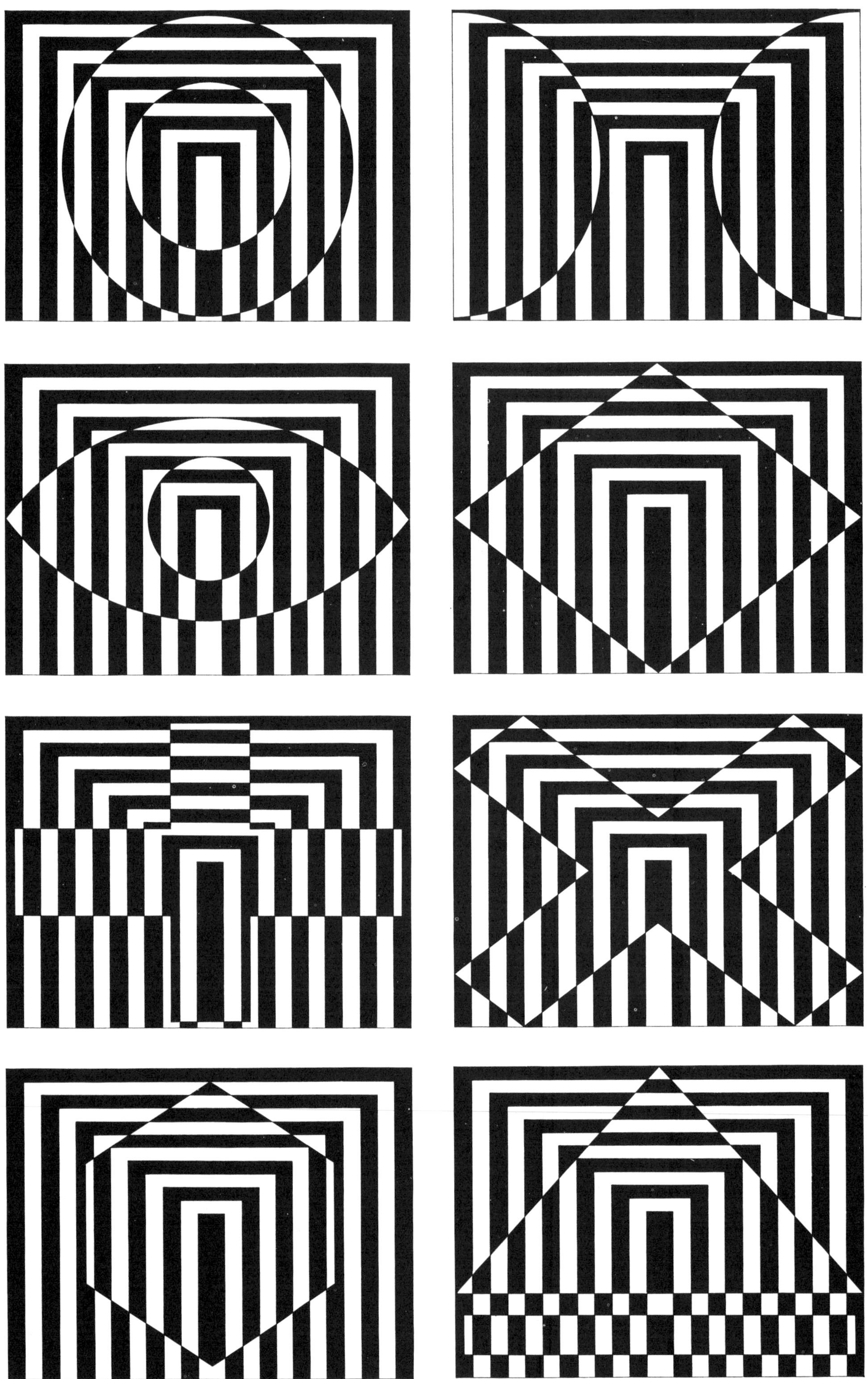

PLATE 52

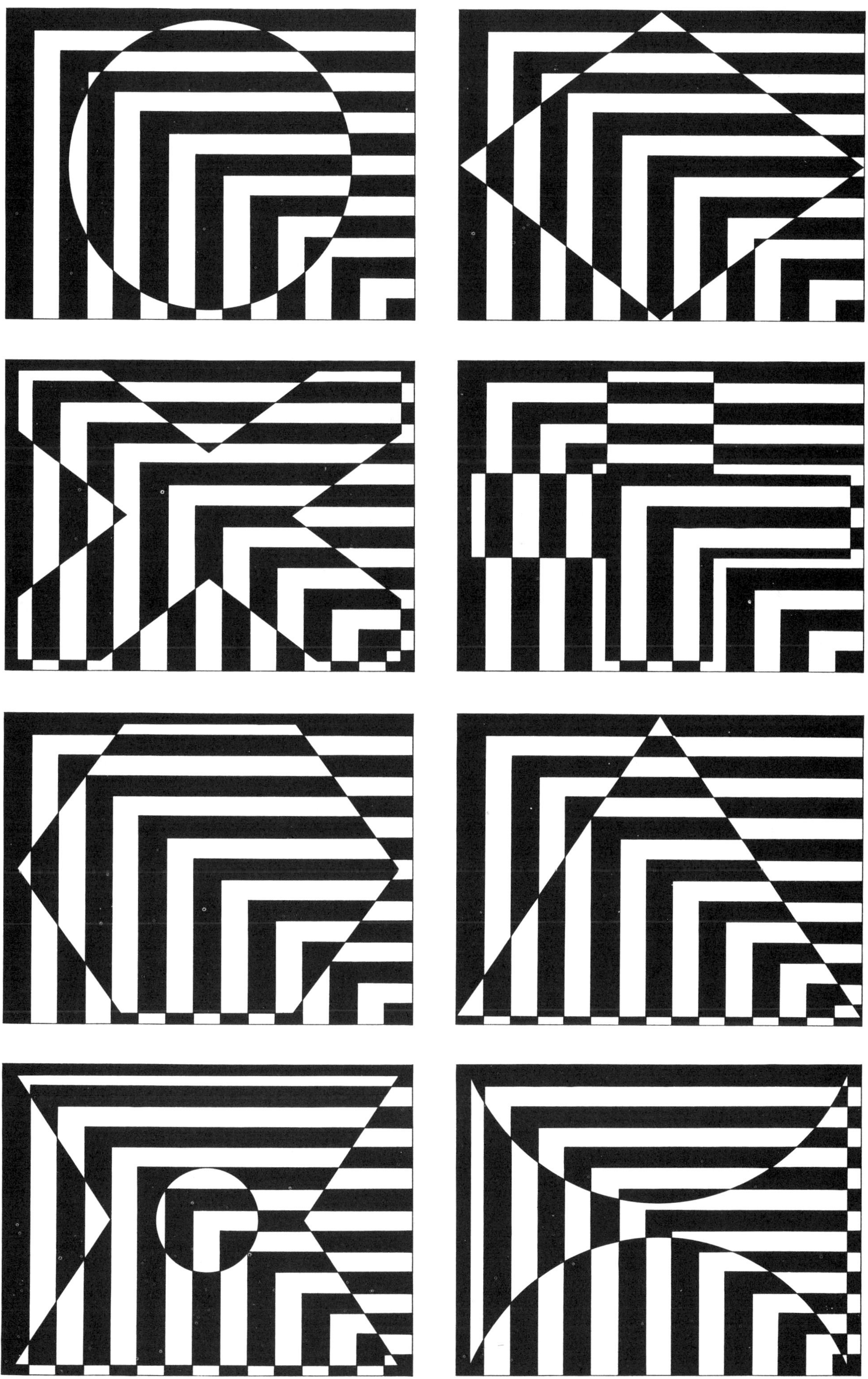

PLATE 53

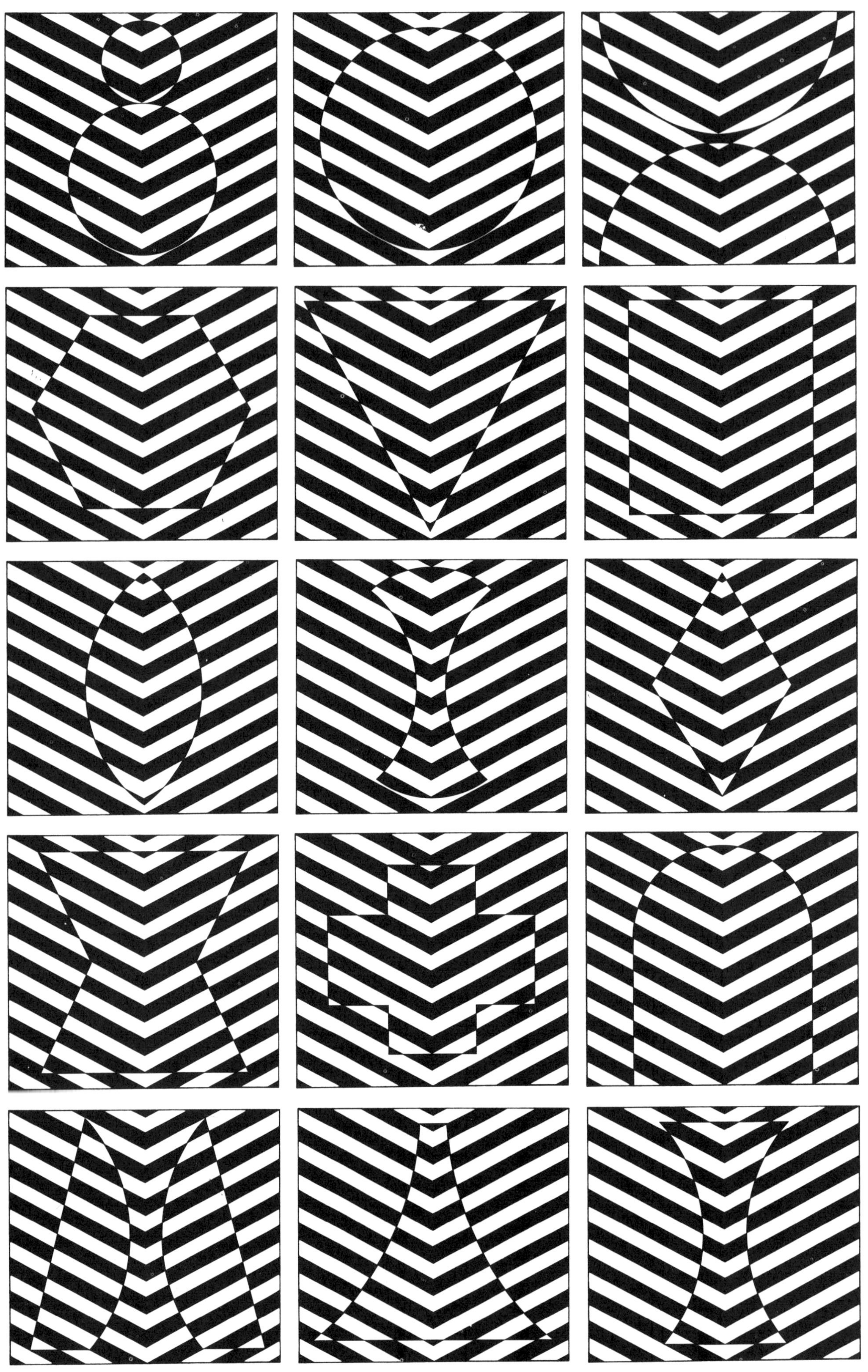

PLATE 54

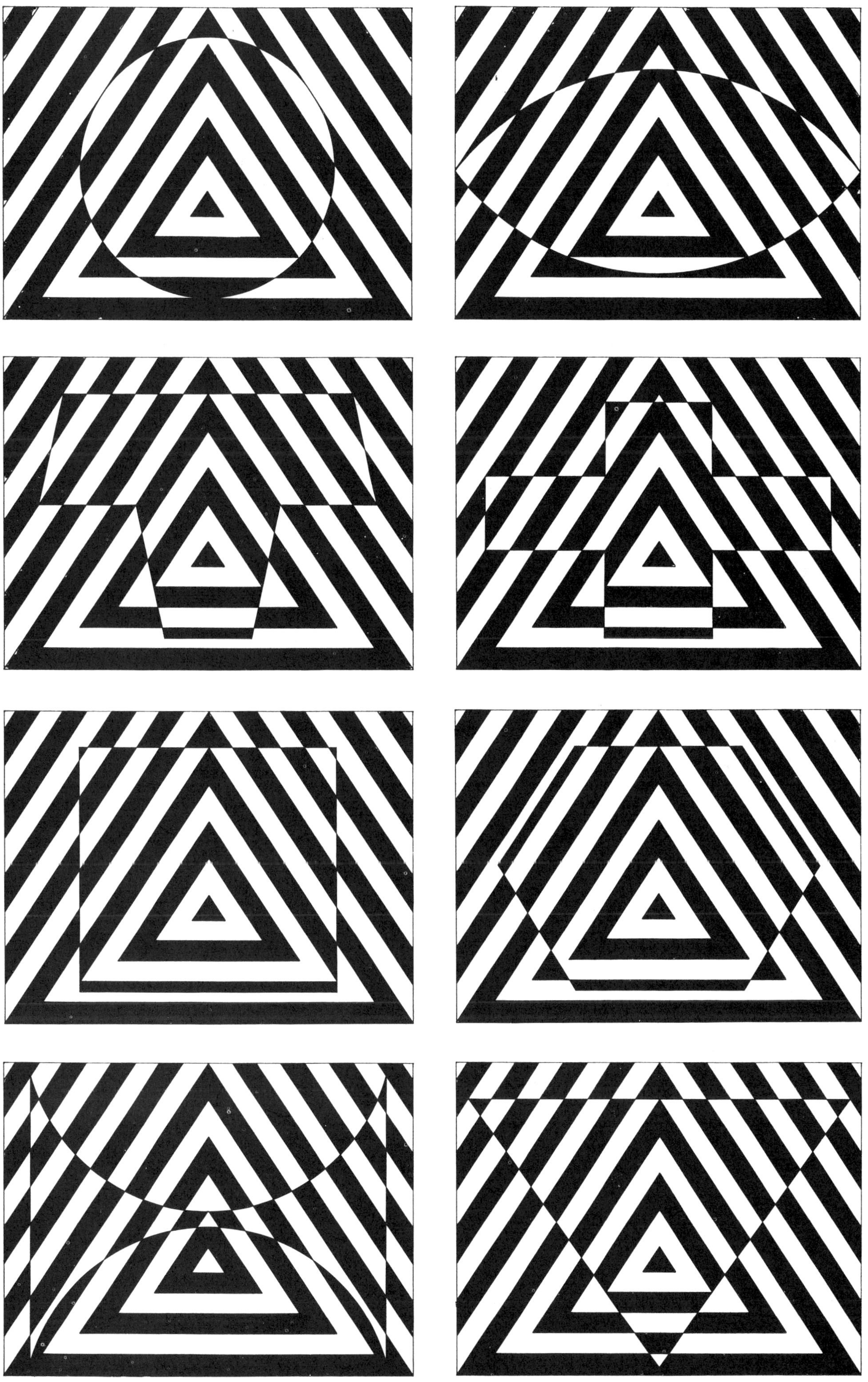

PLATE 55

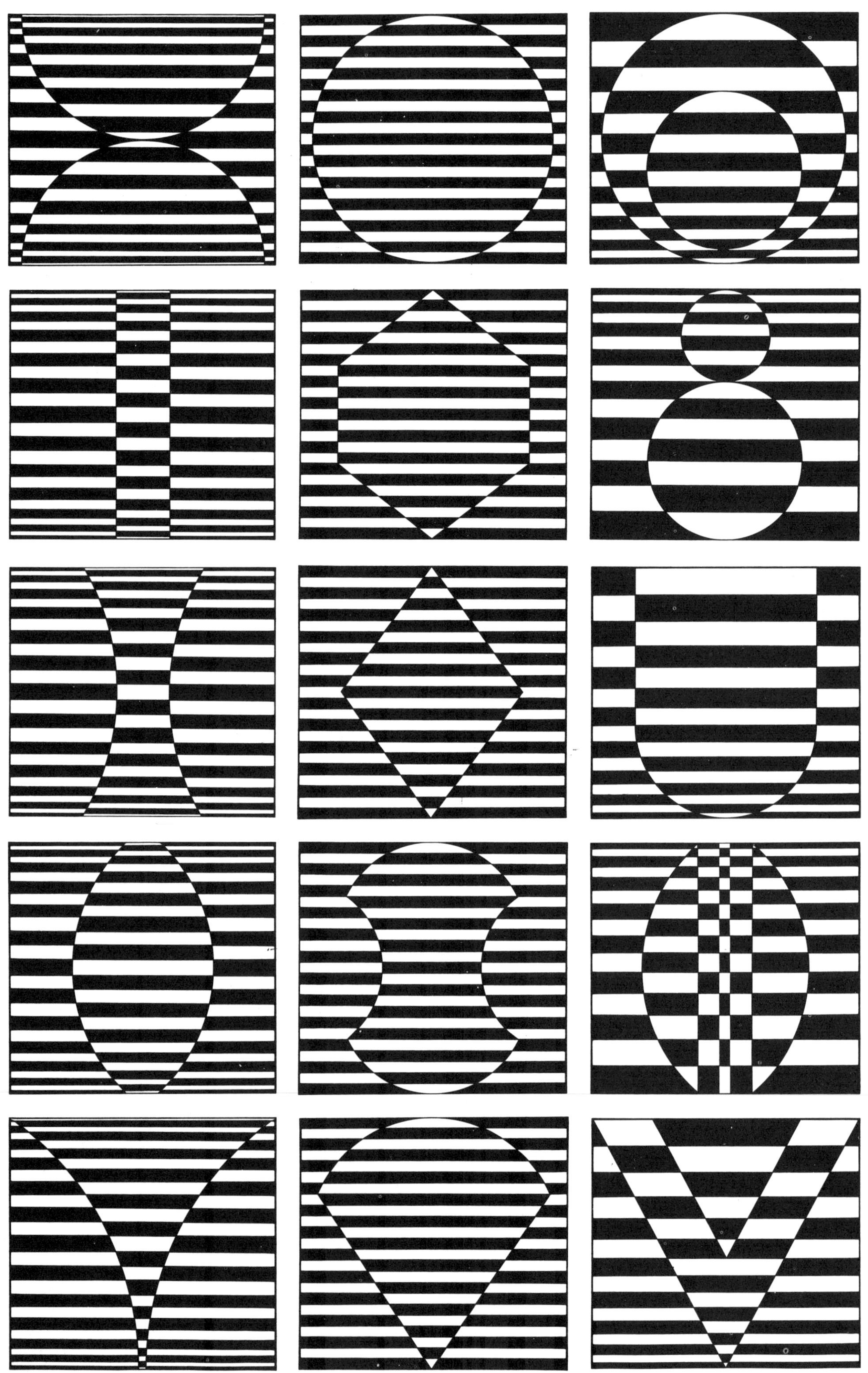

PLATE 56

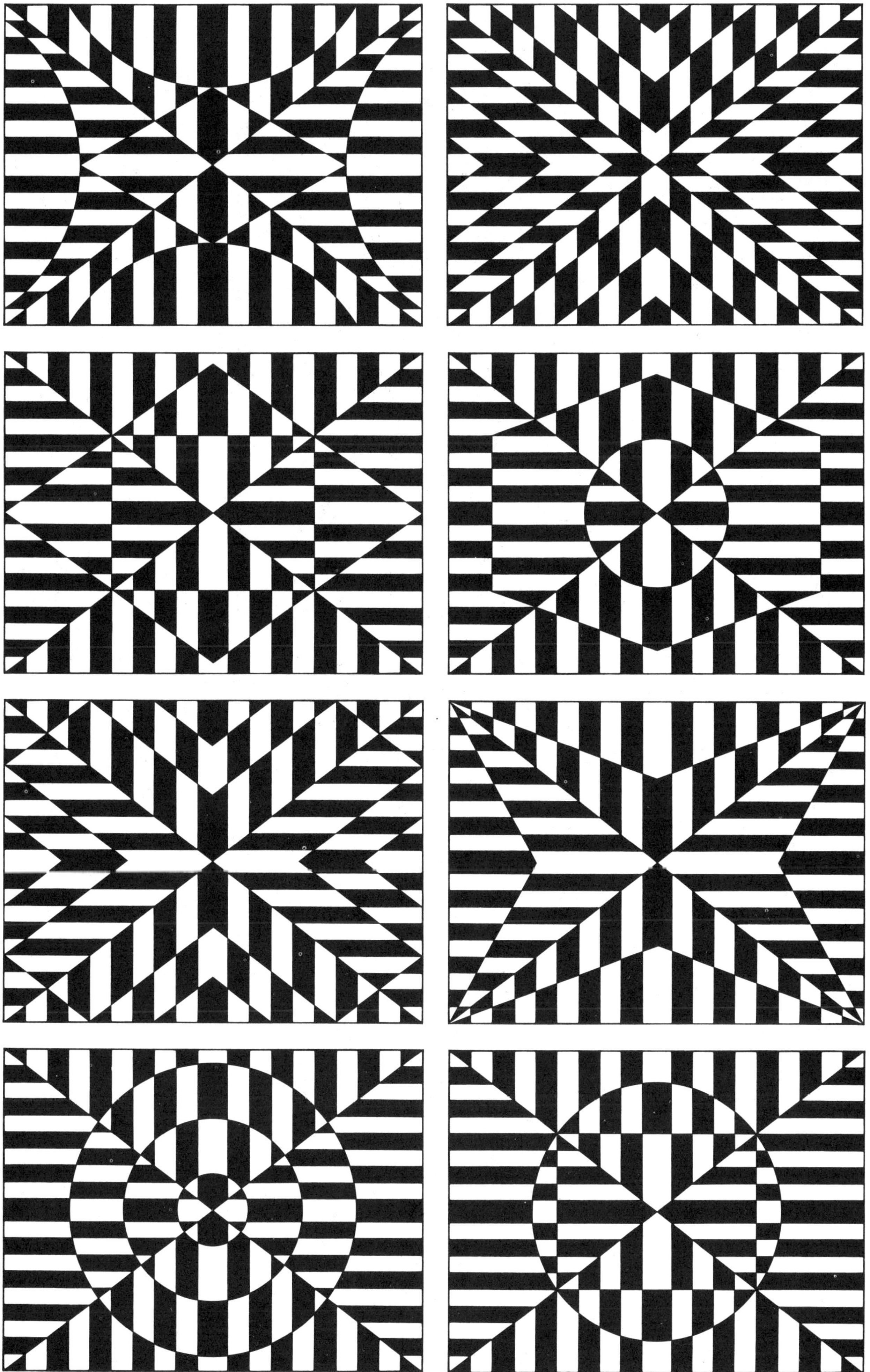

PLATE 57

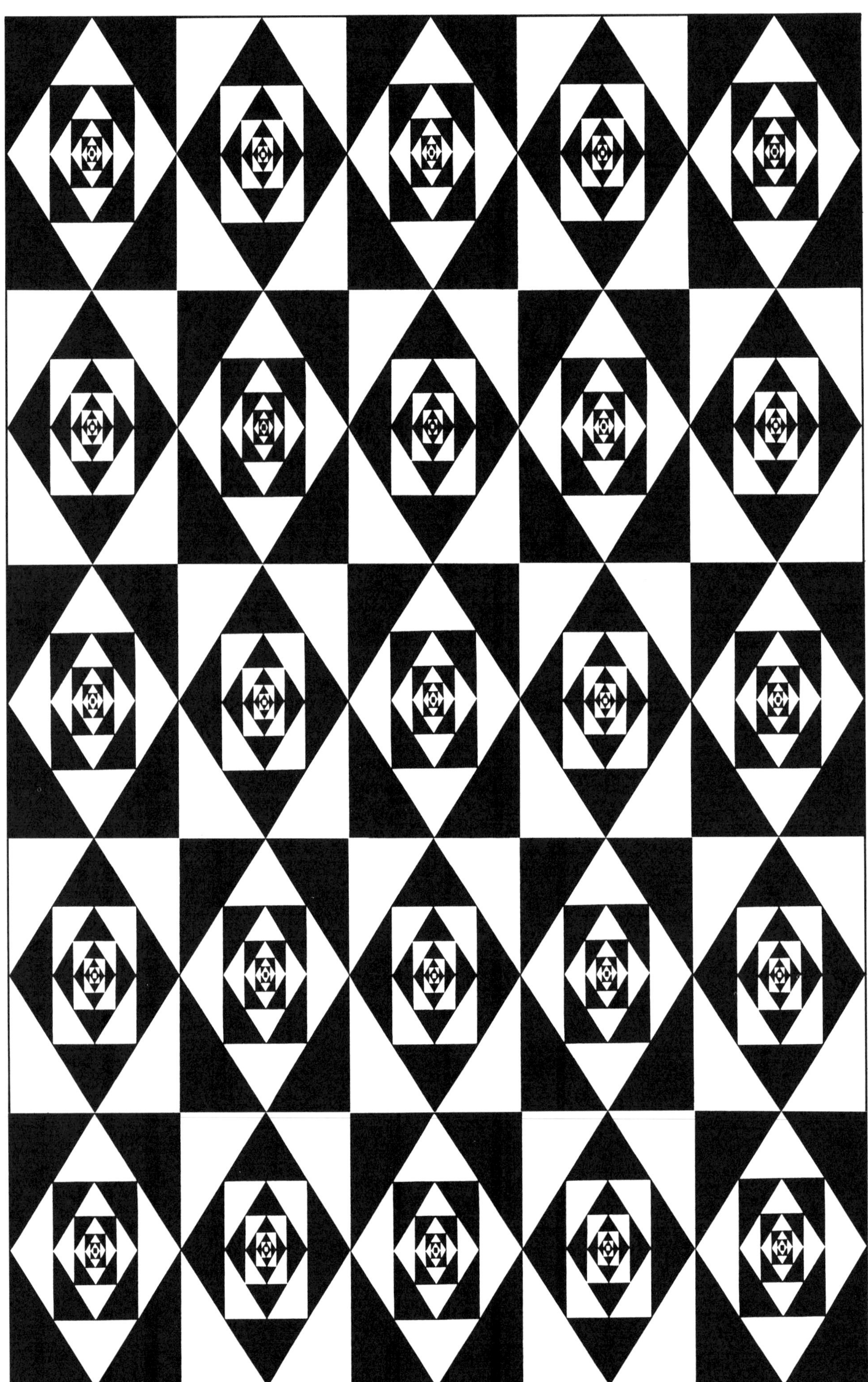

PLATE 58

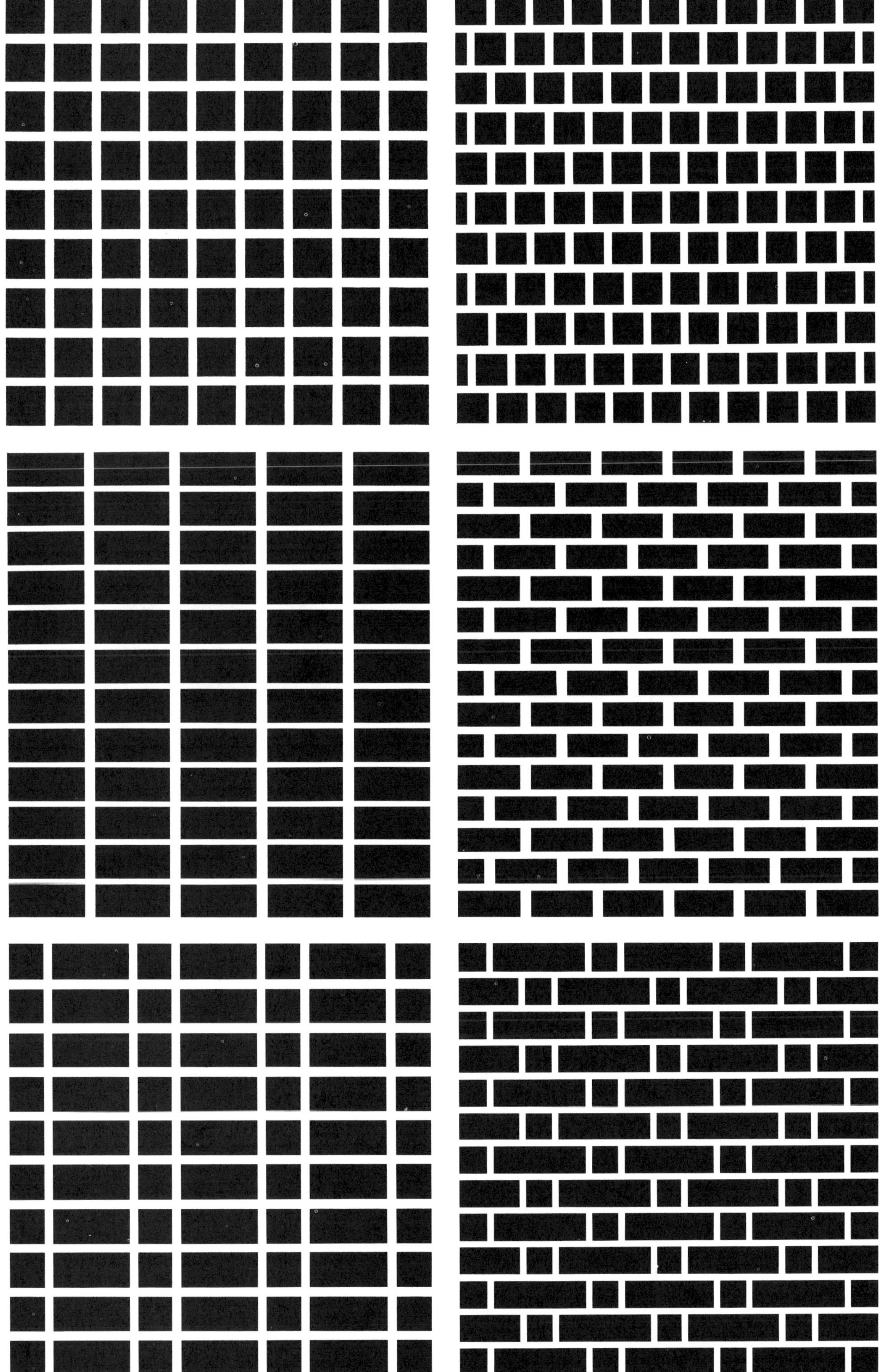

PLATE 59

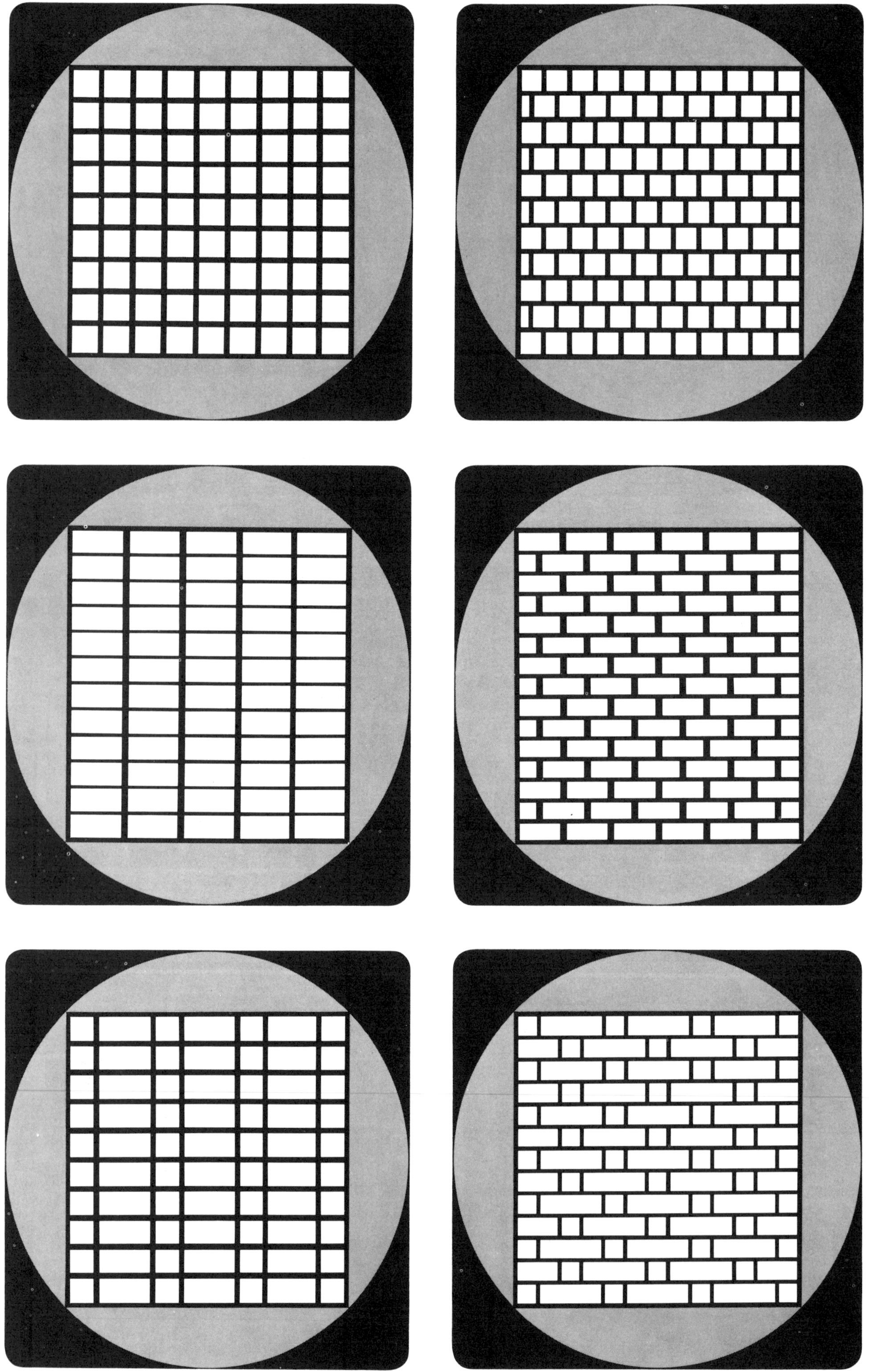

PLATE 60

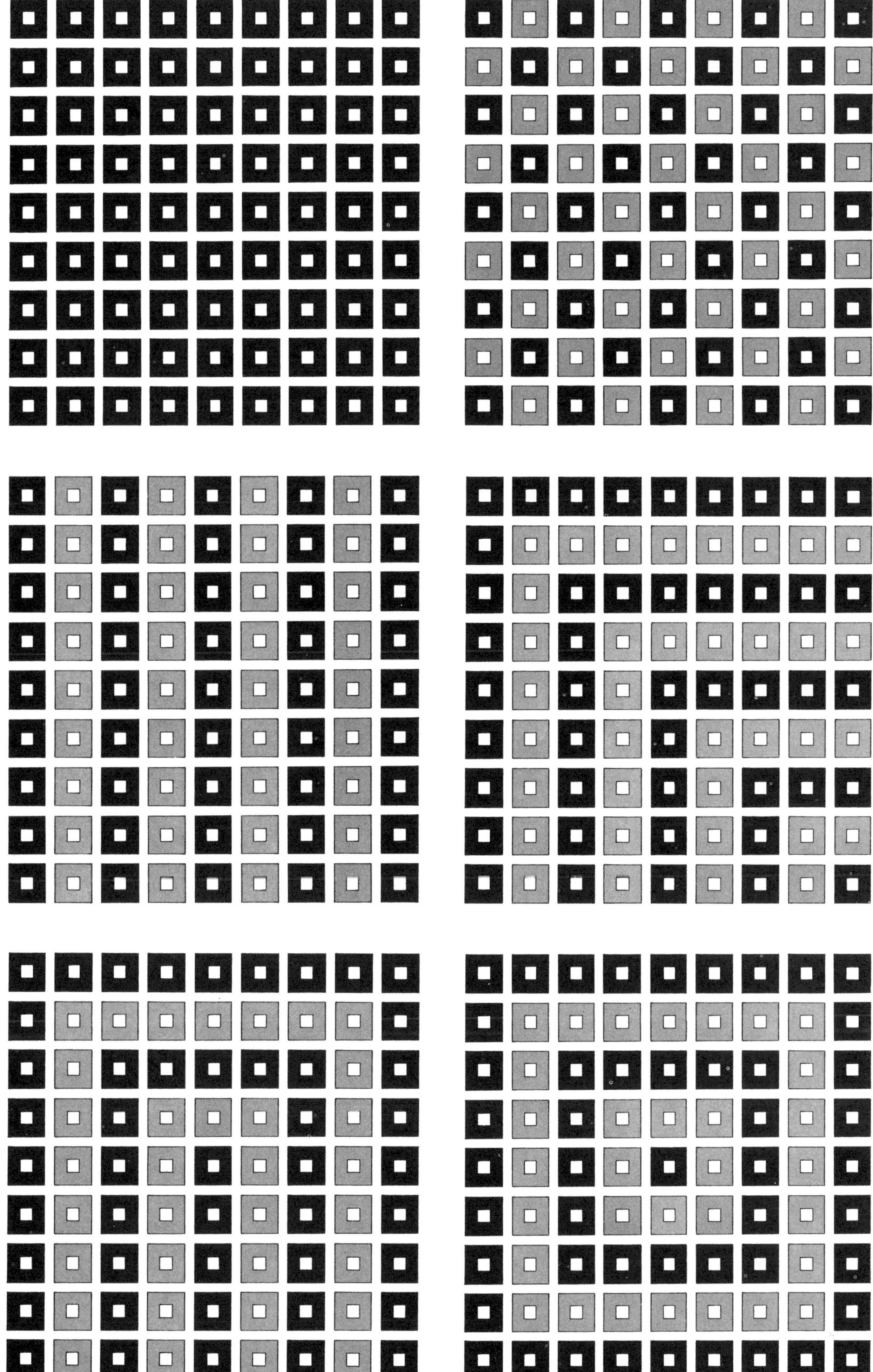

PLATE 61

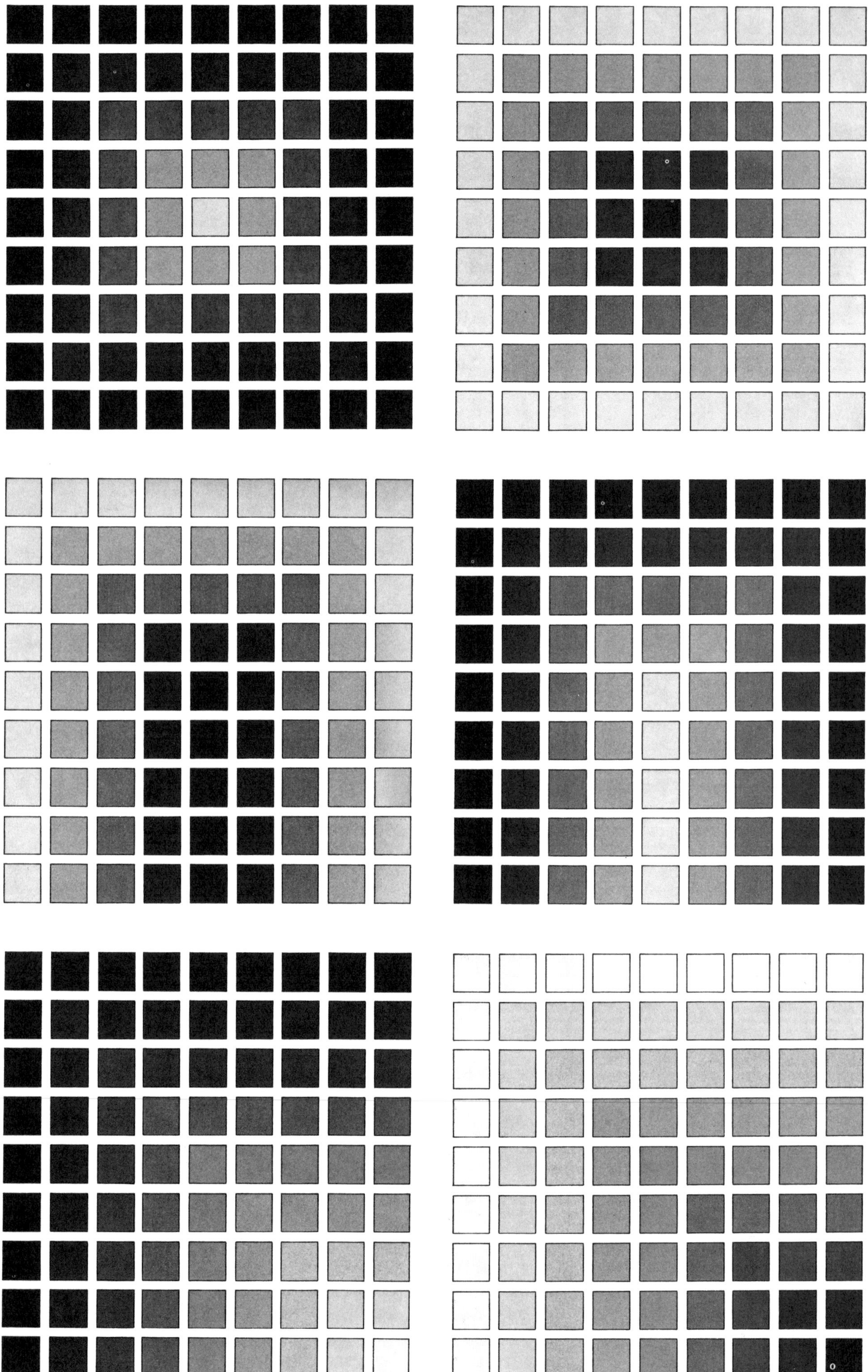

PLATE 62

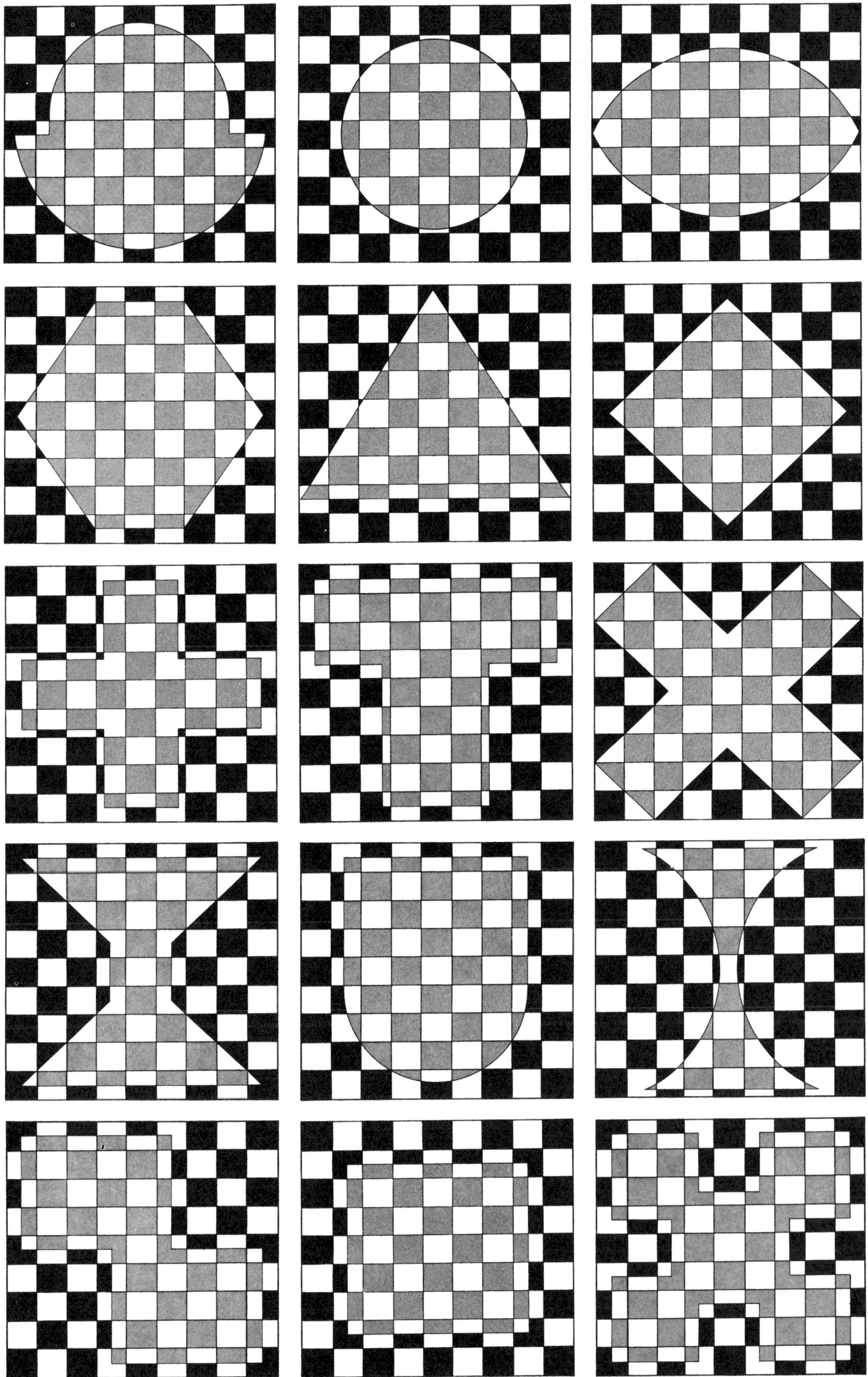

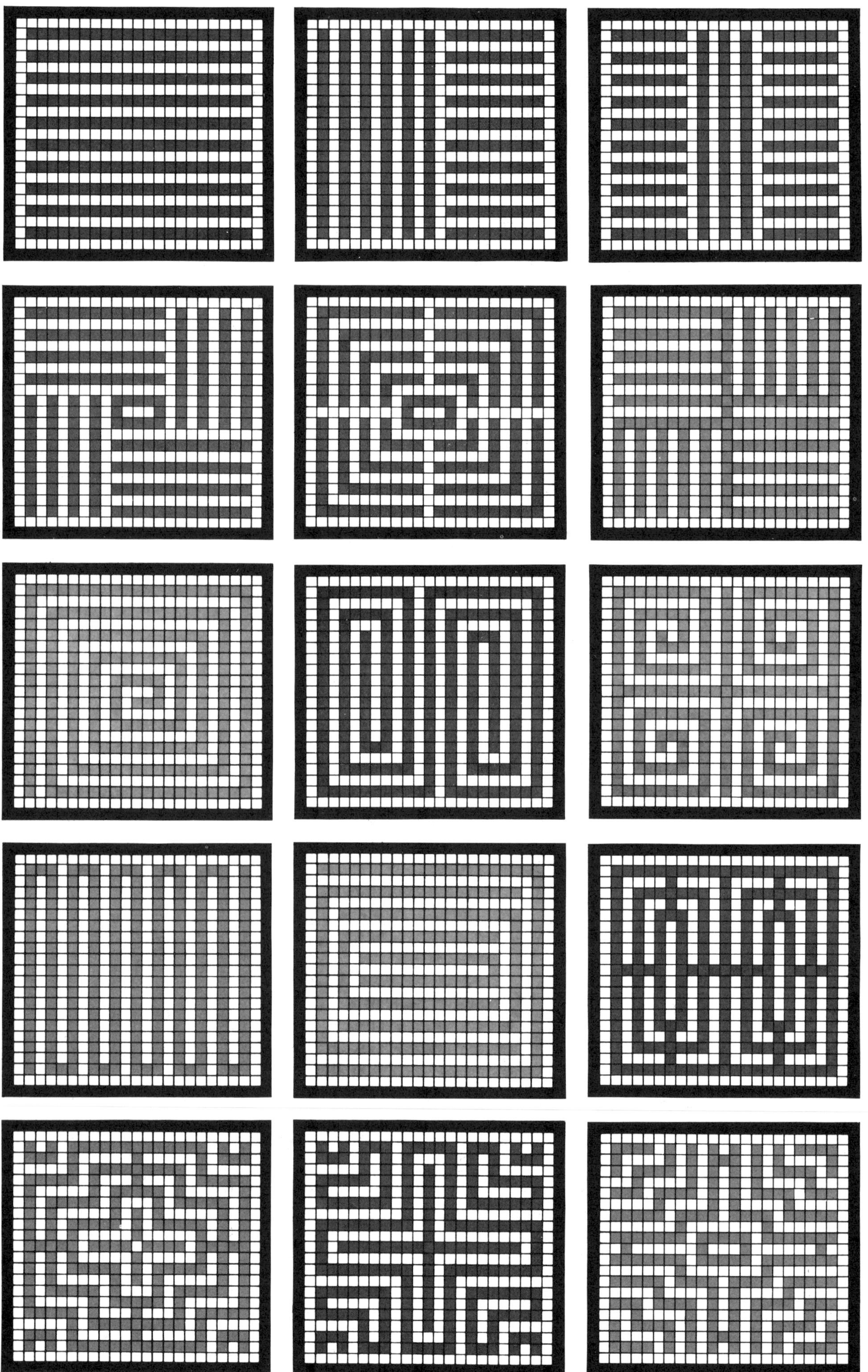

PLATE 64

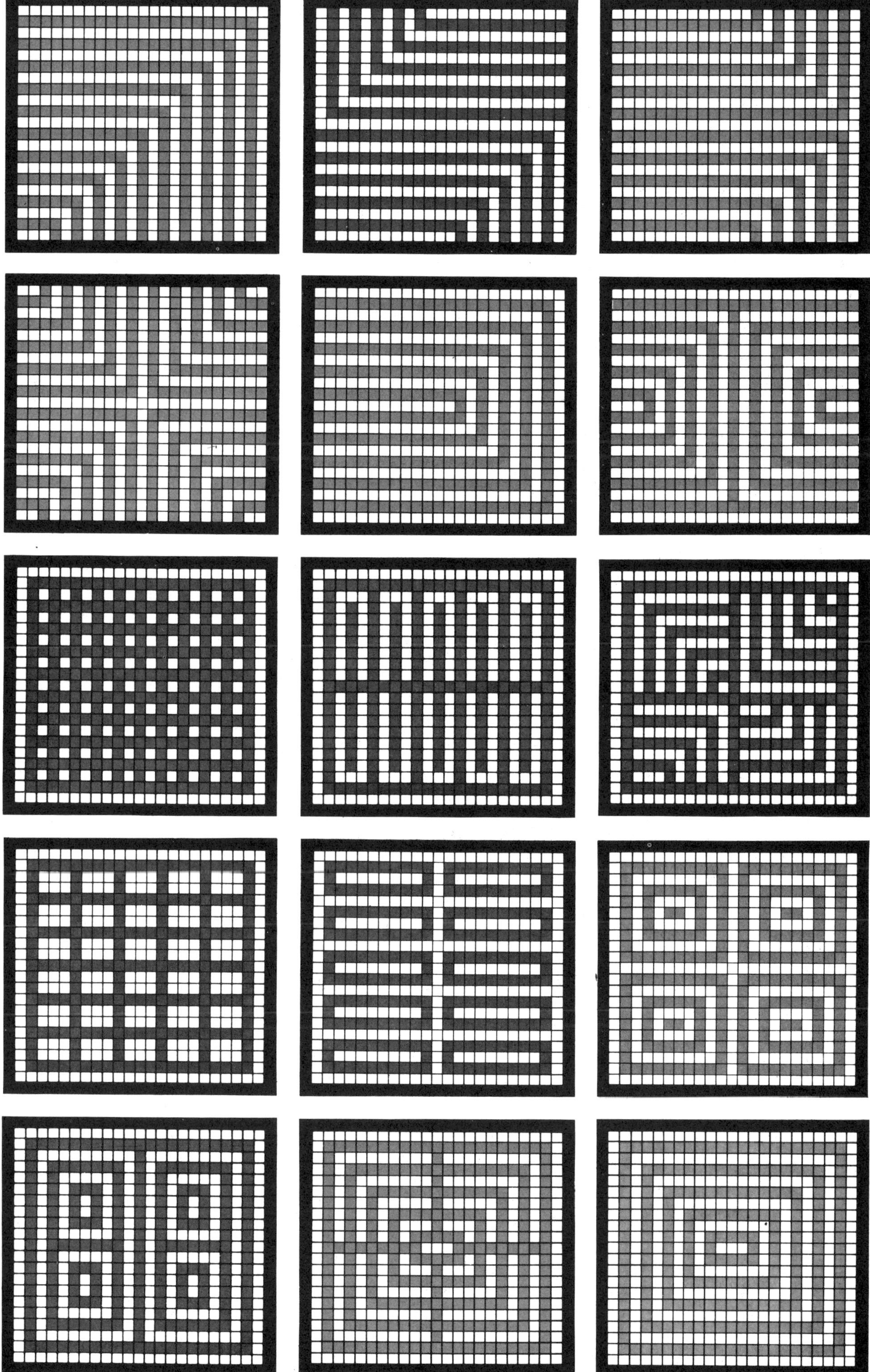

PLATE 65

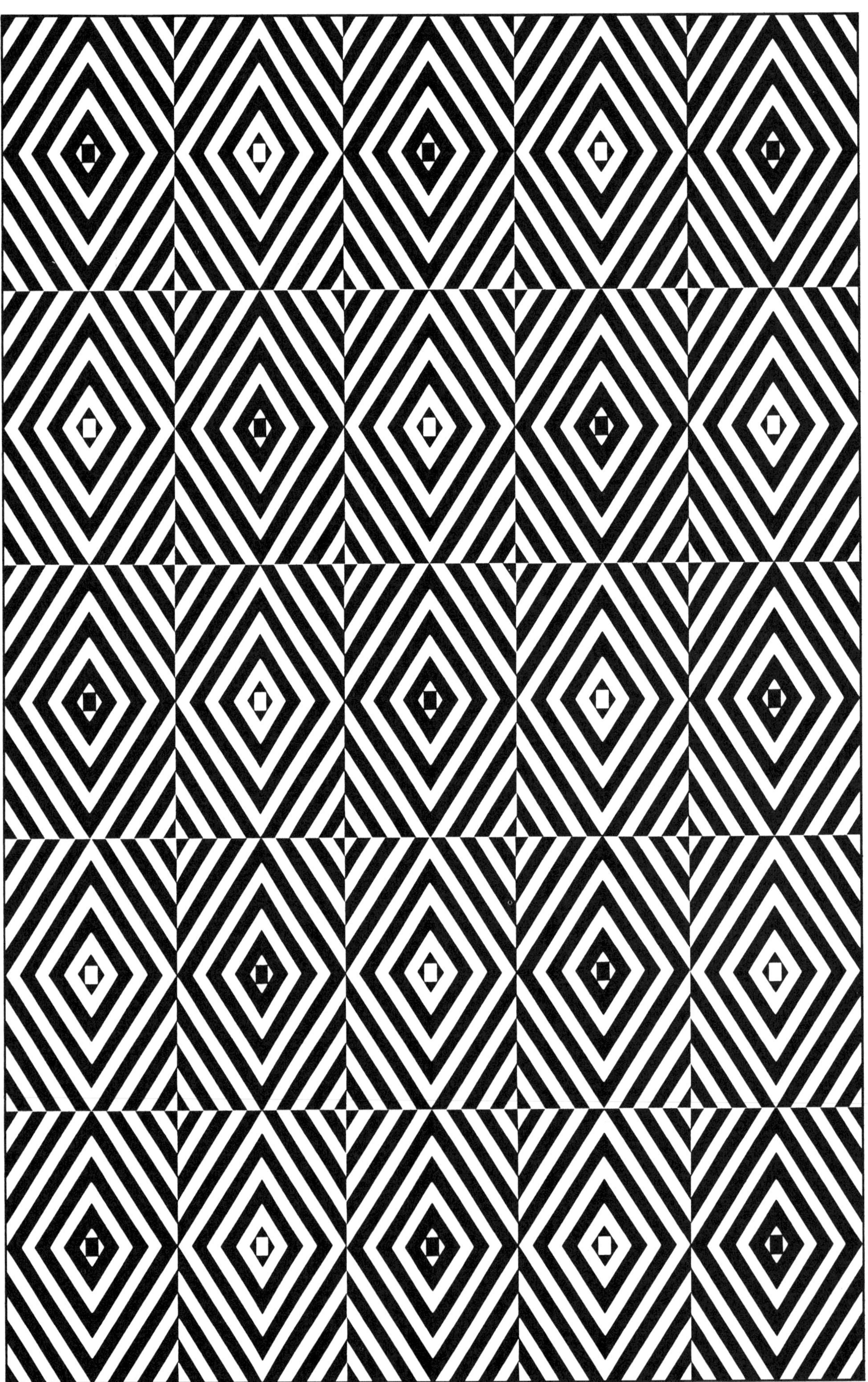

PLATE 66

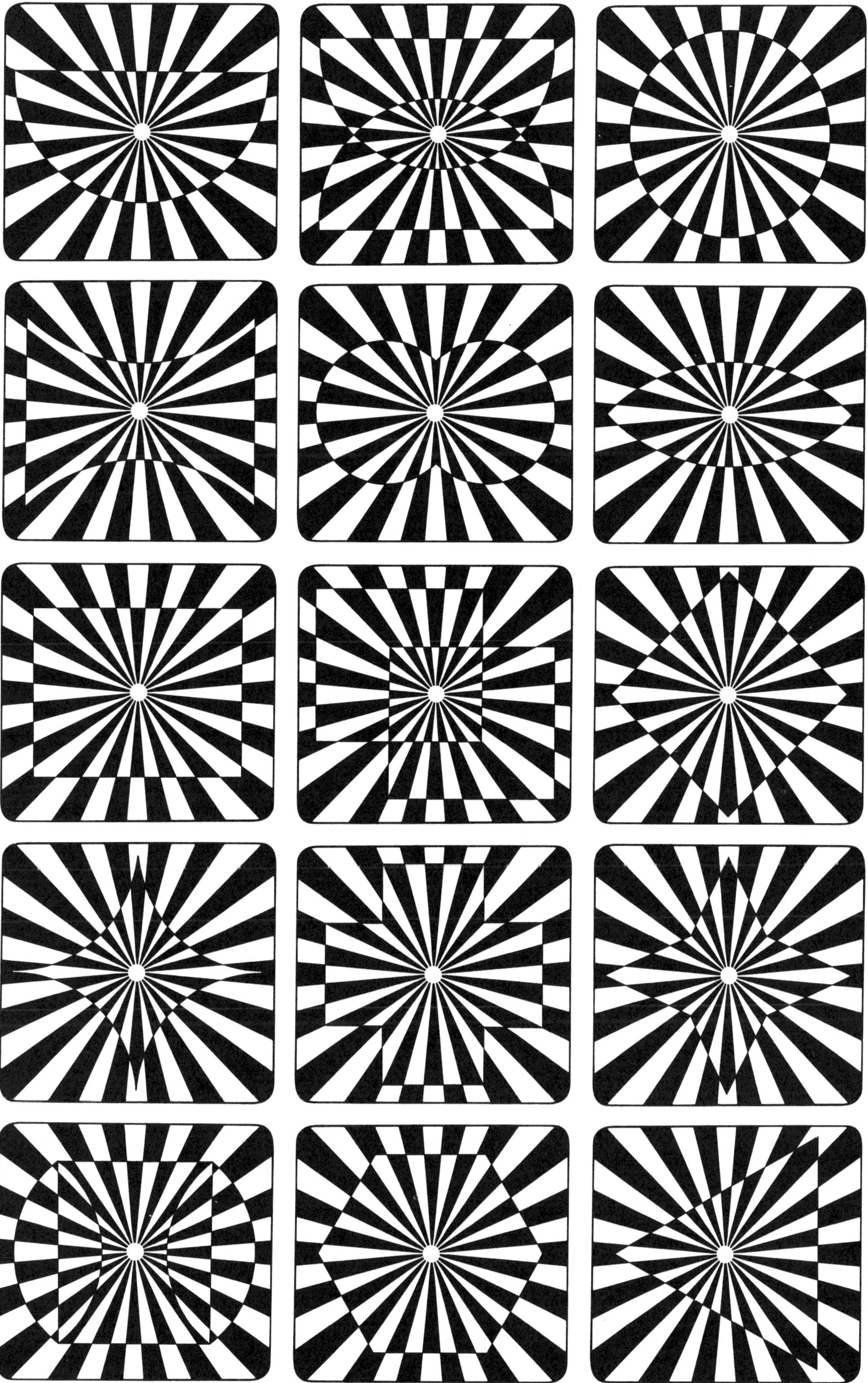

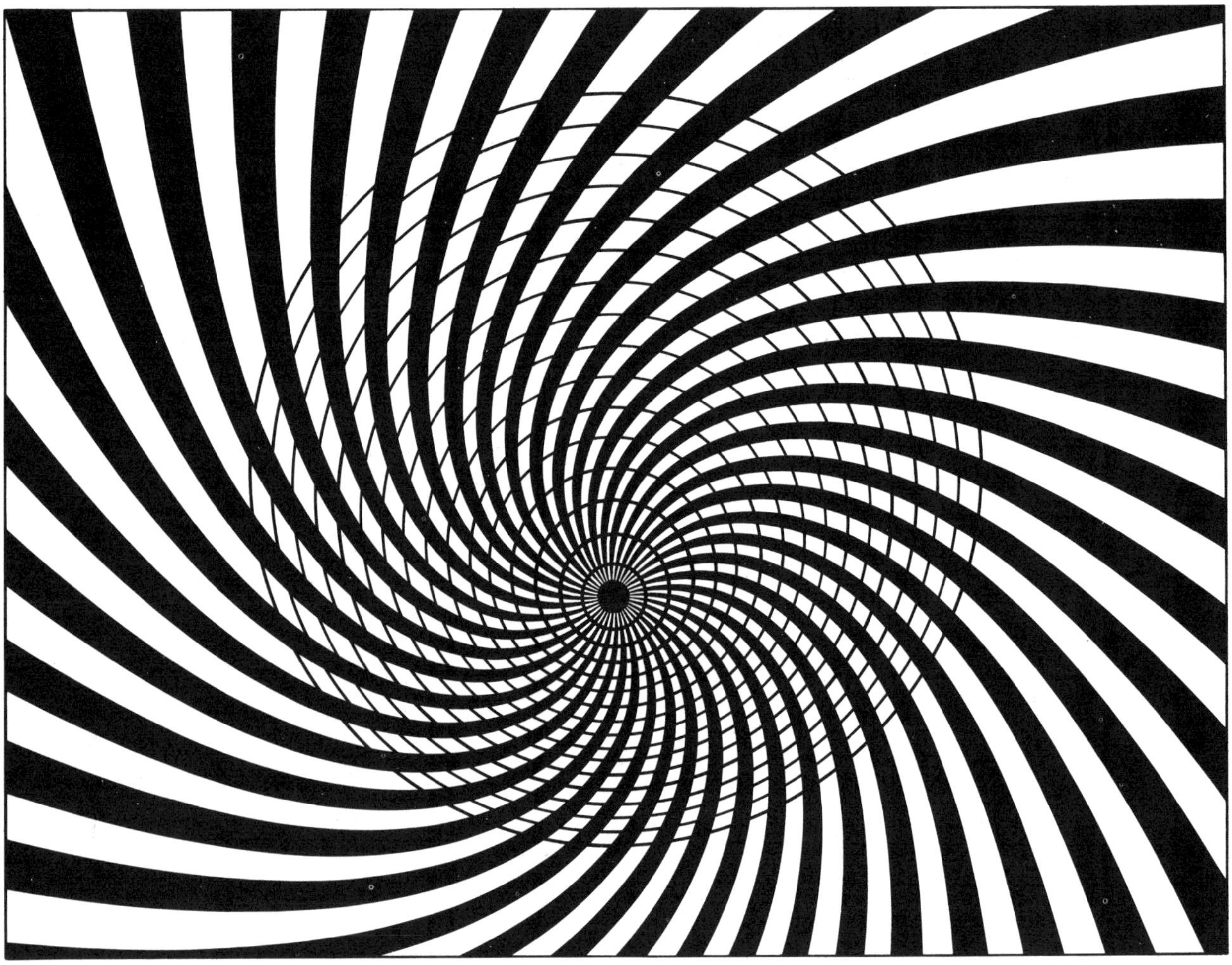

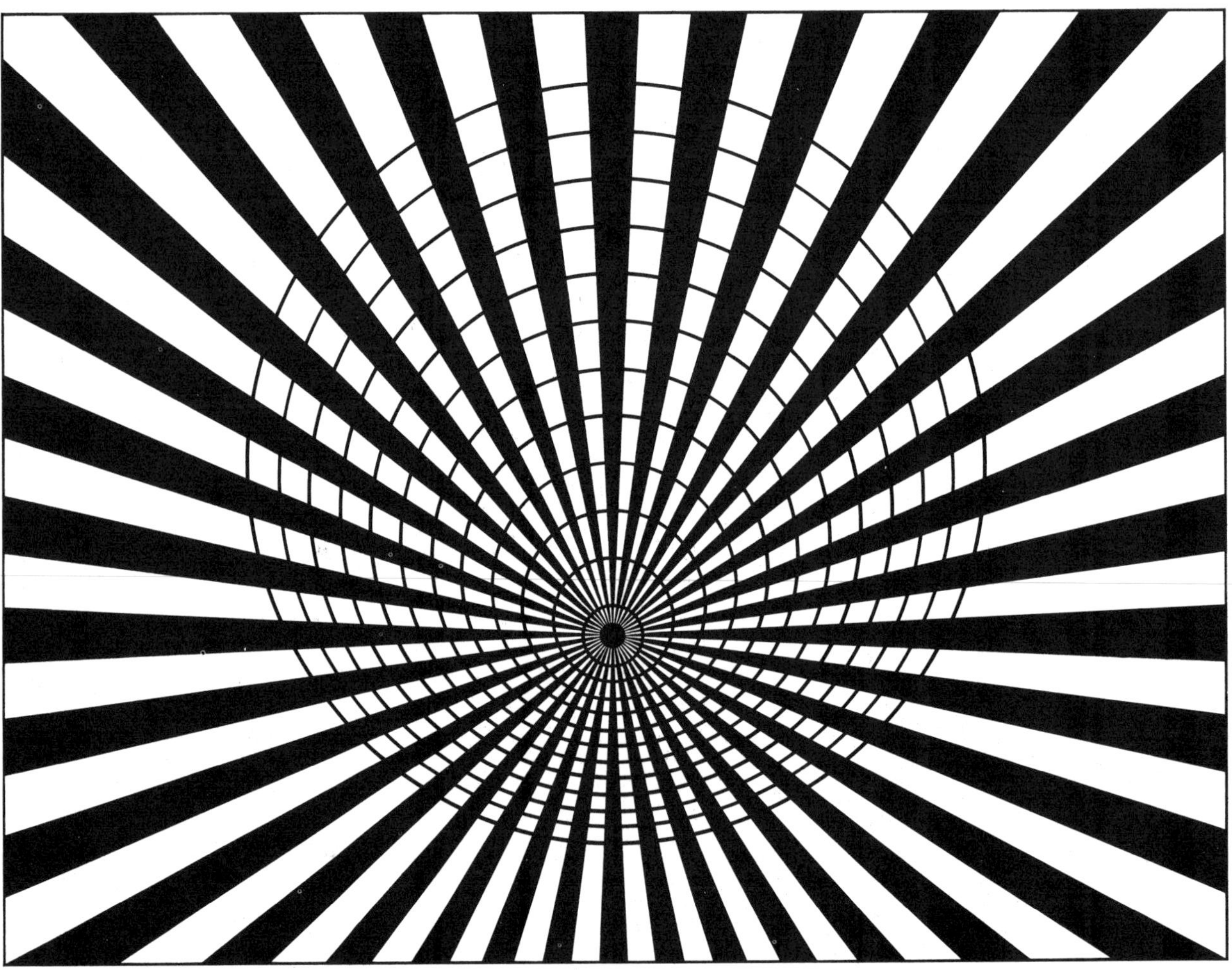

PLATE 68

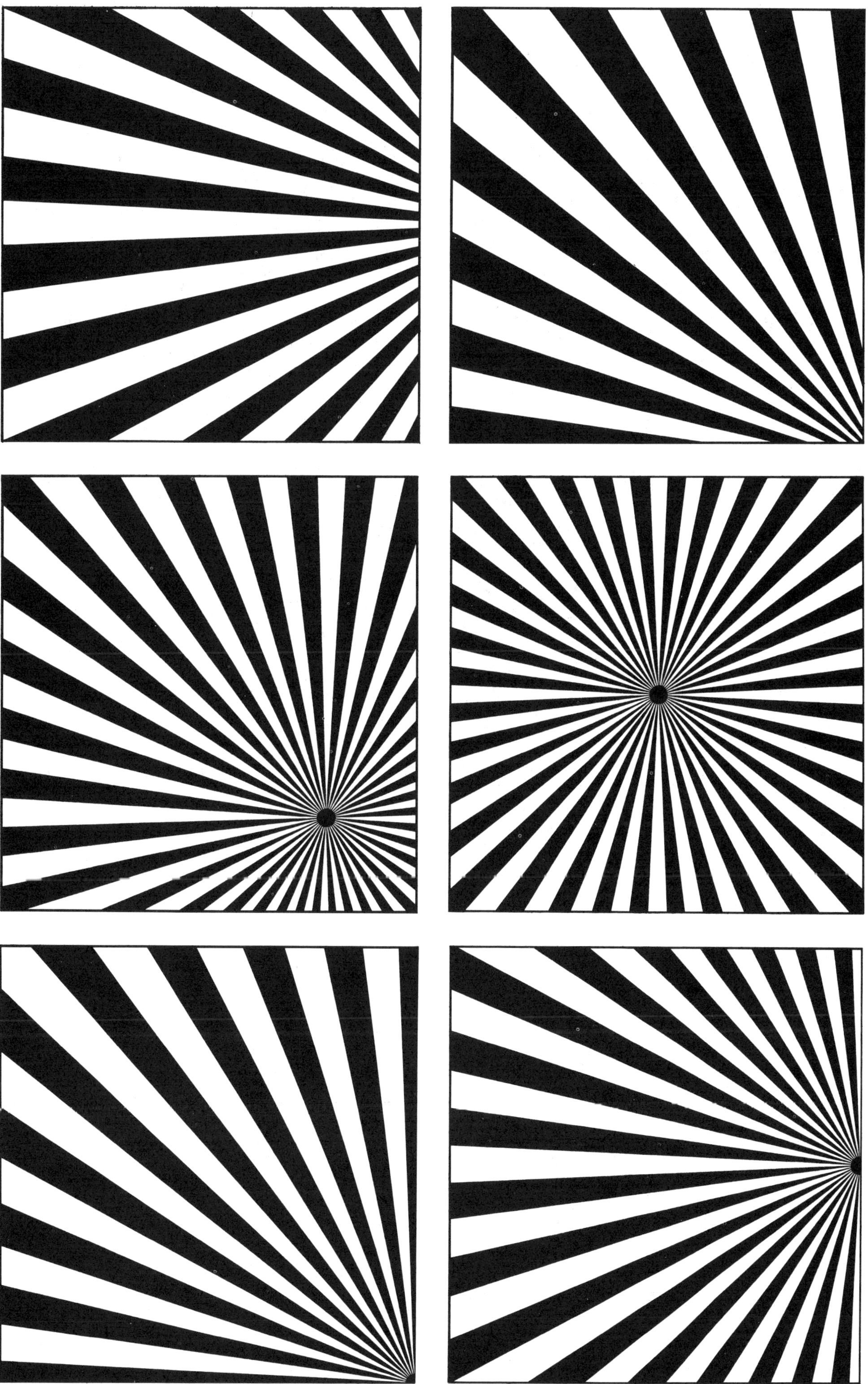

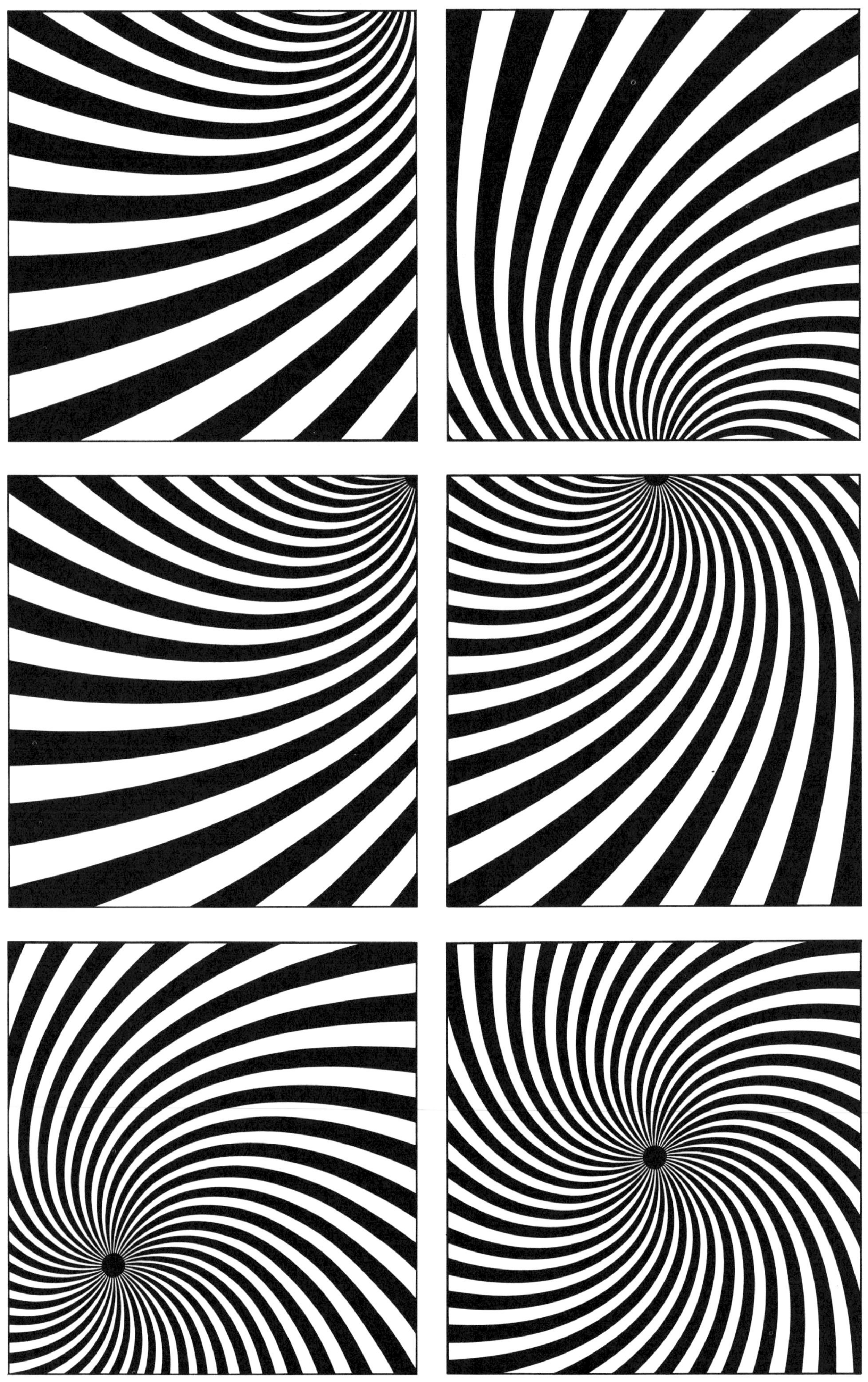

PLATE 70

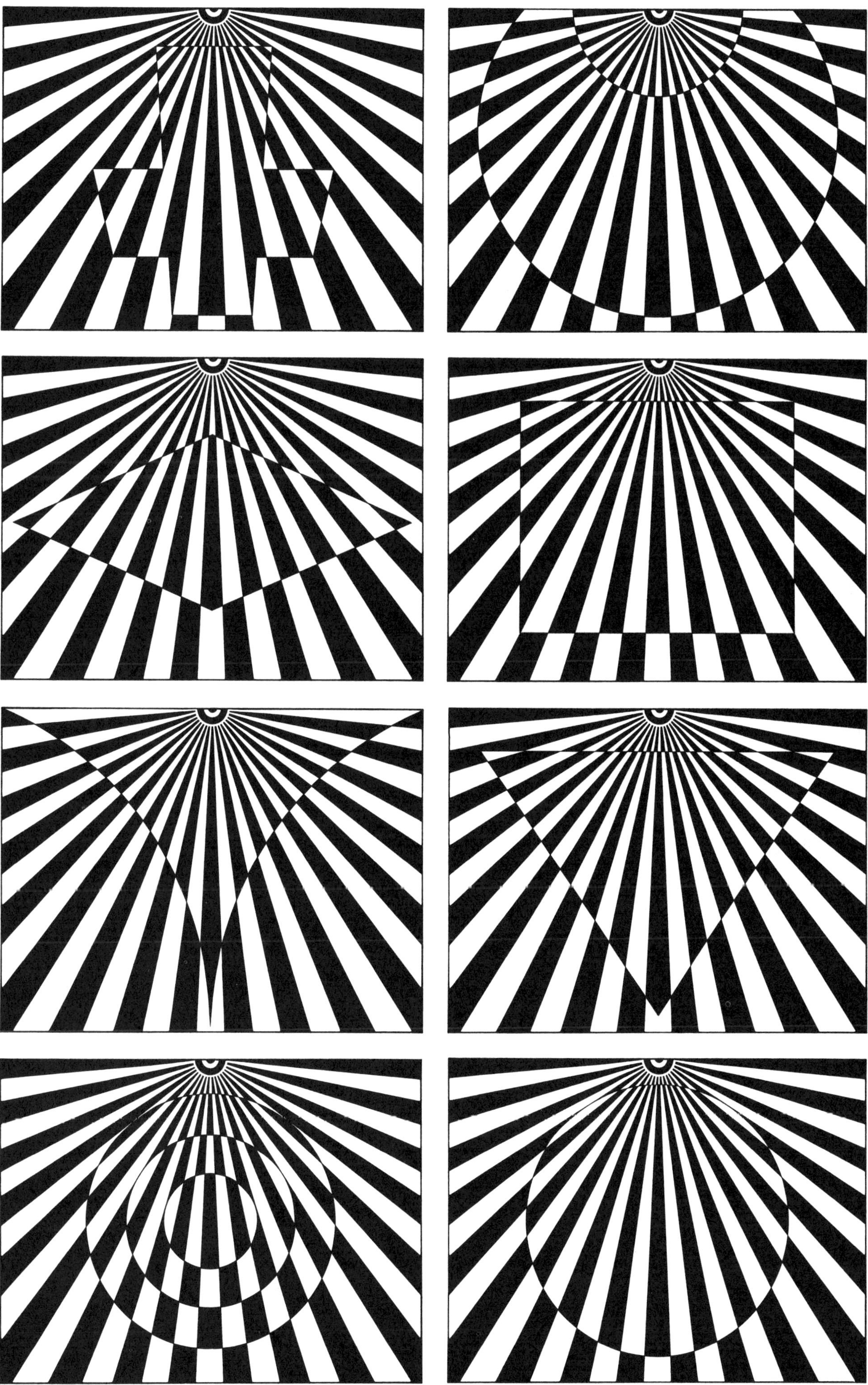

PLATE 71

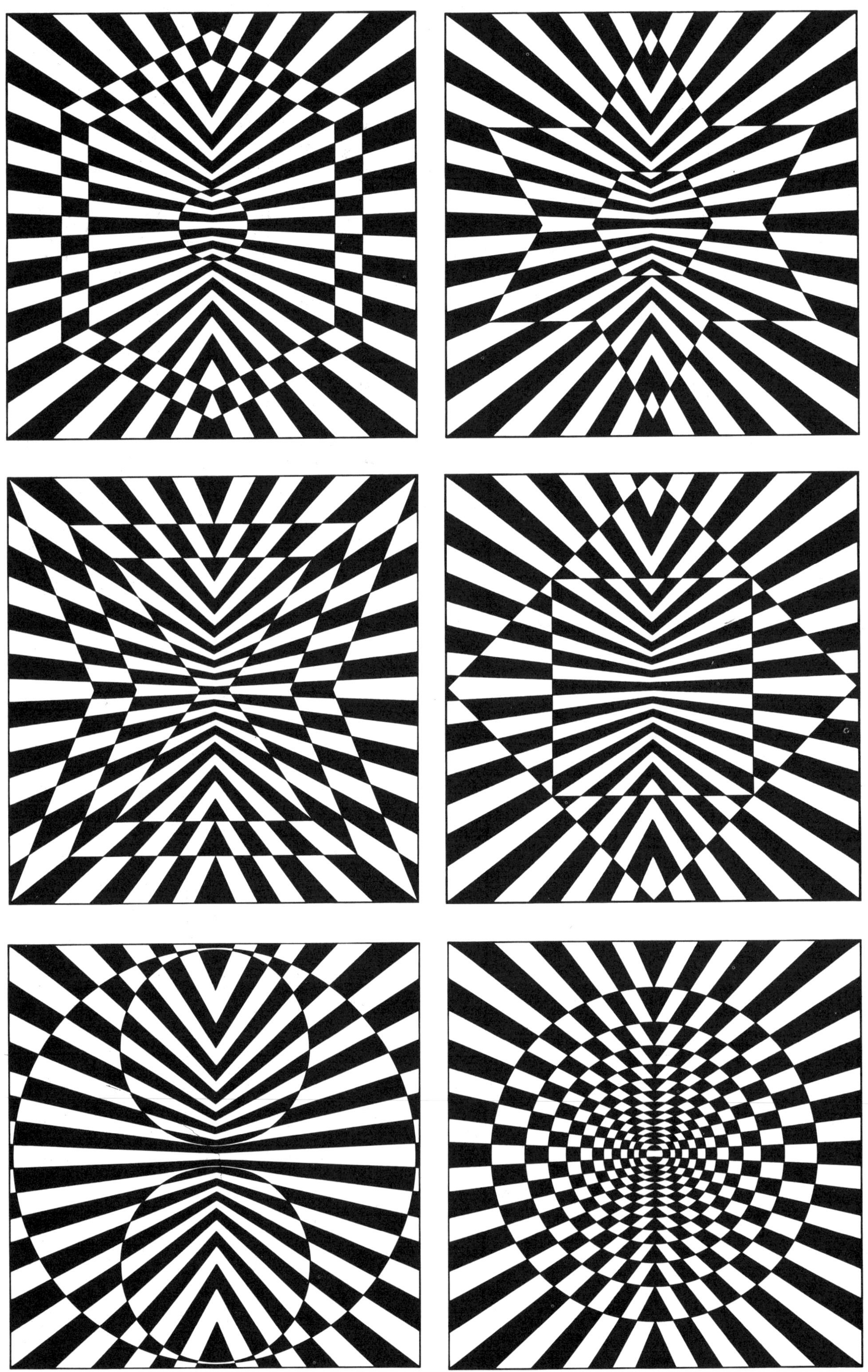

PLATE 72

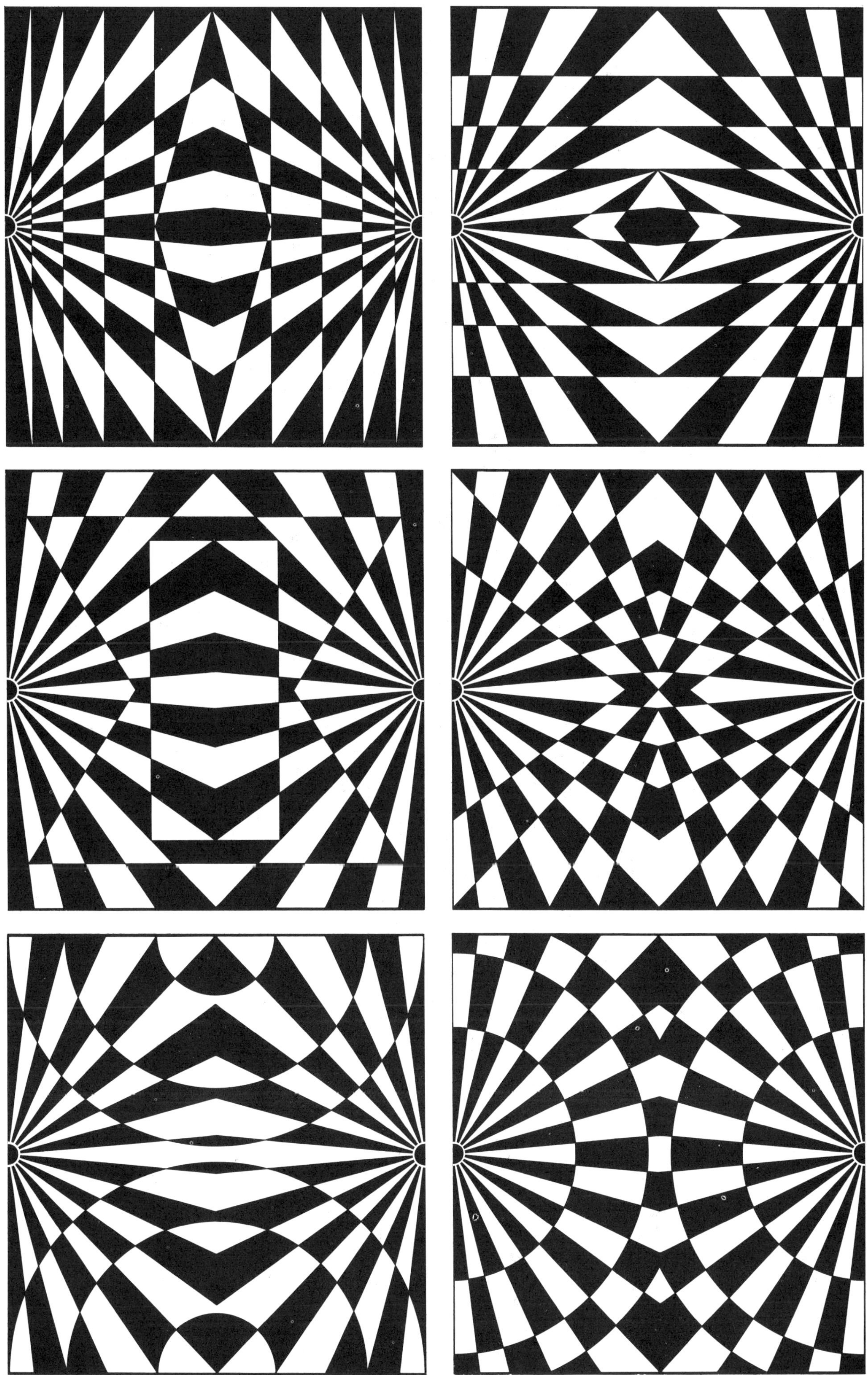

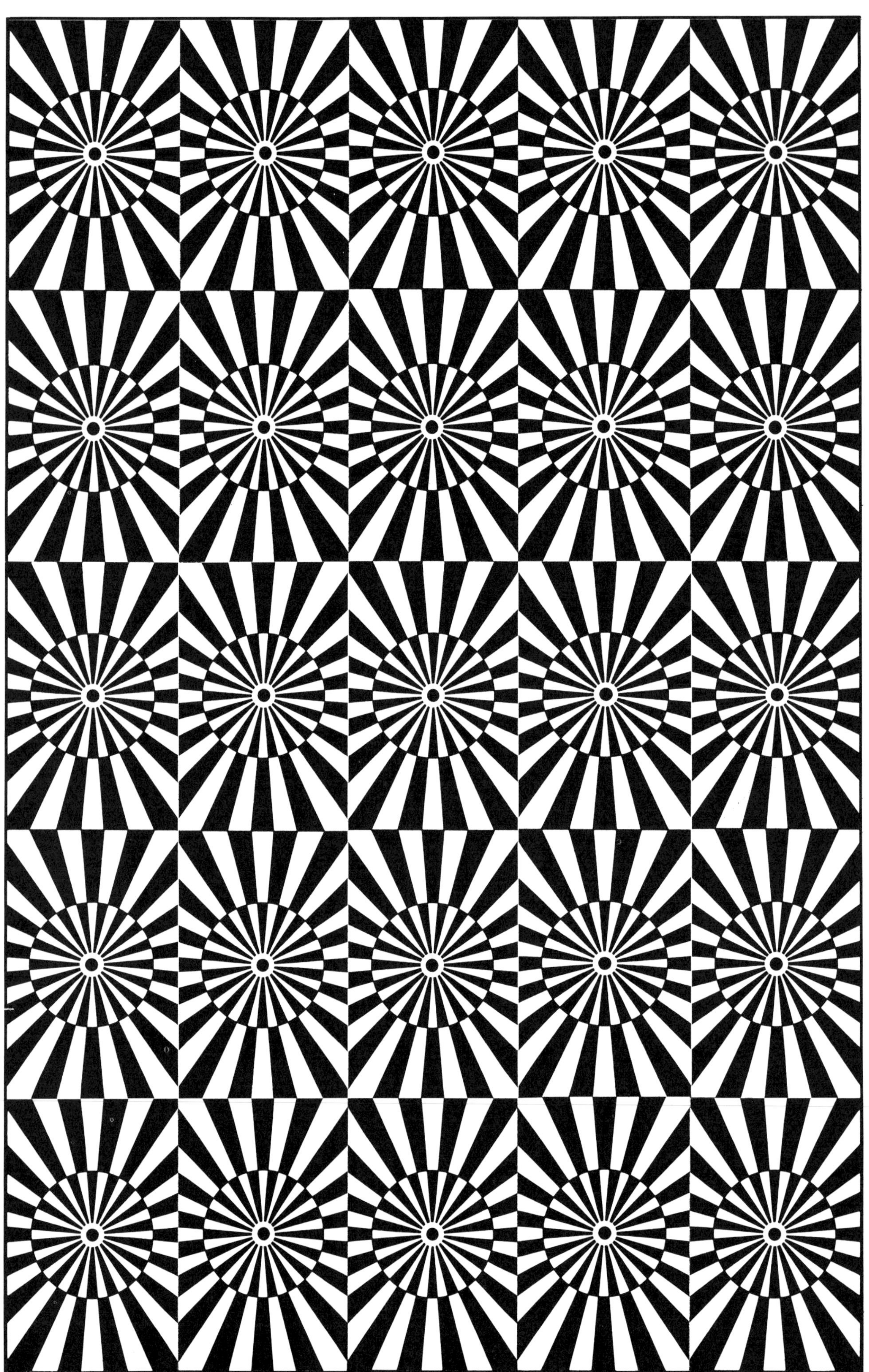

PLATE 74

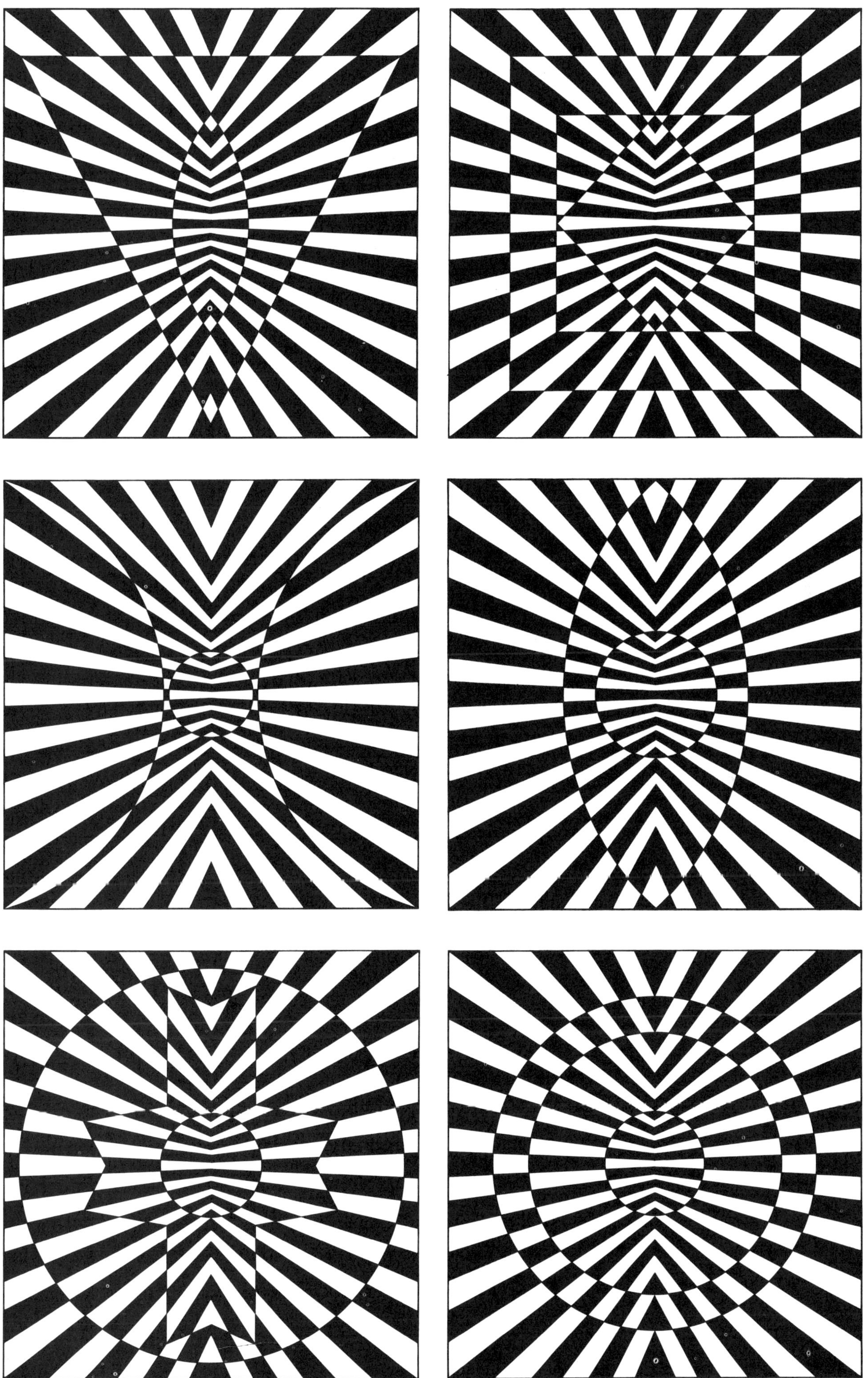

PLATE 75

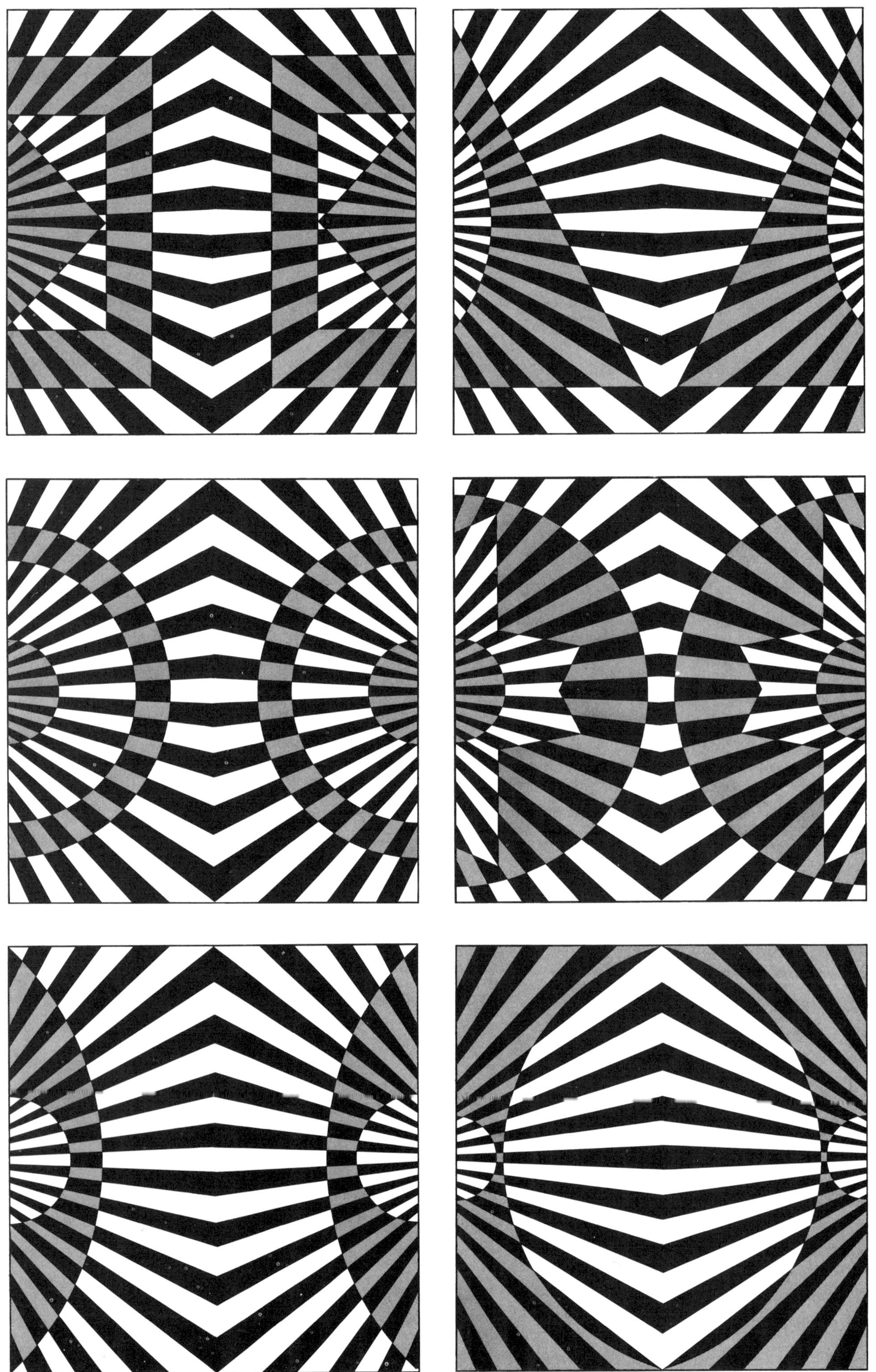

PLATE 76

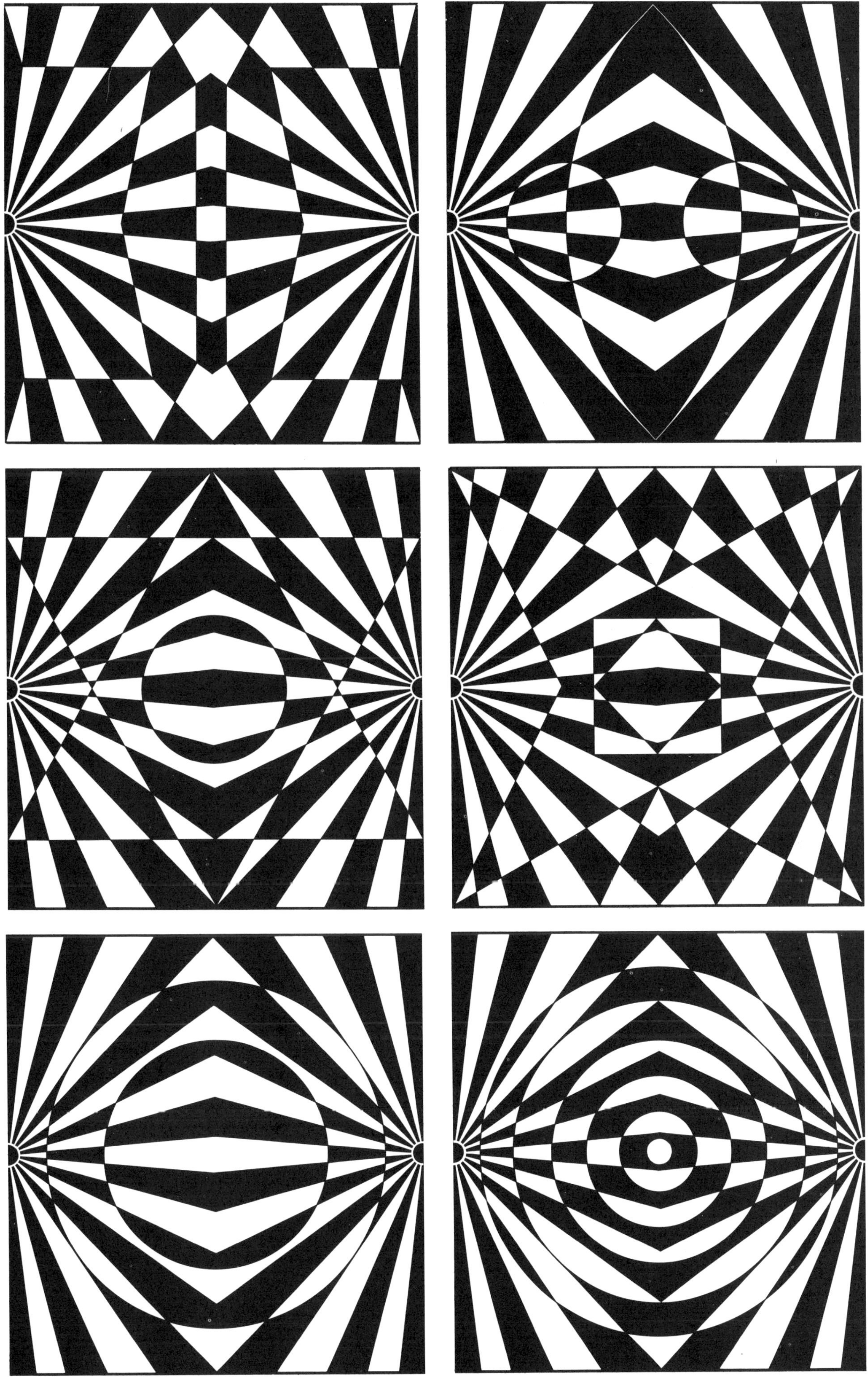

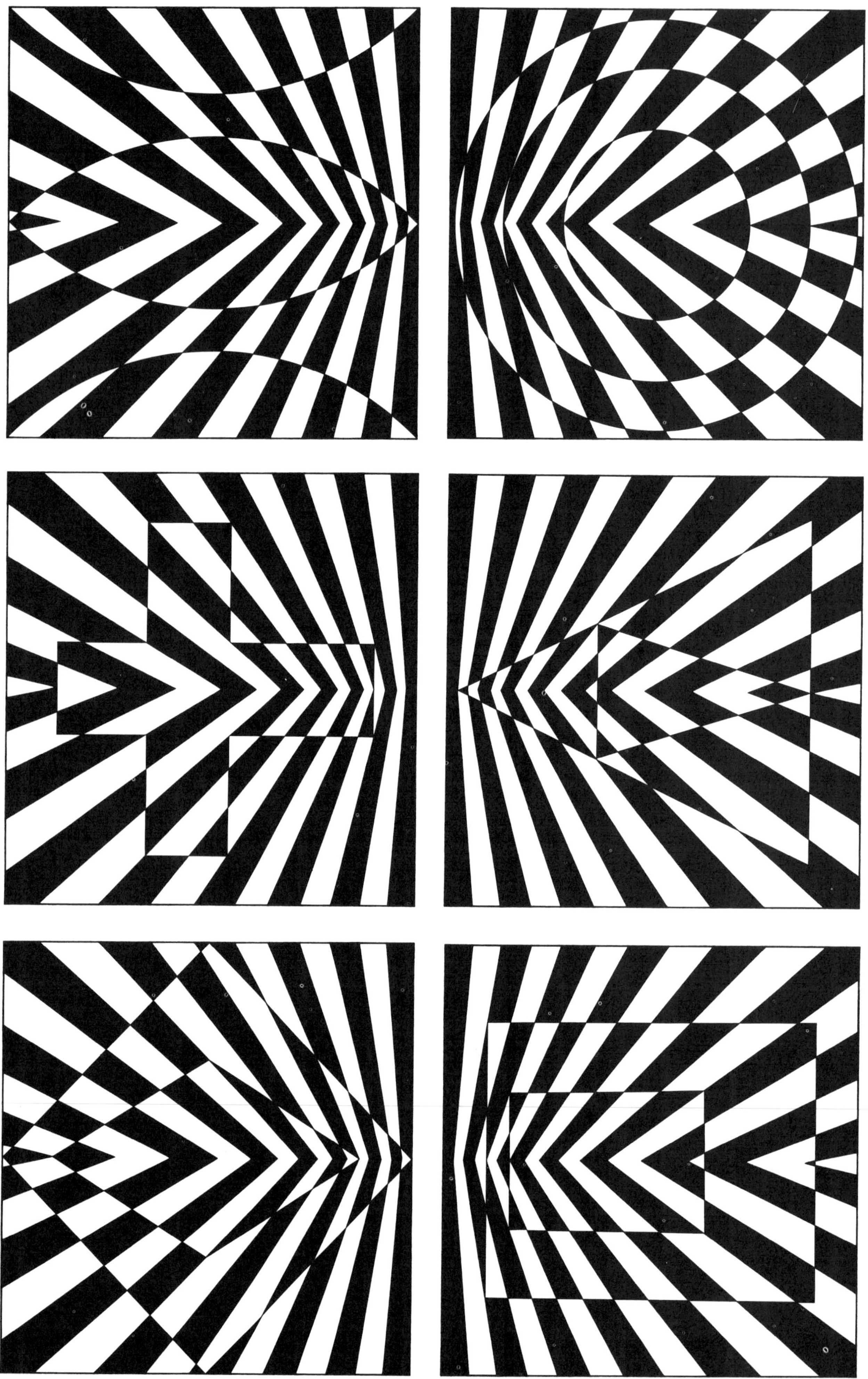

PLATE 78

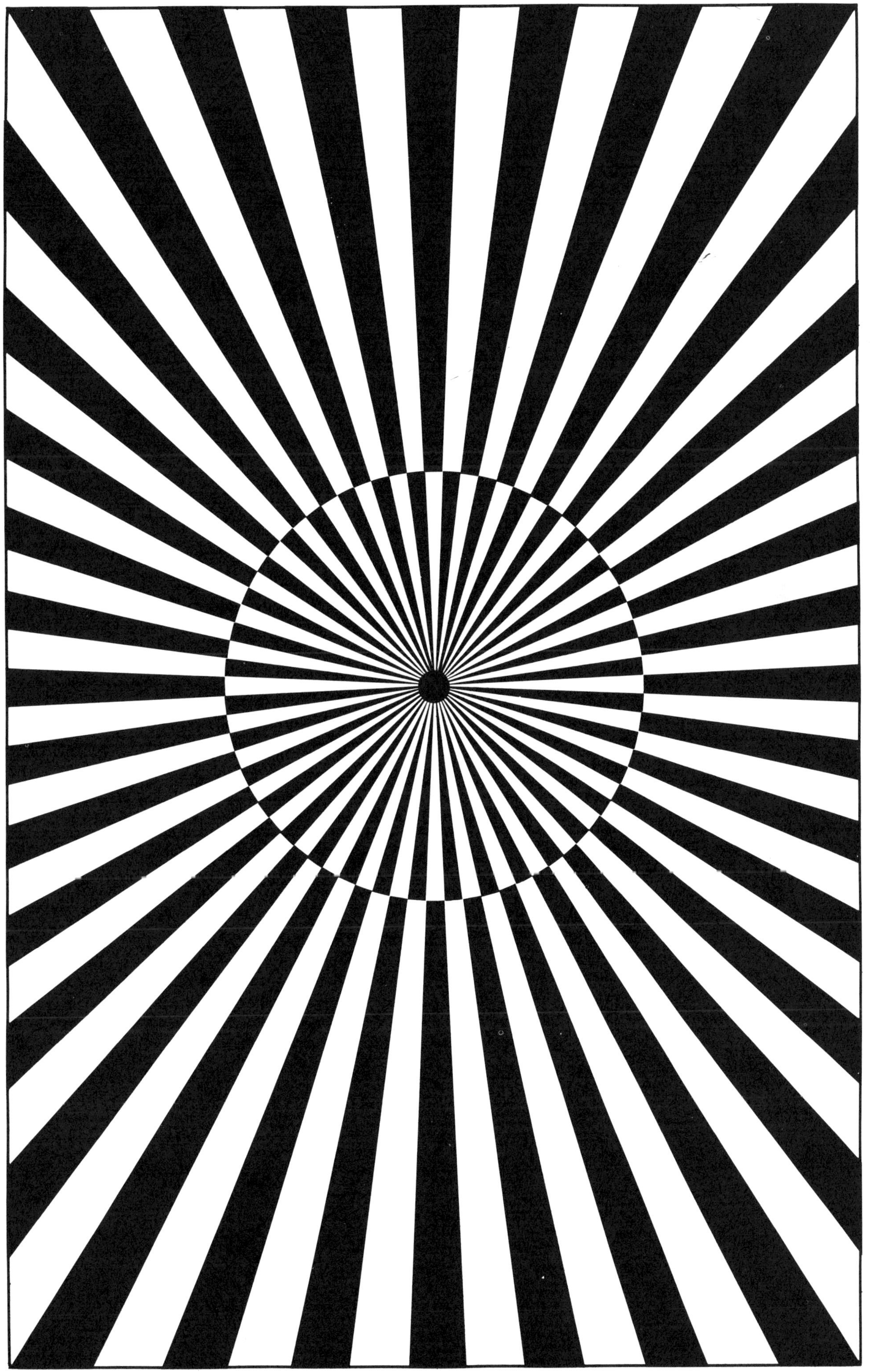

PLATE 79

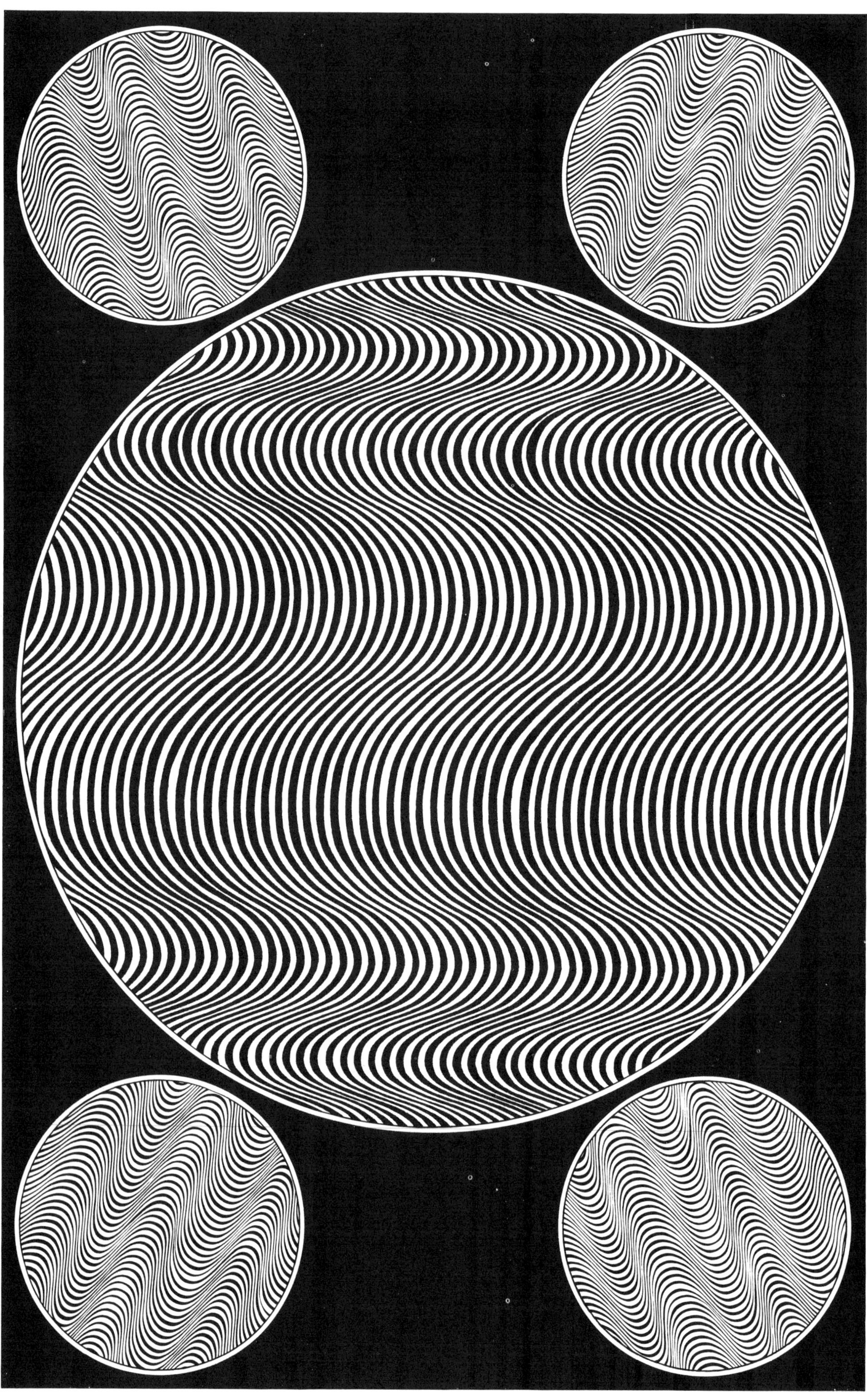

PLATE 80

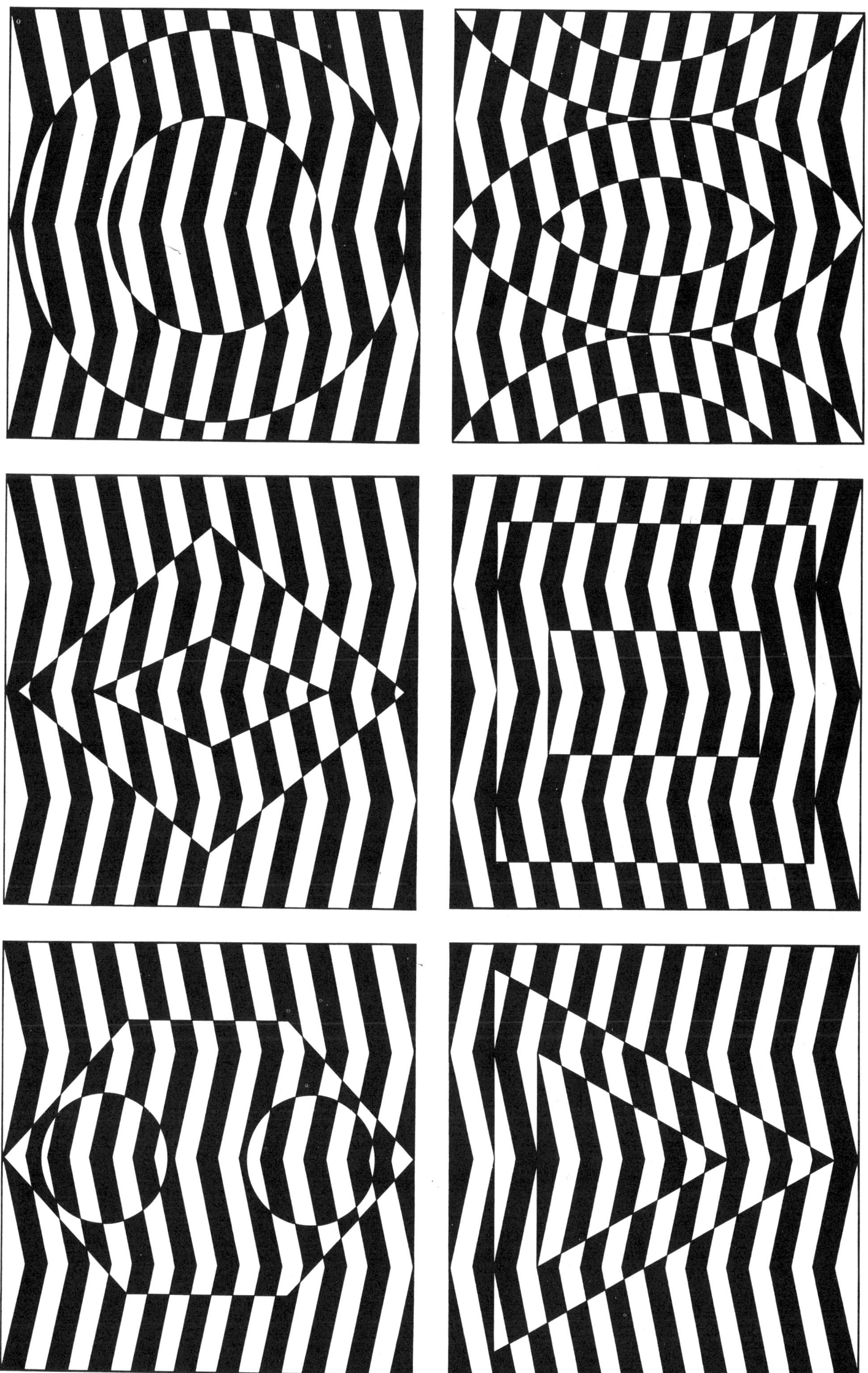

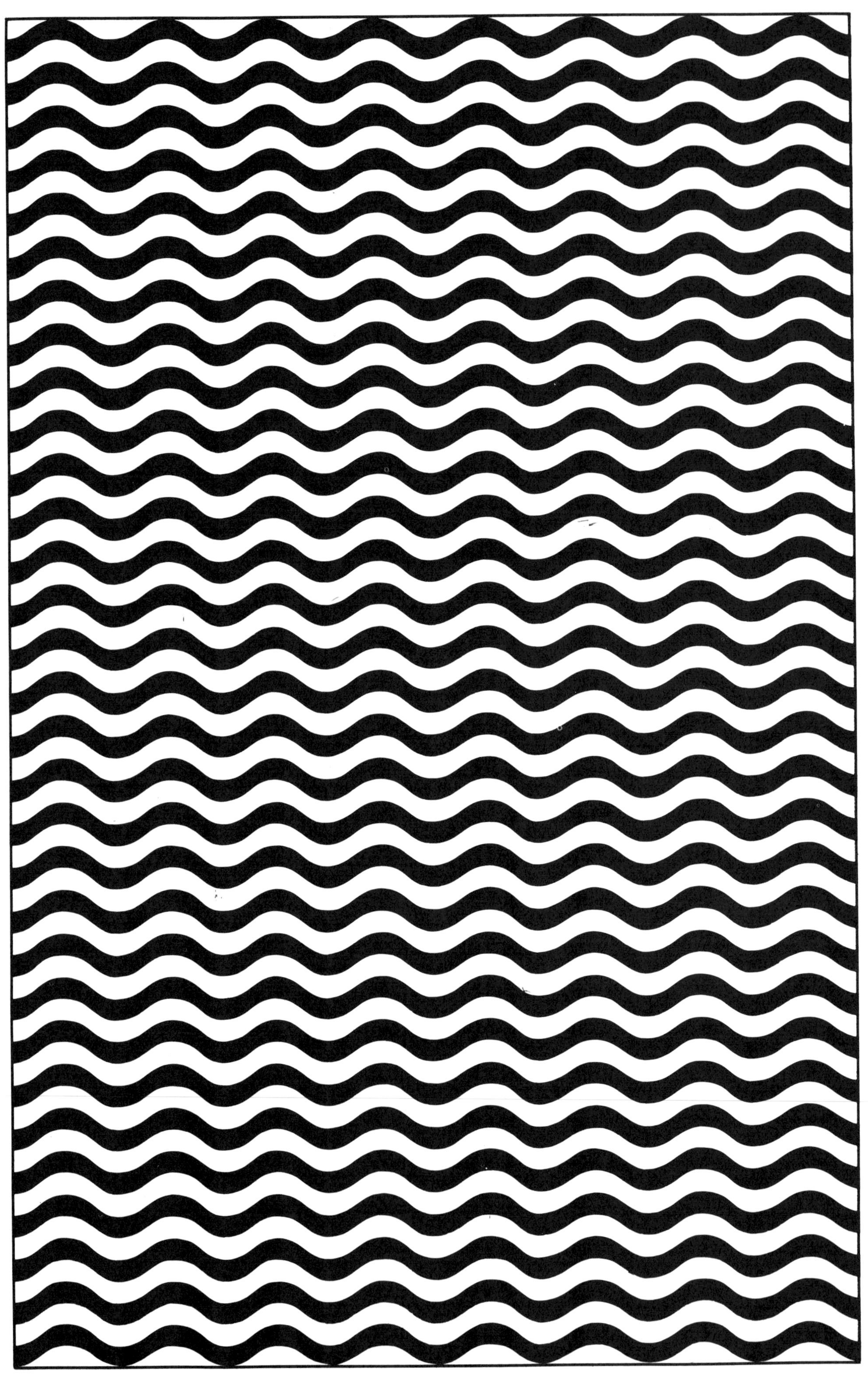

PLATE 82

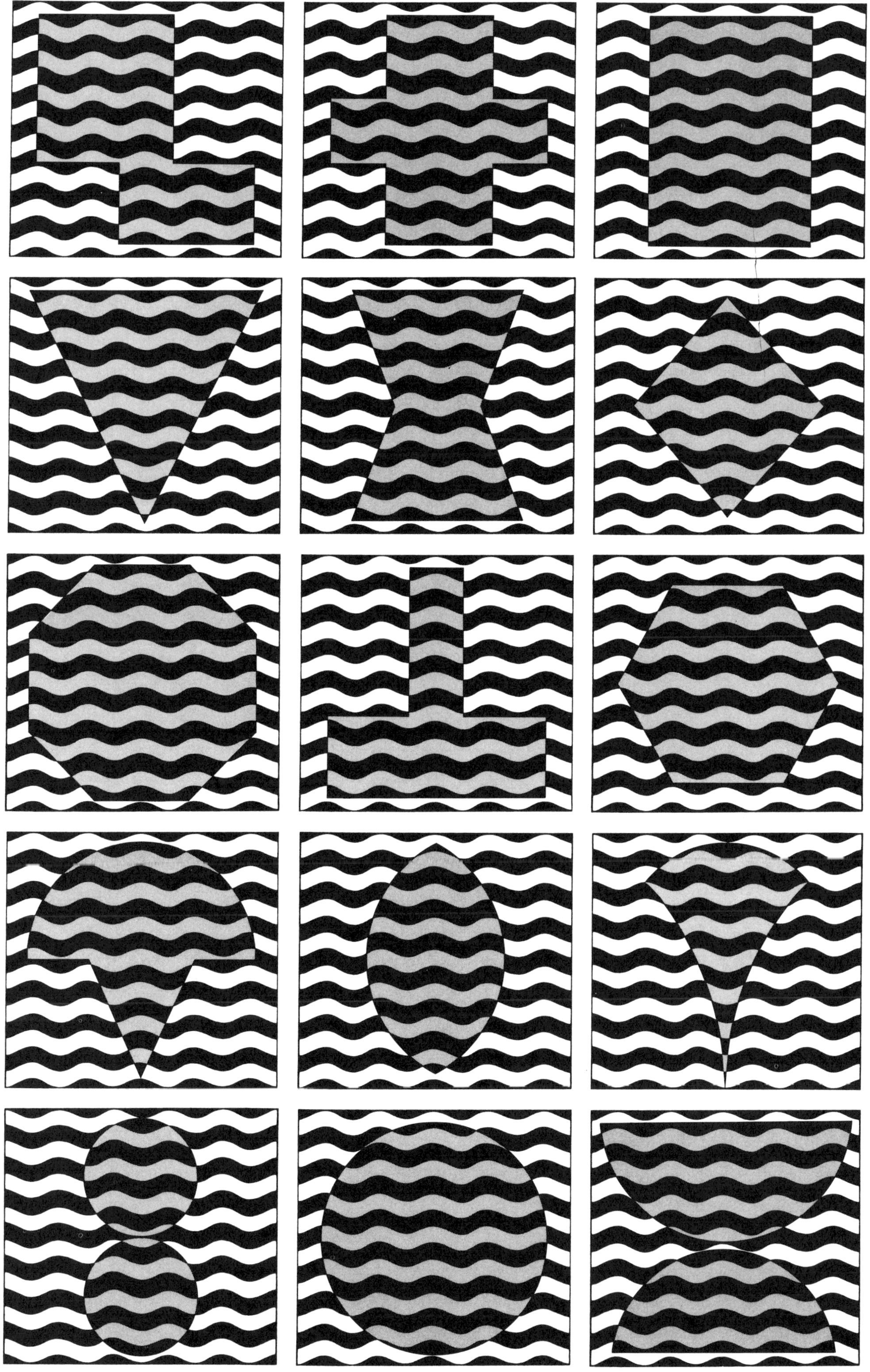

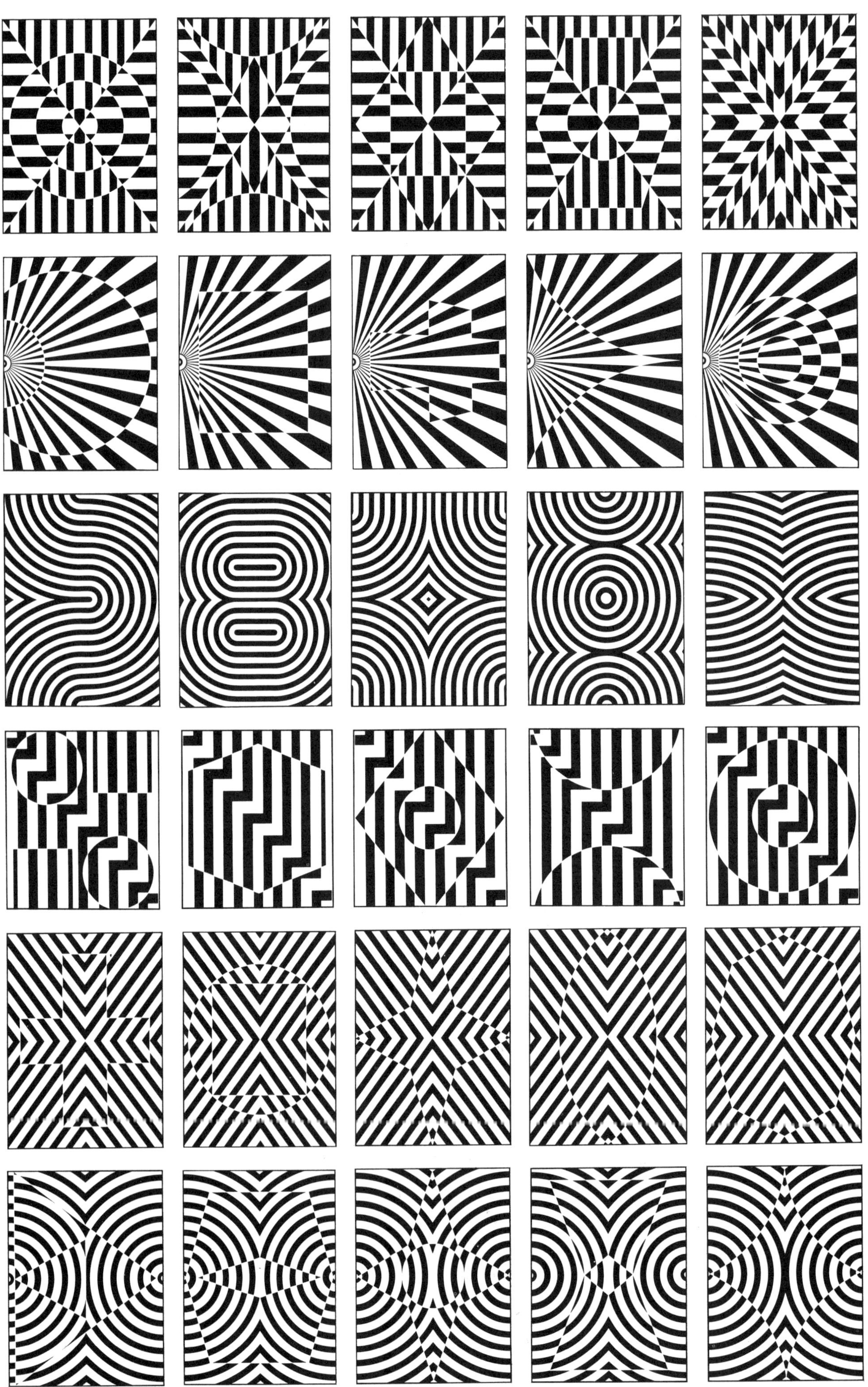

PLATE 84

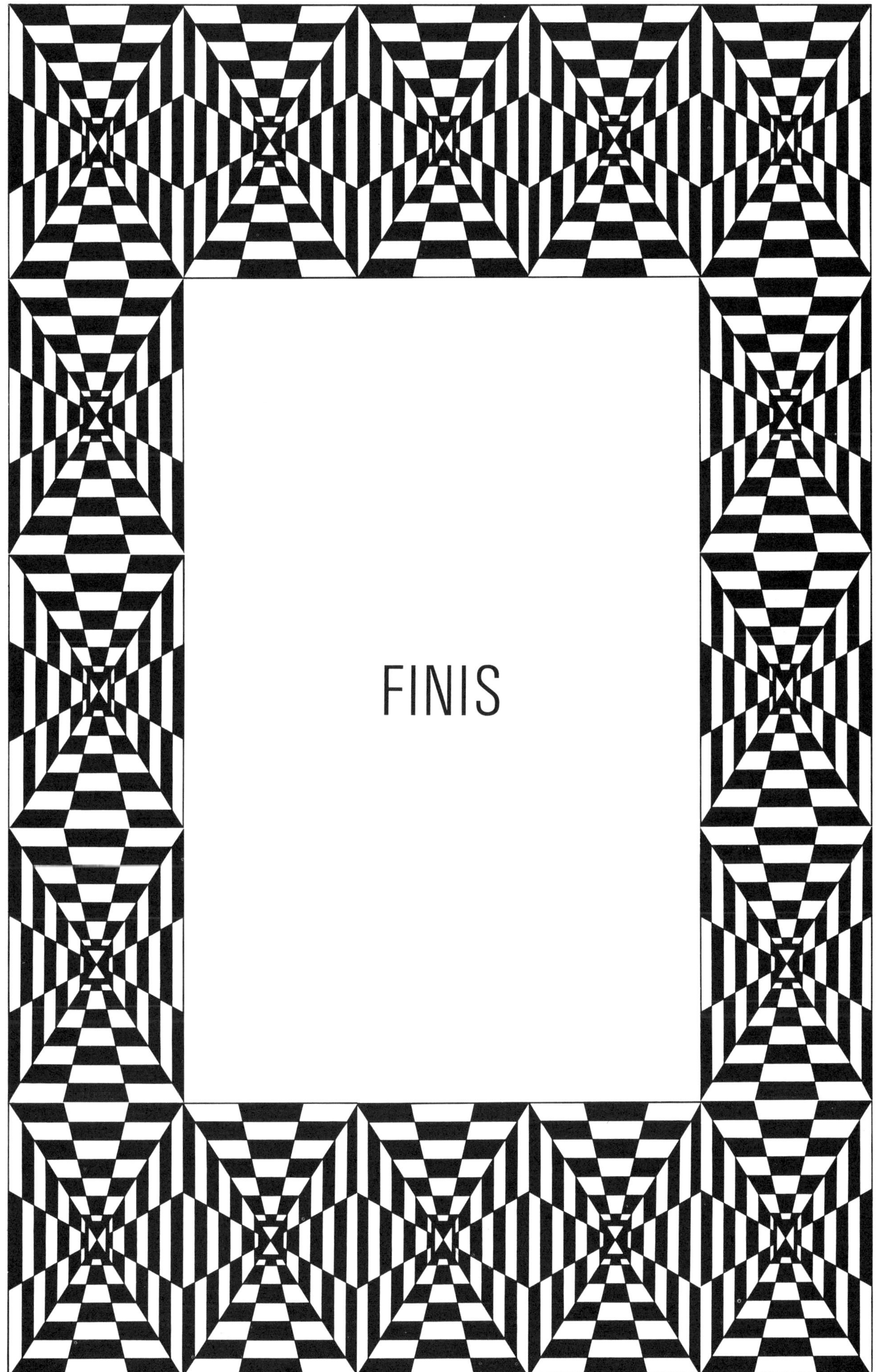

FINIS

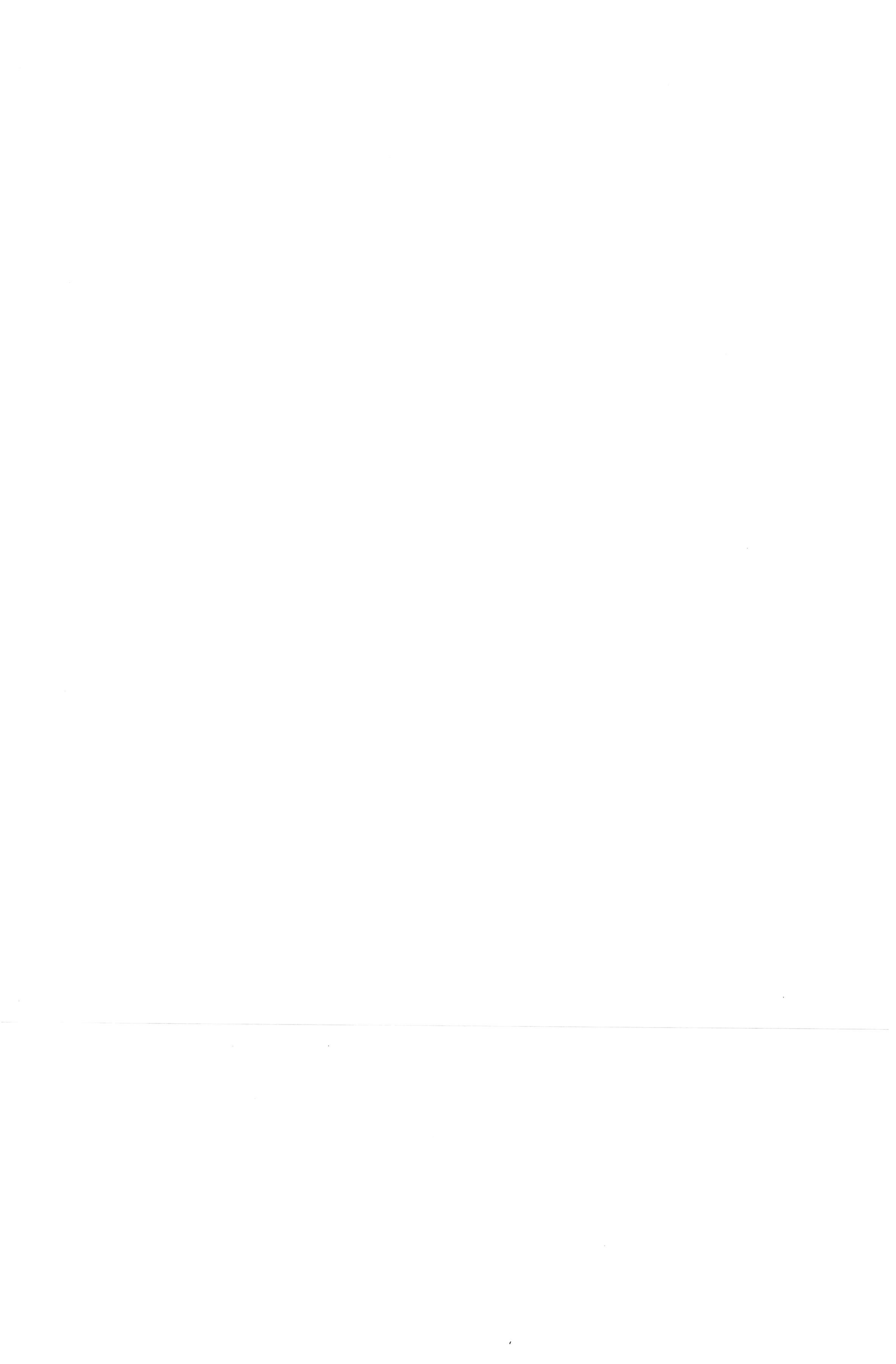